International Economics
The Wealth of Open Nations

Jørgen Ulff-Møller Nielsen

Associate Professor, The Aarhus School of Business

Erik Strøjer Madsen

Associate Professor, The Aarhus School of Business

Kurt Pedersen

Associate Professor, The Aarhus School of Business

Translated from the Danish by
Margrethe Petersen
Lecturer, Department of English
The Aarhus School of Business

McGRAW-HILL BOOK COMPANY

London · New York · St Louis · San Francisco · Auckland
Bogotá · Caracas · Lisbon · Mexico · Milan
Montreal · New Delhi · Panama · Paris · San Juan · São Paulo
Singapore · Sydney · Tokyo · Toronto

Published by
McGRAW-HILL Book Company Europe
Shoppenhangers Road, Maidenhead, Berkshire SL6 2QL, England
Telephone 01628 23432
Fax 01628 770224

British Library Cataloguing in Publication Data

Neilsen, Jørgen Ulff-Møller
  International Economics: Wealth of Open Nations
  I. Title II. Petersen, Margrethe
  337

  ISBN 0–07–707979–5

Library of Congress Cataloging-in-Publication Data

First published in Danish as *International Økonomi* 3rd edn by Forlaget Pareto, Århus 1994. (Copyright © 1994 Jørgen
Ulff-Møller Nielsen, Erik Strøjer Madsen and Kurt Pedersen and Forlaget Pareto, Århus.)

Neilsen, Jørgen Ulff-Møller
  [International økonomi. English]
  International economics: wealth of open nations / Jørgen Ulff-Møller Nielsen, Erik Strøjer Madsen, Kurt Pedersen.
    p. cm.
  Includes bibliographical references and index.
  ISBN 0–07–707979–5
  1. International economic relations. 2. International trade. 3. International finance. I. Title.
  HF1359.N548   1995
  337–dc20

                 94–44975
                    CIP

12345 CL 98765

Typeset by Computape (Pickering) Ltd, Pickering, North Yorkshire
and printed and bound by Clays Ltd, St Ives plc.

Printed on permanent paper in compliance with ISO Standard 9706.

CONTENTS

Preface

The discipline of *International economics* is as relevant as ever. The world economy is increasingly internationalized, which results in political use and abuse of established theory. Old and valid insights should not be forgotten in the process, however. Likewise, the significant fields of analysis which have been added to the discipline in recent years and which will undoubtedly contribute to the understanding and handling of internationalization, should also be taken into consideration.

Theories of comparative advantage are supplemented with theories of competitive advantage, integrating the mobility of goods and services with international factor movements. In the same vein, macro-level political management in a world increasingly dominated by giant trade blocs necessitates the development of theories of economic coordination.

In just under 250 pages we present models, outline political challenges and examine some possible applications of theory. In covering the discipline, we have chosen to rely heavily on graphs and very little on algebra. Readers with a basic understanding of microeconomics and macroeconomics will easily find their way through this book. However, the apparent simplicity of the presentation should not fool anyone as some parts are rather complex.

Suggestions for further reading will provide more detailed knowledge of this discipline, which has fascinated such great economists as Adam Smith and P. R. Krugman. We hope that readers of this book will reap the reward of useful knowledge and feel inspired to gain a genuine interest in the topics covered.

Jørgen Ulff-Møller Nielsen
Erik Strøjer Madsen
Kurt Pedersen
Aarhus, Denmark

ONE

INTRODUCTION

Good economic theory is almost always based on reflections on reality and the structures and problems of real life. Some examples of this kind are Adam Smith's reflections on the economic growth process, Karl Marx's reflections on the laws of development followed by the capitalist system and J.M. Keynes' reflections on the fact that contrary to the assumptions of economic theory economies do not automatically tend towards full employment equilibrium.

Useful economic theory yields fruitful insights into and solutions to the problems presented by reality. The reflections of Adam Smith resulted in a deadly assault on mercantilism and the analyses of J.M. Keynes paved the way for fiscal policy and thus for the full employment period of the sixties.

We are convinced that the branch of knowledge known as *international economics* is useful and therefore worth some effort. It has mainly taken down-to-earth problems as its point of departure and the utility value of the solutions that it suggests is considerable and conspicuous if they are carried out.

1.1 A SEPARATE BRANCH OF KNOWLEDGE

It may rightly be asked whether international economics is an independent branch of knowledge. Its development has not been independent of general theoretical developments. Some of the central figures in international economics have been Adam Smith, David Ricardo and P.A. Samuelson. They are all known for the contributions that they have made to general economic theory, so this, in itself, guarantees some parallelism between international economic theory and the development of general economic theory.

Nevertheless, it makes sense to speak of a separate branch of knowledge, but this is due to real-life conditions, the most prominent one being the existence of *nations* which each have their own economy. *Factors of production* move internationally but they move slowly compared to their intra-national mobility. This puts a restraint on the difference between wages paid in Wales and in London: if the bricklayers in London are paid too much, then bricklayers from Wales will move to the capital and start laying bricks there. This will not apply, however, to bricklayers from Poland, Portugal or Pakistan; even sizeable wage differences will not attract them to London—but of course they will be attracted to Lodz, Oporto and Karachi, respectively.

In addition, each economy has its own *currency*. It is rather troublesome having to buy

1

foreign exchange in connection with international transactions. This would not be problematic if the exchange rates of all currencies were fixed and permanent. Exchange rates vary, however, sometimes unpredictably, so exchange and capital markets are extremely important elements in the international economy. They may be analysed by means of conventional economic concepts, of course; nevertheless, they are something special.

This leads us to a third reason why international economics is a separate branch of knowledge: there is no international monetary authority but a large number of national ones. The unit of analysis is usually a nation, which may cause exchange rate fluctuations of the kind mentioned above by means of its policies. The motives for economic policy include the intention to perform as well as possible, even if it does harm other countries a bit. Therefore the international economy, understandably, contains a strong element of *politics*.

We want to emphasize that international economics does not differ from other kinds of economic theory as regards the aims of analyses. The focus is on efficiency, distribution, stability and employment. The actual order of priorities may of course differ from country to country. Micro-analyses will focus on efficiency and distribution, macro-analyses on stability and employment. The crucial questions are the following:

1. How do international trade and investments influence the division of labour and the allocation of resources in individual countries?
2. How do trade and trade policies influence the distribution of wealth and of income among countries and in individual countries?
3. How do international shocks influence an open economy and what are the effects of different kinds of macro-economic policies?
4. How do international trade and investments influence employment and growth in individual countries?
5. How will increased economic integration in Europe influence our national economies?
6. How will coordination of the monetary and fiscal policies of various countries influence their economic goals?

1.2 INTERNATIONAL DEPENDENCE

International trade is central to the international dependence of a country. Figure 1.1 shows the historical development in the production and trade of selected countries. As can be seen, growth has been subject to strong fluctuations but the level of growth in foreign trade has typically been higher than that of growth in production. The period from 1913 to 1950 is of particular interest: economic growth deteriorated because of two world wars, but the protectionism characteristic of the inter-war period also contributed to this development. From a theoretical perspective, national trade and international trade are explained in parallel fashion. Economic theory explains national trade in terms of the advantages of the *division of labour* among the firms and individuals of a given society, and according to international trade theory countries divide labour among themselves in such a manner that the same optimistic conclusion follows.

Historically, however, the evaluation of international trade has varied. Until the end of the eighteenth century, national and international interests were assumed to conflict. If a country had a trade advantage, then this was seen as something positive since it was assumed to put trade partners in a worse position. Due to Adam Smith (1776) and David Ricardo (1817) this dogma was replaced with a *laissez-faire* policy, which holds that everyone is better off through the international exchange of goods and services. Funnily, on an almost identical analytical

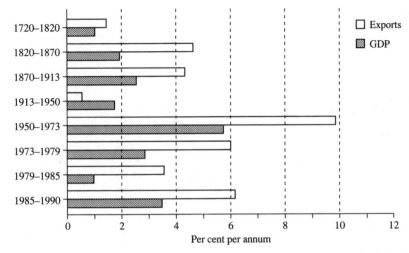

Note: The figures covering the early periods are based on limited and uncertain information from a few countries.

Figure 1.1   The development of growth in production and trade in selected countries, 1720–1990
         Sources: IMF, the World Bank, OECD and Maddison (1982).

basis, some marxist trade theory brands international trade as an imperialist exploitation mechanism.

During recent years international *investments* have become much more prevalent than previously. The liberalization of capital markets has led to daily transfers of hundreds of millions of dollars among the countries of the world. At the same time, investments by firms across national borders have become the most significant mediator of technological and managerial progress. The developing countries are particularly dependent on capital and technology transfers. Yet in spite of these transfers it is foreseeable that the growth levels in the nineties in the world's poorest countries will continue to be hampered by the burdens caused by the combination of borrowing and high-level interest rates in the eighties.

The concept of international dependence is wider, however, and basically covers the fact that practically no country in the world is self-sufficient. Trade is a precondition of continued economic growth and sometimes even of national survival. The following quotation from a Japanese report (MITI, 1982) clearly illustrates the intertwinement of trade, economy and politics:

In the present report, we will review the following three policy goals in the light of Japan's need for economic security as defined in the foregoing: (1) to secure a steady supply of critical materials, (2) to help the world economic system maintain and strengthen its roles in the face of an unsettled international political and economic environment, and (3) to make due contributions to the community of nations through technology development so as to make Japan's role indispensable to the development of the world economy.

Figure 1.2 expresses global dependence straightforwardly. At the same time it illustrates the pivotal and dominant role of the 27 rich OECD countries in the world economy as suppliers of advanced technology and basic foods. In return, the OECD countries receive energy and raw materials, in particular rare minerals applicable in high-technology industries, from the rest of the world. Not only do the OECD countries play a pivotal role in trade among the four groups of countries but, in addition, approximately two-thirds of all trade and three-fourths of all direct investments take place internally *among* the OECD countries.

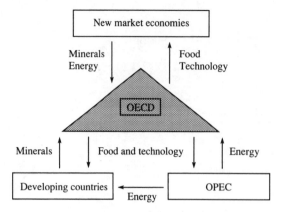

Figure 1.2   International dependence

The triangle symbolizes the OECD: it has become common usage to speak of North America, Japan and Western Europe as a 'triad'. The interaction and differences prevailing among these three areas determine the economic pulse of the world. Accordingly, one of the aims of international economics is to throw some light on the conditions of trade, exchange and management that form part of the basis of international politics.

1.3   NAVIGARE NECESSE EST

If the world economy is conceived of as an ocean, which at times is rough and at times calm, a small open country may be conceived as a ship that has to cross the ocean in the best way possible. Knowing weather conditions and currents is essential, but once they are known the primary problem is the steering of the ship. Theoretical knowledge does not equal practical skill.

Because the more interesting object of study is at times the ocean and at times the ship, the present book will at times take the international 'system' and at times a nation as its unit of analysis. The holistic or system point of view has been chosen, for instance for the treatment of international trade theory and for that of international coordination of economic policies dealt with in the final chapter. Mainly, however, the analyses focus on the small open country. Small open economies generally have a large volume of foreign trade and are in principle unprotected from international trade cycles.

Small open economies may gain considerably from pursuing appropriate policies at both micro-level and macro-level. Pursuing such policies, i.e. good navigation, requires extensive knowledge and considerable insight. It requires knowledge of the results and the underlying motives for international trade and of the effects of trade policy measures. It requires knowledge of the function of exchange and capital markets. It requires knowledge of the short- and long-term effects of the major politico-economic measures including the stabilizing measures resulting from fiscal and monetary policies and the competitiveness-influencing measures resulting from incomes and exchange rate policies.

Of course one should not forget that no country restricts itself to purely economic considerations. For strategic reasons, a country may choose to refrain from the international division of labour and choose to produce its own weapons; for political reasons, it may choose to participate in or abstain from various kinds of international cooperation. A number of small

West European countries have chosen to cooperate within the European Union for political reasons. Likewise, political preferences account for the fact that these countries are under the 'OECD' umbrella shown in Figure 1.2 and do not form part of the new market economies.

1.4 OUTLINE OF THIS BOOK

The two preceding sections have indicated which subjects a textbook on international economics should include. The exposition in the rest of the book falls into three parts, each dealing with a central aspect of economic relations among nations and the dependence of nations.

Chapters 2 to 6 deal with *real* transactions: the flows of goods, services and production factors across national borders. In this connection, the theories of international *trade* have been divided into two chapters: Chapter 2 presents classical foreign trade theory as developed by the classical and neoclassical economists who attempt to explain international trade patterns in terms of different national production factor endowments, while Chapter 3 supplements this with an outline of recent foreign trade theory, which focuses more on conditions at firm and industrial levels in order to explain foreign trade. Chapter 4 looks at international factor movements and the organizational forms that these may assume, including investments by multinational firms. Chapter 5 deals with the tools of international trade policy as well as their welfare effects and distributional consequences. Chapter 6 looks at some developmental trends in trade policy, partly in a multilateral, global perspective and partly in a regional perspective, which involves a description of the functioning and effects of trade agreements.

Chapters 7 to 9 deal with the *monetary* aspect of international transactions. Chapter 7 focuses on the balance of payments and the financial position of a nation *vis-à-vis* the rest of the world. Some features of international development are included and the chapter also contains a discussion of the question of whether foreign debt is a burden and a problem to debtor nations. Chapter 8 deals with exchange markets and gives a preliminary overview of previous and current exchange rate systems. In addition, this chapter describes price formation in the spot market and finally discusses the long-term determination of exchange rates. Chapter 9 deals with international capital markets and explains capital movements; it then looks at forward exchange markets, and finally the links combining exchange rates, interest rates and inflation rates can be clarified.

The remainder of the book, Chapters 10 to 14, focus on the management of a small open economy, i.e. on the macro-perspective. Chapter 10 is based on the assumption of fixed real exchange rates and shows how monetary and fiscal policies, under this assumption, affect economic key variables like incomes, employment and the balance of payments. Chapter 11 deals with policies affecting competitiveness, i.e. incomes and exchange policies, and with the differences and similarities between their effects, in particular between the ways in which they affect inflation and distribution. Chapter 12 is based on the assumption of floating exchange rates. The chapter opens with a discussion of how fluctuations in economic activity are transferred among countries with this kind of exchange rate system. The introduction is followed by an examination of the tools available for economic management, viz. monetary and fiscal policies, and the subsequent conclusions are compared to those reached in Chapter 10. Finally, we present some reasons for the fluctuation of exchange rates.

The exposition in Chapter 13 is more realistic in that it includes an inflationary aspect. The assumption of variable price levels is introduced with respect to both fixed and floating exchange rates, and the kinds of management problems that may be caused by variable price levels are discussed. In addition, the chapter presents arguments for and against floating exchange rates. Finally, Chapter 14 extends economic management to the world economy. The G7 model provides the initial basis of the discussion: the world's leading countries attempt to design world development. The chapter introduces models of coordination of international economic policy. Finally, the experience gained so far from international economic management is summed up and future possibilities are discussed.

REFERENCES

Maddison, J. (1982), *Phases of Capitalist Development*, Oxford University Press, New York.

MITI (1982), *Economic Security of Japan*, Japan Ministry of Trade and Industry, Tokyo.

Ricardo, David (1817), *The Principles of Political Economy and Taxation*, Everyman's Library, New York, 1965.

Smith, Adam (1776), *The Wealth of Nations*, The Modern Library, New York, 1937.

TRADE THEORY: COMPARATIVE ADVANTAGES

This chapter and the following one examine two principal questions: why do countries trade with each other and how does it affect them? In themselves these questions do not differ from the ones that might be posed in connection with interregional domestic trade. Two circumstances have, however, contributed to the development of a specifically international trade theory. Firstly, the cross-border mobility of factors of production is low, consequently, the movement of goods has a decisive influence on the efficiency of the exploitation of *national* resources. Secondly, countries are inclined to impose import restrictions in order to increase domestic production and employment. If the consequences of such political intervention are to be assessed, international trade theory becomes indispensable.

This chapter examines earlier trade theory, which explains international trade in terms of national differences: countries differ with respect to fundamental conditions of production, such as weather conditions, amounts of labour, capital and natural resources, which provide each country with a set of comparative advantages. The following chapter concentrates on modern trade theory, which is capable of explaining the vast part of international trade which takes place among countries with fairly similar production conditions, as is the case in the Western world. The theory explains this in terms of the set of *competitive advantages* which individual firms or industries have developed over time. Such a development is, in particular, possible in markets with imperfect competition.

This chapter is organized chronologically. It opens with an exposition of earlier trade theory, which developed over a period of 200 years during which the original model from the eighteenth century was increasingly refined. The fundamental features of the theory were carved out by classical economists in their refutation of mercantilist trade theory. Sections 2.2 and 2.3 deal with this classical explanation for trade, the key phrase of which is international specialization in the production of goods—each country exploiting its set of comparative advantages. Neoclassical theory, which is presented in Sections 2.4 and 2.5, explains this specialization in terms of the international differences in factor endowment. This leads to an integrated theory allowing for the analysis of the distributional consequences of trade. An evaluation of the empirical validity of the theories concludes the chapter.

2.1   THE MERCANTILISTS

The mercantilists were a varied crowd of writers who expatiated on economic conditions in the seventeenth and eighteenth centuries in various booklets, pamphlets and the like. Mercantilism had no unifying doctrine but the focus of these writings was on international economy. To the mercantilists gold and silver, the means of payment of those days, were expressions of wealth. The national wealth of a country was identical with the amount of gold and silver at its disposal. Consequently, a country could increase its wealth by maintaining a positive balance of trade: an export surplus would be paid for in precious metals.

In general, the mercantilist writers held the view that equilibrium on a country's balance of payments was of no significance for that country since the gold receipts from exports were matched completely by import expenditure. A balance of payments surplus, however, would increase wealth and have the further advantage of forcing other countries into a deficit and thus decreasing their wealth.

For this reason the mercantilist writers were concerned with finding out how a country might increase its export surplus. The answer which they gave was that countries should import inexpensive raw materials while exporting expensive, manufactured goods: the more a country could sell abroad of the value added domestically, the wealthier it would become. They therefore proposed to the rulers of the time that they should restrict imports and stimulate exports through strict foreign trade regulations. Tight import restrictions were imposed on (expensive) luxury goods, while the exports of manufactured goods as well as the imports of raw materials were encouraged through government subsidies and the establishment of governmental or state-subsidized commercial enterprises and production firms. Nevertheless, mercantilist philosophy may not have been all that silly. If some of a country's resources are idle, a money supply increase may affect the level of economic activity.

The mercantilist ideas never died completely. Even today, it is possible to find quite strong elements which are based on them, such as so-called neoprotectionism. Chapter 6 takes a look at this phenomenon. In the course of time the fundamental idea of strong government management of the economy has had its ups and downs. Towards the end of the twentieth century it is very much alive and kicking.

2.2   ADAM SMITH: ABSOLUTE ADVANTAGES

It was the Scotsman Adam Smith who delivered the crucial blow to the mercantilists. Adam Smith (1712–90) was a professor of moral philosophy in Glasgow and is generally considered to be the founding father of economics. His principal work, *The Wealth of Nations*, from 1776, was the first major survey of economics and was characterized by a fundamentally liberal attitude. In particular, Adam Smith opposed the view that global wealth is independent of trade and the volume of trade. He showed how total production and wealth would increase in countries that specialized in the production and exports of the goods that they produced most efficiently. If these countries used their export receipts to pay for the imports of goods that they produced less efficiently or could not produce at all, then this would ensure that they would spend their productive resources where the gains would be the largest.

In Table 2.1 a fictitious example illustrates the argument with figures. The table shows labour productivity in the production of bacon and cloth in the UK and Denmark: a Dane produces less cloth in a working day than does someone in the UK, but he produces more bacon.

Table 2.1 Absolute advantages

Country	Production per person per working day	
	Cloth	Bacon
Denmark	10 m	8 kg
UK	12 m	4 kg

Consequently, Denmark has an absolute advantage in the production of bacon while the UK has an absolute advantage in the production of cloth. If, in the initial state, both countries produce goods of both kinds, then reallocating production factors from the production of cloth to the production of bacon in the case of Denmark, and vice versa in the case of the UK, will result in specialization gains. Each time both countries reallocate one person, cloth production increases by $12-10=2$ metres and bacon production by $8-4=4$ kilograms. So the total volume of production to be shared by the two countries will have increased.

According to Adam Smith free trade automatically results in specialization: goods will be produced where productivity is the highest and costs consequently the lowest. In other words, freedom of competition ensures that goods are produced at the lowest costs possible in precisely the same way as competition in individual countries does. Politically, the conclusion drawn from the economic analysis was that a policy of *laissez-faire* should be given priority.

On Adam Smith's analysis, international trade would only take place if a country had at least one absolute advantage, i.e. one industry in which labour productivity was higher than in any other country. Table 2.2 illustrates a situation in which this is *not* the case: in both industries the absolute advantage lies with Denmark since labour productivity in both of them is twice as high as in the UK. Again, if, as above, one person is reallocated to cloth production in the UK, and vice versa in Denmark, cloth production will change by $12-24=-12$ metres of cloth, while bacon production will increase by $8-4=4$ kilograms. So the result is more bacon but less cloth. Later on we shall see that, in this case, international specialization holds no advantages.

Table 2.2 Absolutely no advantages

Country	Production per person per working day	
	Cloth	Bacon
Denmark	24 m	8 kg
UK	12 m	4 kg

2.3 DAVID RICARDO: COMPARATIVE ADVANTAGES

Nevertheless, the situation is not beyond imagination in which a highly developed country is the best at producing both kinds of goods and in which international trade still holds its advantages. However, Adam Smith's theory of absolute advantages does not explain why, in a situation of this kind, it would still pay for two countries to trade with each other. Forty years were to pass from the publication of Adam Smith's work until a theoretically fully satisfactory explanation for trade was delivered by David Ricardo (1772–1823), an English economist and landowner. The international trade theory which he launched is to be found in his principal

Table 2.3   Comparative advantages

| Country | Production per person per working day | |
	Cloth	Bacon
Denmark	16 m	8 kg
UK	12 m	4 kg

work, *The Principles of Political Economy and Taxation*, from 1817. His analysis is restricted to one factor of production, which may have been justifiable at the time since labour was the entirely dominant factor.

David Ricardo showed that trade is not determined by absolute advantages, but by relative ones, for which he coined the term *comparative advantages*. As appears from Table 2.3, in which both the goods and countries of Tables 2.1 and 2.2 have been repeated, the argument is fairly simple: the assumption is that Denmark possesses an absolute advantage in the production of both kinds of goods, but, unlike the situation in Table 2.2, Denmark is not equally better in both industries. In cloth production Danish productivity is 33 per cent higher and in bacon production 100 per cent higher than that in the UK. It is precisely this difference in relative productivity that explains why both countries will profit from trading with each other.

Since UK cloth production is doing relatively better, the UK ought to specialize in this field, while the Danes with their particularly good knack of handling pigs ought to concentrate on this industry. Again, if we imagine that in the UK one person is reallocated from pig production to cloth production, and vice versa in Denmark, the joint specialization gain will be $12 - 16 = -4$ metres of cloth and $8 - 4 = 4$ kilograms of bacon. So the accumulated gain is 4 kilograms of bacon at the expense of 4 metres of cloth.

Would this be an advantage? Yes, it would. Assume that the marginal 8 kilograms of bacon produced in Denmark are shipped to the UK and sold there. For the amount that they fetch it will be possible to buy $(8 \div 4) \times 12 = 24$ metres of cloth, i.e. 50 per cent more than the 16 metres of cloth that the exchange value in Denmark would represent. If we ignore transaction costs, international specialization has increased the consumption possibilities of the Danes by 8 metres of cloth.

Is the implication then that the UK population have been fleeced? The mercantilists claimed so. Nevertheless, this is not the case: in our example the bacon was traded at UK prices, so the people there are just as well off as they were before the transaction took place. Typically, however, such transactions are carried out at relative prices which are somewhere between the price relations in each of the two countries. Consequently, the transaction will make everybody better off, so Adam Smith's theory was extended to include trade between countries of generally high productivity and ones of generally low productivity.

From Figure 2.1 it is obvious that both countries will gain from international trade since their production possibility curves do not coincide with their consumption possibility curves, so both countries will be able to consume beyond their production possibility. First of all, the figure shows the production possibility curve per person employed in each of the two countries. The fully drawn lines are the relevant curves, which show that a Dane can produce either 16 metres of cloth or 8 kilograms of bacon a day (or some combination of these commodities represented by the curve). Someone from the UK can produce 12 metres of cloth or 4 kilograms of bacon. Without trade the two production possibility curves represent the set of consumption compositions which the two countries have to choose from.

However, if it is possible for the Danes to trade at UK prices then this will increase their

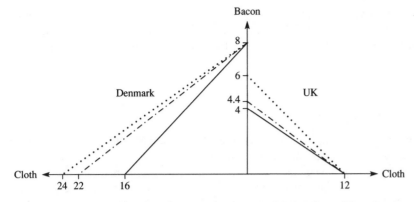

Note: The curves illustrate the situation per person employed. Curves illustrating the situation for the UK as a whole will be further from the origin than the corresponding curves for Denmark since the population of the UK is larger.

Figure 2.1   Production and consumption possibility curves

consumption possibilities since relative prices are not the same in the two countries. In Denmark the exchange value of two metres of cloth is one kilogram of bacon, since one person can produce either 16 metres of cloth or 8 kilograms of bacon. In the UK, by contrast, 3 metres of cloth are worth 1 kilogram of bacon, so relative bacon prices in the two countries are as follows:

$$p^{DK} = \frac{16 \text{ m cloth}}{8 \text{ kg bacon}} = 2 \text{ m cloth per kg bacon}$$

$$p^{UK} = \frac{12 \text{ m cloth}}{4 \text{ kg bacon}} = 3 \text{ m cloth per kg bacon}$$

These prices determine the slopes of the two production possibility curves in Figure 2.1. If the Danes specialize in bacon production, bacon being relatively more expensive in Denmark, they will be able to trade their daily production of 8 kilograms of bacon for 24 metres of cloth in the UK market, which will increase their consumption possibilities from the fully drawn curve to the dotted curve. Likewise, the UK will be able to increase their consumption to the dotted consumption possibility curve if they specialize in cloth production and trade at Danish prices.

If we ignore the costs incidental to international trade, trade between the two countries will offset the price differences, leaving only one set of international prices. These prices will not correspond precisely to the prices ruling in any one of the two countries prior to trade. As an increasing number of Danes bring bacon to the UK and British people bring cloth to Denmark, these business people will gradually reduce the price of the goods they are offering.

Consequently, the Danes will have to settle for less than 3 and the British for a bit more than 2. The international price will be somewhere in between and, generally, it will be closer to the relative prices of the larger country (in this case, the UK). The dashed lines in Figure 2.1 represent international terms of trade of 2.75 metres of cloth per kilogram of bacon. This allows Denmark to trade its daily production of bacon for 22 metres of cloth, while the UK's daily production of cloth can be traded for 4.4 kilograms of bacon.

On this analysis, the countries whose production and consumption structures differ the most from those of the rest of the world will gain the most from international trade since prior to trade their internal price relationships differ the most from the subsequent international price relations. In sum, comparative advantages result from differences in the relative labour productivity of various industries. Table 2.2 depicts a situation in which this is not the case: Denmark's absolute advantage is the same in both industries, so it will have no comparative advantages to exploit.

2.3.1 The nominal wages trap

David Ricardo's theory is fairly simple and, once you have realized the truth of it, even evident. Nevertheless, when it comes to international trade, views that conflict with his theory can easily be found in almost any newspaper. This goes for such statements as: 'free trade is only of benefit to countries that can hold their own in international competition', 'competition from imports is unfair if they are due to lower wages abroad', 'a great many small countries have no competitive advantages whatsoever', 'the level of efficiency in quite a number of poor countries is so low that they will be outsold if the current restrictions on imports were to be abolished'.

We have shown above that both countries will be able to benefit from trading with each other, but, in order for trade to be reciprocal, wages, prices and exchange rates have to be suitably matched. Using the example in Table 2.3 above, we can illustrate this if, in addition, we assume that, in Denmark, a day wage is DKK 800, in England it is GBP 60, and that the exchange rate is DKK 12 against the GBP. On these assumptions trade will not be reciprocal since the prices of both bacon and cloth will be higher in the UK:

$$P_{Ba}^{DK} = \frac{800}{8} = DKK\ 100$$

$$P_{Ba}^{UK} = 12 \times \frac{60}{4} = DKK\ 180$$

$$P_{Cl}^{DK} = \frac{800}{16} = DKK\ 50$$

$$P_{Cl}^{UK} = 12 \times \frac{60}{12} = DKK\ 60$$

As the UK is uncompetitive in both kinds of goods, prices have to be adjusted. This can be achieved either through devaluation of the GBP or through an increase in the Danish wage level relative to the UK one. For instance, if the value of the GBP decreases, i.e. if the GBP is devalued, and the resulting exchange rate is 9 against the GBP, then $P_{Ba}^{UK} = DKK\ 135$ and $P_{Cl}^{UK} = DKK\ 45$, so trade between the two countries will be resumed in accordance with the pattern described above.

Table 2.3 shows that in the UK the level of real wages is somewhere between 50 per cent and 75 per cent of the Danish one, namely somewhere between the levels of relative productivity in the two industries: if it is above 75 per cent, UK competitiveness in cloth will disappear, and if it is below 50 per cent, Danish competitiveness in bacon will do the same. It is intuitively obvious that real wages will be lower in the country in which the general level of productivity is lower.

As was mentioned above, the claim is often made in industrialized countries that competing with developing countries is impossible since their wage levels are only a fraction of those of the industrialized countries. Contrariwise, developing countries claim that their industries should be protected since productivity is much lower than it is in industrialized countries. David Ricardo's theory shows that both claims are wrong. International trade is determined by relative levels of productivity and wages. Any country can compete successfully internationally if the levels of nominal wages and productivity are reasonably matched for a given exchange rate. Thus the government and the labour market parties have to ensure that they do not walk into the nominal wages trap. If they do, the country will be excluded from the gains of international trade and everybody will be worse off.

2.4 HECKSCHER–OHLIN: FACTOR ENDOWMENTS

David Ricardo's explanation of international trade was based on some ascertained differences in the levels of productivity per person per day in various industries in different countries. However, one might ask what the underlying reason for these differences in labour productivity is. In David Ricardo's model, with only one factor, such differences might be due to differences in climate or in the levels of technological development. However, the differences may also be explained exclusively on the basis of differences in national endowments with factors of production. This was first shown at the beginning of this century by Eli Heckscher and Bertil Ohlin, two Swedish economists. The Heckscher–Ohlin theory, which is presented in this section, is a distinctly neoclassical analysis. Although the original formulation still underlies the theory today, it has been subjected to numerous extensions and refinements over the past half century.

The point of departure of the theory is that countries differ in their endowments with factors of production and that these differences affect costs in individual industries. For example, countries with a great deal of capital are the most efficient producers of capital-intensive industrial products, while agricultural countries with a great deal of farm land are the most efficient producers of foodstuffs.

It is presumably obvious that national endowments with factors of production differ: Figure 2.2 illustrates the extent to which a number of countries differed in their endowments with the three fundamental factors of production—land, labour and capital—in 1978. The sides of the triangle measure the ratio between two factors of production on a logarithmic scale. Therefore countries on a random axis starting from any one of the three corners of the triangle are relatively equally endowed with the two other factors of production. Consequently, France (FRA) has approximately the same distribution between land and labour (land/labour) as the countries as a whole (TOT), namely 0.9 hectare (1 hectare (ha) = 2.47 acres) per person. Jamaica (JAM) and the United States (US) have approximately the same ratio between capital and land (capital/land), namely $13 000 per ha. Both Spain (SPN) and Israel (ISR) have the average capital/labour ratio (capital/labour) of $12 000 per person.

The figure shows that countries in the upper part of the triangle are richly endowed with land, countries in the left-hand corner are labour-abundant, while countries in the right-hand corner are capital-abundant.

2.4.1 The Heckscher–Ohlin Theorem

It is intuitively obvious that if we place individual commodities in the triangle in accordance with the ratio by which the factors enter the production of these commodities then we will receive an impression of how comparative advantages can be derived from national factor endowments. Obviously, Hong Kong (HKG), where land is extremely scarce, cannot have comparative advantages in grain-growing, which must necessarily be placed in the upper part of the triangle, for example in Canada (CAN) or Australia (ASL). Correspondingly, Japan (JAP),

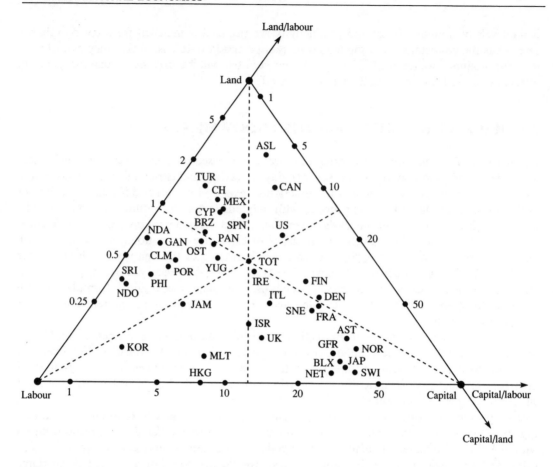

Figure 2.2   Factor endowment triangle—1978
Source: Adapted from Leamer (1987)

Belgium, the Netherlands and Luxembourg (BLX), and others, have comparative advantages in capital-intensive industrial commodities.

If David Ricardo's production function is extended to include three factors, it becomes evident that factor endowments affect comparative advantages:

$$Q = f(\text{labour, capital, land})$$

where the commodity (Q) is produced by means of the factors of labour, capital and land. Labour productivity can now be specified as follows:

$$\frac{Q}{\text{Labour}} = g\left(\frac{\text{capital}}{\text{labour}}, \frac{\text{land}}{\text{labour}}\right)$$

where the amounts of capital and farm land available per person employed affect labour productivity. (Strictly speaking, this formulation presupposes that f is homogeneous of the first degree, i.e. that returns to scale in production are constant so that an increase of x per cent in all input increases production by x per cent.)

In general, the Heckscher–Ohlin theory is presented in a $2 \times 2 \times 2$ version, i.e. in a version with two factors of production, e.g. capital and labour, two commodities, for instance pharmaceuticals (Y) and textiles (X), and two countries, an industrialized country (I) and a developing country (D). As indicated above, two assumptions underlie the theory:

1. Each country has its specific factor endowment. Some are particularly capital-abundant, others labour-abundant, etc.
2. A specific ratio of production factors enters the production of each commodity. For given factor prices, for example, the production of pharmaceuticals is capital-intensive and that of textiles is labour-intensive.

In addition, it is generally assumed that the two commodities are produced under perfect competition, that consumers in the two countries have identical preferences, and that the two countries have access to the same techniques of production. Further, constant returns to scale are assumed. This means that if the contribution of all production factors is increased by 1 per cent then production will rise by 1 per cent. This assumption excludes economies of scale, which are considered in Chapter 3.

Figure 2.3 illustrates the production possibilities with respect to the two commodities. As industrialized countries are more capital-abundant, their advantage lies in the production of capital-intensive pharmaceuticals (Y): in country I the high level of labour productivity pushes the production possibility curve further up the Y axis. With the same production techniques the labour-abundant developing countries have comparative advantages in the production of labour-intensive textiles (X), so their production possibility curve starts further to the right on the X axis.

However, on these assumptions the production possibility curves are no longer linear as in David Ricardo's one-factor model. Assume that in the initial situation only commodity X is produced. As production of the capital-intensive commodity Y is increased, production of the labour-intensive commodity X has to be decreased, and, consequently, the production point moves up along the production possibility curve. Yet the resources released from the production of textiles do not directly match the needs of pharmaceutical production, which has much larger capital requirements. This means that as the nation produces more of commodity Y, it must use resources that become progressively less efficient for the production of that commodity. In consequence, the nation must give up more and more of X to lease just enough resources to produce each additional unit of Y. Increasing opportunity costs and a concave production function is the result.

On these somewhat restrictive conditions the most important features of neoclassical foreign trade theory can be illustrated as in Figure 2.4. Prior to trade the countries are forced to

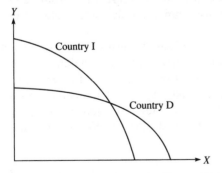

Figure 2.3   Production possibilities in the Heckscher–Ohlin model

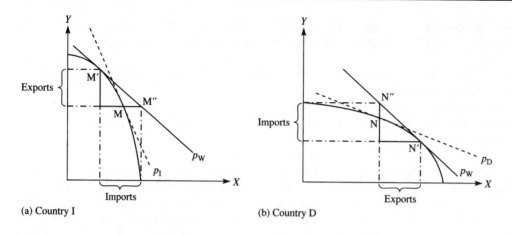

(a) Country I   (b) Country D

Figure 2.4 Specialization advantages in the Heckscher–Ohlin model

consume in accordance with their production possibility curves. Assume that the consumption and production composition of the industrialized country corresponds to the point M, while that of the developing country corresponds to the point N. The slopes of the production possibility curves reflect the exchange value of the two commodities with respect to each other, and thus also the price relationship between them. Since 1 metre of cloth will buy more pharmaceuticals in the industrialized country than in the developing country, i.e. in country I industrial products are cheap as compared to textiles, the price line p_I is steeper than the price line p_D.

In a situation with free trade, international trade levels out these pre-trade price differences, barring the costs incidental to trade. The result is a world market price of p_W, as was illustrated in Figure 2.1, so that trade causes an increase in the price of pharmaceuticals in the industrialized country and an increase in the price of textiles in the developing country.

This change in relative prices as a consequence of trade changes the production composition in the two countries. In the industrialized country production shifts from M to M', i.e. in favour of pharmaceuticals, while it shifts from N to N', i.e. in favour of textiles, in the developing country. Unlike the situation in David Ricardo's model, however, full specialization does not occur, since both kinds of goods are still produced in both countries. This is precisely due to the concave production possibility curves, which reflect that, factor proportions being driven to inefficiency, unit costs in the industry increase with production increases. This is more consistent with actual observations: countries only rarely obtain full specialization.

If the countries exploit the possibilities of trade they are no longer obliged to choose their consumption compositions from their production possibility curves. Instead, making use of the international terms of trade allows them to choose any point on the p_W line. For example, country I may choose the point M'', which is available through exports of industrial goods and imports of textiles. Correspondingly, the point N'' is available to country D if, by contrast, it exports textiles and imports industrial goods. This illustrates the *Heckscher–Ohlin theorem*:

Any country exports goods which have a high content of that country's abundant production factor and imports goods which have a high content of the country's scarce production factor.

2.4.2   The factor price equalization theorem

According to the Heckscher–Ohlin theory international trade increases the consumption possibilities of a country and, consequently, its level of welfare. In this case, however, the conclusion rests on a much more precisely formulated theoretical basis than did the classical theory of comparative advantages. It is therefore possible to draw a whole range of conclusions from the Heckscher–Ohlin theory. We have already mentioned the Heckscher–Ohlin theorem, which offers an explanation for the international pattern of trade. In this section we deal with the factor price equalization theorem, which concerns changes in functional income distribution (i.e. the relative return on production factors) as a consequence of trade.

The income distribution among factors of production is analysed in Figure 2.5, which summarizes the key concepts of the Heckscher–Ohlin theory. The relationship between the prices of the two production factors, i.e. real wages divided by profit rate, w/r, are measured on the abscissa. The relationship between capital and labour (K/L) is measured on the positive branch of the ordinate, while its negative branch measures the relationship between the prices of the finished goods X and Y, viz. P_X/P_Y. As mentioned above, both kinds of goods, X and Y, are produced by means of the production factors of labour and capital, and the lines XX' and YY' express the production functions $Y(K,L)$ and $X(K,L)$. The lines are upward sloping since, if wages increase relative to profit rates, then a more capital-intensive production method will be introduced, and the K/L ratio of production will increase. This kind of factor substitution in production is an assumption which is absolutely central to neoclassical theory. The fact that the line YY' is above the line XX' expresses the greater capital intensity of the production of Y as compared to that of X: the capital intensity K/L is higher for any value of w/r. As regards the factor endowments of the two countries, country D is more sparingly endowed with capital, symbolized by the horizontal line DD', than country I, whose more abundant capital endowment is symbolized by the line II'.

If prices are determined by the price mechanism, a set of factor prices exist which allow exactly the full employment of factors in the economy before trade. Assume this to happen at

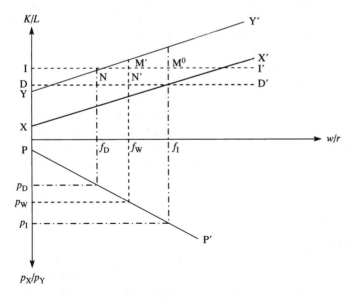

Figure 2.5   Factor price equalization

point N in country D at the relative factor price (w/r) of f_D. Since N states the average K/L ratio in the economy it has to be between the lines XX' and YY'. Correspondingly, the relative factor price is f_I in country I given an average K/L ratio at M.

In a situation without trade, wage earners obtain a higher level of remuneration in the capital-abundant country I, where labour is a relatively scarce factor. It is immediately obvious that production of the labour-intensive commodity X is relatively more expensive in country I, where labour is relatively expensive. The line PP' in the lower half of Figure 2.5 illustrates this argument. By contrast, production of the labour-intensive goods is relatively cheap in country D, where labour is abundant.

If the countries start trading with each other the relative prices of goods are equalized, thus leading to a common world market price of p_W. Since the capital-intensive commodity Y is more expensive in the world market, country I exports commodity Y and imports commodity X. The increase in the production of Y causes a derived demand for capital, while the demand for labour decreases. As a result w/r decreases and f_I shifts to the left. In entirely parallel fashion, w/r increases in the developing country as a result of the increased production of commodity X and f_D shifts to the right.

Figure 2.5 shows that trade induces equalization of relative factor prices and that f_W holds for both countries. This illustrates the *factor price equalization theorem*:

Trade in goods and services induces equalization of differences among countries in relative factor prices.

One implication of the theorem is that factor prices are equalized solely as a consequence of trade in goods. It is therefore not necessary for factors of production to move among countries in order to exploit comparative advantages in factor endowments. Commodity movements can replace factor movements since commodities contain production factors, so to speak, to varying degrees. Factor movements among countries being relatively limited, this is of great significance with respect to the distribution of return among factors. In Chapter 4 we revert to this subject.

Paul Samuelson (1949) showed that equalization also applies to absolute factor prices. While it is immediately comprehensible that imports of textiles into industrialized countries reduce the demand for labour and hence the relative remuneration of labour in industrialized countries, it may be more difficult to accept absolute factor price equalization, which implies the same hourly remuneration in industrialized and developing countries. In fact, what recent years have actually shown is a tendency in the direction of increasing the significant absolute difference still persisting between industrialized countries and many of the world's poorest countries. Of course, this is due to the fact that the assumptions of the Heckscher–Ohlin model are not satisfied. Apart from the restrictions on free trade among industrialized and developing countries, the assumptions relating to identical technology and homogeneous labour are not satisfied. In the industrialized countries labour is much more efficient and better educated, and labour productivity is higher because of more advanced technology and better production management.

2.4.3   The Stolper–Samuelson theorem

Above, we have seen how trade affects factor prices in both countries. From the one-to-one correspondence holding between prices in the commodity market and prices in the factor market (the line PP' in Figure 2.5) it is easy to see that changes in demand affect the distribution between the two factors of production. With trade, the demand in country D for the labour-intensive commodity increases as a consequence of exports. This leads to an increase in the price of commodity X and to a relative increase in the demand for labour, labour being applied intensively in the production of X, and hence to an increase in wages relative to return on capital. This effect is reinforced as the imports of capital-intensive goods simultaneously reduce the demand for capital and, consequently, the remuneration of this factor.

In country I trade increases the demand for commodity Y, thus leading to an increase in the demand for capital, which is employed intensively in the production of Y, and to an increase in the relative remuneration of capital. This illustrates the *Stolper–Samuelson theorem* (1941):

Remuneration increases as regards the factor that is employed the most intensively in the commodity whose price increases.

Changes in demand and, by implication, in the prices of commodities have considerable distributional consequences. Obviously, it comes as no surprise that organized labour in industrialized countries often fights competition from abroad. When imports of textiles and other labour-intensive products are reduced through import restrictions in industrialized countries, remuneration of labour increases.

2.5   MODEL EXTENSIONS

The neoclassical analysis described above is a powerful tool which leads to a great many clear-cut and unambiguous conclusions. As is apparent from the next section, the conclusions are not always quite in agreement with the actual development of the economy, the reason being, of course, that reality contains more aspects than the assumptions of the Heckscher–Ohlin theory take into account. In this section some of the assumptions are weakened but the assumption of *perfect competition* is not abandoned until Chapter 3.

According to the theory, relative prices are equalized in both factor markets and commodity markets (see f_W and P_W in Figure 2.5). If we take into account transportation and other *trade costs*, the amount of trade is reduced and no full equalization of commodity prices and, consequently, of factor prices takes place.

We assumed that the two countries applied *identical technologies* in their production of the two commodities. In fact, however, developing countries often use a primitive technology with a considerably lower level of productivity than that of the advanced technology of the industrialized countries. In addition, labour in the industrialized countries is better educated and more efficient. Consequently, labour productivity in the developing countries is often no more than a fraction of productivity in the industrialized countries, and this is reflected in a correspondingly lower wage level, as was seen in David Ricardo's theory. Commodity trade cannot equalize these *absolute* wage and income differences between industrialized and developing countries, which are rooted in technological and educational differences. However, the analysis of Figure 2.5 is fully valid, given the modification that only *relative* factor price differences are equalized.

The Heckscher–Ohlin model is static since we assumed a given factor endowment. Over a period of time, however, demographic development changes the labour supply, just as net investments may alter the amount of real capital. How does such a *dynamic process* affect production, distribution and trade?

Consider a small developing country which cannot affect international prices and whose demographic development results in a marked increase in labour supply, while the amount of capital is assumed to be constant. In Figure 2.5 the curve DD′ shifts downwards since the amount of capital per worker is reduced. World market prices being left unaffected, relative factor prices (f_W) remain unaffected, too, and N' shifts downwards towards the curve XX'. Therefore a shift in production away from the capital-intensive commodity Y and towards the labour-intensive commodity X takes place. This yields the somewhat paradoxical result that an unbalanced growth in factor supply leads to a fall in the production of one of the commodities. This illustrates the *Rybczynski theorem* (1955):

Growth in the supply of one factor of production results in a decrease in the production of the commodity that employs the other factor the most intensively.

As production of the labour-intensive commodity increases and the capital-intensive one decreases, an increase in international trade is derived, if we assume that the demand structure in country D remains unaffected in respect of the two commodities. If, however, the K/L ratio had been increased through a rise in investments, production would have shifted towards the capital-intensive commodity. This would have made country D more similar to country I and would have reduced the need for trade.

In sum, an unbalanced growth in factor endowments may be either *trade expanding* or *trade reducing*. In the case of industrialized countries, the reverse situation holds: an increase in the K/L ratio strengthens their comparative advantages and, in turn, increases trade, while a fall in the K/L ratio reduces trade.

In the case of the Heckscher–Ohlin theory above, we explicitly assumed that *preference structures* were identical in the two countries involved. This situation can by no means be taken for granted, however, and how do changes in the structures affect trade? Figure 2.6 illustrates this: we assume that technologies and factor equipments are identical in the two countries, e.g. France and the UK, which yields identical production possibility curves. If, likewise, their demand structures are identical, then, prior to trade, the price relationship in the two countries is also identical, so there is no basis for trade. For example, each country both produces and consumes at E_0.

Assume that France has a larger consumption of clothes and the UK a larger consumption of pharmaceuticals. In a situation with free trade these differences in consumption structure do not necessarily result in differences in production composition in the two countries. If we assume production is at E_0, consumption in the two countries will be placed on the

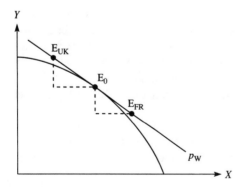

Figure 2.6 Differences in demand structure.
Source: MacDougall (1951).

international price curve p_W. The conditions of production being identical, the UK's imports of pharmaceuticals and exports of textiles are in this case solely the result of differences in demand structures.

2.6 THEORY AND EMPIRICAL VALIDITY

In his explanation of patterns of trade and the advantages of international trade, David Ricardo focused on productivity differences among countries. His theory is simple and elegant, but is it also capable of explaining the actual development in trade?

The answer is affirmative: all analyses show a strong correlation between productivity in individual industries and their share of exports. Figure 2.7 presents the results from the first investigation of this area. In the case of 20 industries in the United States and UK, MacDougall (1951) compared average labour productivity (AP) and export volume with those of third countries. The figure shows a clear positive correlation between relative labour productivity in individual industries and their relative export volumes. This is precisely what David Ricardo's theory predicts. For instance, the United States has a larger volume of exports of cars and steel than does the UK, while the volume of UK exports of margarine and textiles is larger than that of the United States. This reflects the fact that American labour productivity is about three times as high in the steel and car industries, but only slightly higher than in the UK as regards the production of margarine and textiles.

The figure also illustrates that *comparative* and not *absolute* advantages are decisive for trade. In all industries, American labour productivity is higher, so the United States enjoys the absolute advantage. However, at that time American real wages were about twice as high as in the UK, so the UK had the comparative advantage in the industries in which the American level of productivity was not twice as high as the UK level of productivity. It appears that in those industries in which the American export is bigger, American productivity is also more than twice UK productivity Nonetheless, the figure also indicates a weakness in David Ricardo's model. Comparative advantages do not result in full specialization: both countries maintain a certain volume of exports in the industries in which they have a comparative disadvantage. The

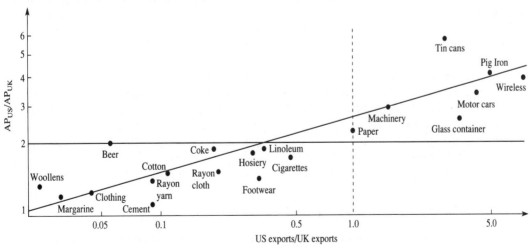

Figure 2.7 Comparative advantages in the United States and England
Source: MacDougal (1951)

lack of perfect competition in these industrial markets may be an explanation. Imperfect competition often leads to intra-industrial trade. This is discussed in Chapter 3.

2.6.1   Leontief's paradox

The American economist Wassily Leontief was the first to test the factor endowment theory. He did so at the beginning of the fifties and the result was negative. Leontief investigated American foreign trade in order to examine the Heckscher–Ohlin theorem, according to which the capital-abundant United States ought to be an exporter of capital-intensive goods and an importer of labour-intensive ones. Leontief's result (1956) was paradoxical: American imports contained 30 per cent more capital per labour unit than American exports did.

Since that time, several explanations have been offered for this paradox. One explanation holds that American labour is more efficient because it is better trained and educated. If education is considered an investment and if a part of wages is considered remuneration to the capital invested in education, then American exports are more capital-intensive than Leontief's calculations showed.

Another explanation points to the technological gap existing between the United States and its trading partners. The result of this gap is that the United States primarily exports highly advanced products, and often patented ones. Obviously, there is foreign demand for these, irrespective of their factor intensity. Research and product development being highly labour-intensive, the technology gap results in labour-intensive exports. It stands to reason that there is a close connection between the level of education, on the one hand, and research and product development efforts, on the other. To some extent the technology gap is a result of the investments in education mentioned above.

A third explanation is that, in fact, the world actually offers more than two factors of production. It also offers raw materials, for example. The United States being relatively poor in some raw materials, imports commodities with a large content of raw materials. However, this also basically forces the United States to import capital-intensive goods since mining, oil extraction, etc., are highly capital-intensive.

In fact, establishing the capital content of a commodity requires very precise measuring. Later investigations have shown that precise measurements of the capital content of imported and exported goods resolve the paradox and that commodities flow as stated by the theory.

The US Department of Labor has carried out an investigation (1980) which confirms the conclusions of the theory with respect to trade between industrialized and developing countries. The more capital-abundant a country is, in terms of US$ per worker, the more capital-intensive its exports are as compared to its imports. This is shown in Figure 2.8.

The vertical axis measures capital intensity in the exports of a country relative to capital intensity in its imports. Korea being at 0.5 illustrates that the capital intensity of its exports are half that of its imports. Basically, Korea imports capital and exports labour. The factor endowment theory is confirmed by the figure in that countries like India, Brazil and Hong Kong, which are poor in capital, primarily export labour-intensive goods, while countries like Canada and Sweden, which are capital-abundant, primarily export capital-intensive goods.

2.6.2   Explaining world trade

For the time being, the classical and neoclassical theories of trade cannot be invalidated on the basis of Leontief's doubts. However, they only explain the part of world trade that takes place between countries with widely diverging factor equipments, for instance between developing

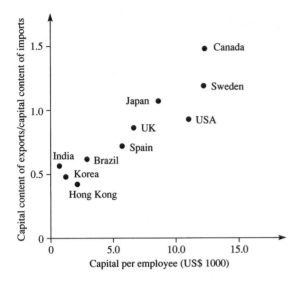

Figure 2.8   An illustration of the factor endowment theory
        Source: US Department of Labor (1980).

and industrialized countries. Table 2.4 shows that this is characteristic of little more than one third of world trade, while trade among industrialized countries is responsible for almost half of world trade. The industrialized countries may be differently equipped with natural resources, but their capital equipments are rather homogeneous (see Figure 2.2). Differences in factor endowment can hardly offer an explanation for the absolutely predominant trade in industrial goods.

In addition, examining individual industries leaves the impression that, among the

Table 2.4   Network of world trade, 1991, by groups of countries (%)

Origin	Destination				
	Industrialized countries	*OPEC*	*Developing countries*	*Socialist countries*	*World*
Industrialized countries	55.0	2.5	11.3	2.3	71.7
OPEC	3.0	0.1	1.0	0.1	4.7
Developing countries	10.1	0.7	4.1	1.3	16.4
Socialist countries	2.8	0.1	1.9	2.2	7.1
World	70.9	3.4	18.5	5.9	100

Note: Figures are compiled from the source, minor imprecisions carried over.
Source: UNCTAD (1993).

industrialized countries, goods are sold in all directions: German factories buy measuring equipment from Dutch suppliers, while equipment of the same kind is bought in Germany by Dutch firms; Swedes buy Danish textiles, and vice versa. If trading countries have approximately identical factor endowment structures, the question of who develops and produces which products receives an arbitrary answer, just like the question of what trade pattern applies among these countries.

Since the sixties a number of theories of international trade have been proposed, which supplement the traditional ones. While, in this chapter, trade has been explained in terms of the comparative advantages of individual countries, recent theories are founded on the assumption that individual firms or industries can establish competitive advantages.

SUMMARY

1. The concept of comparative advantages relates to national resources. For centuries comparative advantages have been scrutinized both from a theory point of view and from a policy point of view.
2. Opposing earlier mercantilist theory, Adam Smith formulated the 'absolute advantages' explanation of foreign trade: a country would export if and only if its labour productivity in one or more products was higher than that of any other country.
3. David Ricardo proved that trade is determined by relative, or comparative, advantages, assuming that wage levels and/or exchange rates adapted sufficiently.
4. Heckscher and Ohlin introduced neoclassical trade theory and showed that trade is determined by factor proportions: each country will export goods with a high content of its abundant factor. In this process, relative factor prices are equalized.
5. Leontief unsuccessfully tested the Heckscher–Ohlin model, thus giving name to the Leontief paradox, which since then has led to numerous further tests.
6. Theories dealing with comparative advantages mainly attempt to explain trade among countries with widely different factor endowments, which amounts to 30–40 per cent of world trade.

REFERENCES AND FURTHER READING

Heckscher, E. F. (1919), 'Utrikeshandelns verkan på inkomstfördelingen', *Ekonomisk Tidsskrift*, **21**, 1–32. Reprinted in English translation in Ellis, H. S. and L. A. Metzler (eds) (1950), *Readings in the Theory of International Trade*, Homewood: Ill; Irwin.

Leamer, E. E. (1987), 'Paths of development in the three-factor, *n*-good general equilibrium model', *Journal of Political Economy*, **95** (5), 961–999.

Leontief, W. W. (1956), 'Factor proportions and the structure of American trade: further theoretical and empirical analysis', *Review of Economics and Statistics*, **38**, 386–407.

Lerner, A. P. (1952), 'Factor prices and international trade', *Economica*, Feb., **19** (73), 1–15.

MacDougall, G. D. A. (1951), 'British and American export: a study suggested by the theory of comparative costs', *Economic Journal*, **LXI** (244), 697–724.

Ohlin, B. (1933), *Interregional and International Trade*, Harvard University Press.

Ricardo, D. (1817), *The Principles of Political Economy and Taxation*, Everyman's Library, New York, 1965.

Rybczynski, T. M. (1955), 'Factor endowment and relative commodity prices', *Economica*, **XXII** (84), 336–41.

Samuelson, P. A. (1949), 'International factor-price equalisation once again', *Economic Journal*, **LIX** (234), 181–97.

Smith, A. (1776), *The Wealth of Nations*, The Modern Library, New York, 1937.

Stolper, W. F. and P. A. Samuelson (1941), 'Protection and real wages', *Review of Economic Studies*, **9**, 58–73.

UNCTAD (1993), *Handbook of International Trade and Development Statistics 1992*, United Nations, New York.

US Department of Labor (1980), 'Changes in the international pattern of factor abundance and the composition of trade', Washington DC.

THREE

TRADE THEORY: COMPETITIVE ADVANTAGES

In his *Essays in Positive Economics* from 1953 Milton Friedman claims that the real test of any theory is the exactness of its predictions rather than the realism of its assumptions. Therefore, in considering the international trade theory which reigned supreme until 1980, i.e. the Heckscher–Ohlin theory, we should, in Milton Friedman's words, not worry about the lacking realism of the assumptions—everybody seems to agree on this point—but instead worry about the ability of the theory to explain and predict reality. As shown in the final section of Chapter 2, 'theory and empirical validity', the results are mixed. The weak explanatory force may follow from the fact that central assumptions had not been satisfied. Consequently, there may be a need for examining the specific assumptions more closely.

As early as in the sixties a series of attempts were made to disengage international trade theory from the neoclassical framework: Vernon (1966) with its emphasis on differences in production techniques and Linder (1961) with its emphasis on demand are both examples of these attempts. However, the disengagement process was not systematized until around 1980 with the arrival of the so-called *new international trade theory*. This theory was inspired by industrial economics and attached great importance to imperfect competition caused by economies of scale and product differentiation.

In this chapter our main purpose is to focus on contributions made by theoretical development. The contributions of interest are able to explain international trade on the basis of theories that differ from those of the Heckscher–Ohlin and Ricardo models. When assumptions are shifted from perfect competition, the models of interest will be ones that focus on *similarities among countries* rather than *differences between them*. Likewise, the factors of interest will be at the level of *industry or firm* rather than *national* ones.

In the Heckscher–Ohlin theory comparative advantages and hence national differences were determined solely on the basis of differences in national factor endowments. Quite generally, comparative advantages (and disadvantages) are also determined by national differences in technological knowledge and consumption patterns. These cause factor prices and production methods to differ among countries so that some countries have cost advantages on some products and cost disadvantages on others.

By contrast, competitive advantages (or disadvantages) are factors that lend a firm or an industry with some competitive advantages (disadvantages) relative to the competition abroad. These advantages may result from the history of the firm (chance), from product or process development, from the firm's choice of cost and marketing strategy, from the synergy effect caused by the firms in the industry, etc. In general, perfect competition cannot be assumed in

Table 3.1. Economies of scale and product differentiation

	No economies of scale	*Economies of scale*
Homogeneous products	Chapter 2: perfect competition and inter-industry trade	Sections 3.1 and 3.2: perfect competition and monopoly, inter-industry trade Section 3.3: oligopoly and intra-industry trade
Heterogeneous products	Section 3.5: perfect competition and intra-industry trade	Section 3.4: Monopolistic competition and intra-industry trade Section 3.6: oligopoly and intra-industry trade

such cases, since, under perfect competition, firms are assumed to have (largely) identical production conditions, and trade is explained by factors that influence all firms in the industry to the same extent. Imperfect competition, on the other hand, focuses on the firm. Imperfect competition may be ascribed to two main elements: economies of scale and product differentiation (Table 3.1), which also indicates the division of this chapter into sections.

In a situation with a *homogeneous* product and *constant returns to scale* the conditions required for perfect competition are satisfied. In a competitive environment of this kind individual firms cannot possess specific competitive advantages and the pattern of international trade will be exclusively determined by national characteristics, as discussed in Chapter 2. The kind of international trade involved when countries export from some industries and import from others is called *inter-industry trade*. However, perfect competition breaks down if *economies of scale* are available, unless they are external to the firm with national firms in an industry benefiting each other. This situation is analysed in Section 3.1. Firm-internal economies of scale will often occur in small national markets and lead to the emergence of national monopolies, but under global free trade perfect competition will re-emerge. However, if the economies of scale are of a global nature the result will be a global monopoly. These two situations are dealt with in Section 3.2. If the size of the global market relative to the economies of scale leaves room for very few producers the market structure will be oligopolistic. While the situations discussed in Section 3.2 lead to inter-industry trade, oligopoly *may*, as illustrated in Section 3.3, result in a country's exporting and importing the same kinds of products. This kind of bilateral trade, which is particularly surprising in the case of homogeneous products, is termed *intra-industry trade*.

If the products of an industry are *differentiated*, economies of scale are available, and if, in addition, no barriers to entry into the industry exist, then monopolistic competition will result; oligopoly will be the result if the barriers are considerable. Both situations lead to intra-industry trade. The case of monopolistic competition is analysed in Section 3.4. Section 3.6 touches on the case of oligopoly in a dynamic situation with technological progress, and Section 3.5 on product differentiation without economies of scale. The latter case is particularly fit for illustrating trade among industrialized countries and less developed ones because the exchange of goods within industries takes place in the form of product differentiation according to quality. The distinction between inter-industrial and intra-industry trade is completed in Section 3.7. This final section also shows that comparative and competitive advantages often accompany each other in the explanation of a country's international trade pattern. Finally, the appendix to this chapter provides a survey of international trade theory.

3.1 ECONOMIES OF SCALE EXTERNAL TO THE FIRM

We are faced with *industrial* or *external* economies of scale if unit costs in individual firms fall when total production in the industry rises. Various reasons may underlie industrial economies of scale. Joint localization may provide the firms in an industry with the advantage of similarly trained labour. Labour trained in one firm can be hired by other firms in the same industry in the region. At the same time the region will be attractive to the individual worker, as total demand for their specific qualifications is large and reduces the probability of unemployment. A typical example of an industry in which these considerations play a role is the production of semi-conductors in Silicon Valley in California. (For present purposes we are only concerned with industrial economies of scale of a national nature. With respect to the international perspective, see Section 3.6.)

At the same time the geographical concentration and the size of the industry may provide fertile soil for a range of services from which all firms may profit. In addition, suppliers of raw materials, semi-manufactured goods, production equipment, etc., will be able to supply large quantities, allowing them economies of scale, and there will be room for a larger number of competitors than would otherwise have been the case, which increases competition and reduces prices. One example of an industry in which dynamics of this kind have led to a situation with merely one dominant producer is the pharmaceutical firm Novo-Nordisk in Denmark. One of the reasons for the international position of this firm within the fields of enzyme and insulin production is the early existence of well-developed slaughtering, dairy and beer production industries in Denmark (Porter 1990). The development of advanced fermentation methods for beer production at the Carlsberg laboratories and the development of an advanced machine industry with deliveries to dairies and slaughterhouses provided a solid foundation for the establishment of Novo-Nordisk: together, these different firms (dairies, slaughterhouses, producers of refrigerating equipment, breweries, enzyme and insulin producers) form a *cluster* in which progress in one part supports progress in another.

Although economies of scale usually lead to imperfect competition, this is *not necessarily* the result in the case of industrial economies of scale. In this section, we shall, for the sake of simplicity, assume perfect competition and hence constant returns to scale at firm level. Figure 3.1 illustrates cost curves with industrial economies of scale, e.g. in the case of production of insulin.

In a situation *without trade* in the two countries under consideration, viz. H and F, prices will, in the long run, correspond to minimum total unit costs since perfect competition excludes excess profits. It might be asked whether the implication is that pre-trade prices are identical in the two countries. If the two countries have identical levels of demand, the size of the populations, income distribution and preferences in the two countries being identical, then the answer to this question is the affirmative. Under these conditions the two industries are of the same size in the two countries (Q_0 in Figure 3.1(a) in the case of insulin production), and, consequently, the producers in the two countries will be at the same point on the same unit cost curve (AC) represented in Figure 3.1(b), e.g. at the point $H_0 = F_0$. However, if one of the countries has a higher level of demand for insulin, then it will be in a better position to exploit the industrial economies of scale (point H_1 in Figure 3.1) and to obtain lower pre-trade prices. In the case of identical pre-trade prices *international specialization* can be explained as pure

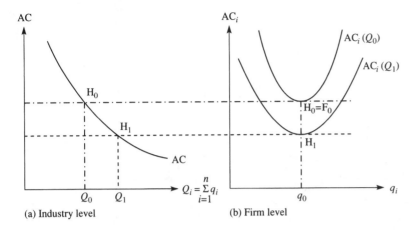

Figure 3.1   Industrial economies of scale

chance, since it will be the firms in the country that initiates production expansion that will have the lower production costs.

Irrespective of whether the cause for specialization is chance or differences in the demand structure, the result will be a global gain since the concentration of insulin production in one country will allow it to be produced with lower factor input. It is not only in the country with economies of scale that a welfare gain can be reaped. On account of economies of scale, the price of insulin will go down so that the productivity gain will accrue to consumers and, consequently, be transmitted to trade partners (Helpman and Krugman 1986). (It should be added, however, that Helpman and Krugman (1986) also show that the country that does not specialize in the production with industrial economies of scale *may* have a welfare loss since two opposing effects have to be considered: a fall in productivity and lower import prices.)

It should be emphasized that this result presupposes perfect competition. For example, if insulin producers possess market power then the welfare result in the case of each of the two countries depends on who reaps the monopoly profit. However, since monopoly and imperfect competition tend to be caused not by *firm external* economies of scale but rather by *firm internal* ones, we now turn to the latter case.

3.2   MONOPOLY: ECONOMIES OF SCALE INTERNAL TO THE FIRM

Internal economies of scale occur when the long-run unit cost curve decreases. This is explained by a more elaborated division of labour at a higher production potential. In such a situation it is not possible to maintain perfect competition. Consequently, we must address the issue of imperfect competition, and in this section we take a look at the case of monopoly.

3.2.1   National economies of scale

Small, closed national markets make national monopolies possible; Figure 3.2 shows how free trade can destroy them. D_H indicates domestic demand for cement, for example, which is considered a homogeneous product in this case. Given the marginal cost curve (MC) and the unit cost curve (AC), we see that without international trade a monopolistic situation results, the unit price being P_H and the quantity q_H on the assumption that marginal revenue (MR)

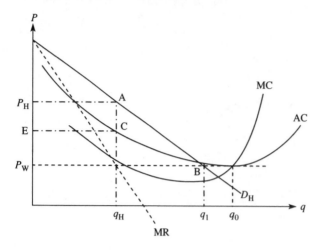

Figure 3.2 Monopoly destruction

equals marginal costs (MC). Since the price is higher than unit costs a monopoly profit of P_HACE is reaped.

If the cost curves are *common* to all producers of cement irrespective of nationality, then a production of q_0 tonnes of cement from each producer is required if the economies of scale are to be fully exploited. This can take place under free trade if the volume of global demand is so large that the number of producers will ensure perfect competition internationally. In this situation the world market price, excepting transportation costs, will correspond to minimum unit costs, i.e. P_W. Any (surviving) cement producer will then produce the quantity of q_0. However, it is impossible to predict in which countries production will take place. If the producer in H survives the introduction of international trade and increased competition, then according to Figure 3.2 this producer will sell the quantity of q_1 in the home market and export $q_0 - q_1$, since the market will force the producer to act as price taker. By contrast, if cement production ceases in H then country H will import the quantity of q_1 from foreign producers.

It follows that international trade leads to the destruction of national monopolies, to lower prices and to an increase in global efficiency. Whether production is maintained in a country, turning this country into an exporter, or whether it is discontinued, thus turning the country into an importer, is of no consequence to the welfare gain of the country. In both situations the fall in price from P_H to P_W will increase the consumers' surplus by the area of P_HABP_W and reduce the producer's profits by the area of P_HACE, so the net gain will be the area of $ECABP_W$.

3.2.2 Global economies of scale

The possibility that international trade leads to monopoly destruction depends on the volume of global demand compared to the volume of production that would exploit the economies of scale fully. In the following we will consider a situation in which the economies of scale are not fully exploited. This might, for example, be the case of the production of supersonic jet planes with room for 300 passengers (Figure 3.3).

We assume the existence of two countries (H and F) which are identical as regards demand for and costs of supersonic planes. The figure represents the conditions in country H. In the *pre-trade* situation the monopoly price and monopoly quantity in this country are P_H and q_H,

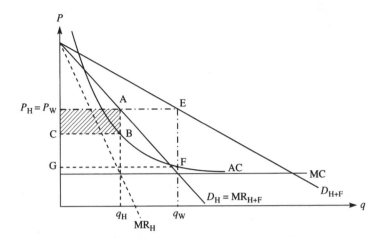

Figure 3.3 A global monopoly

respectively. The figure shows that the monopoly profit corresponds to the area of $P_H ABC$. Price, quantity and profit being the same in country F, international *free trade* will result in *full specialization* in one of the countries since the constantly decreasing unit costs are not exploited in full by total demand. However, we cannot predict where production will be localized, demand and hence pre-trade prices in this example being identical in the two countries. Thus chance determines where production will be localized. If the producer in H captures the world market, his demand curve will be D_{H+F} and marginal revenue will be MR_{H+F}. The quantity sold will be doubled to q_W, the price will remain P_W and the profit will be $P_W EFG$. In the example illustrated in Figure 3.3, where the demand curve is rectilinear and marginal costs are constant, $P_W = P_H = P_F$ and $q_W = 2q_H$.

Globally, the improved exploitation of the economies of scale will result in a welfare gain. Country F, which in this example loses its plane production, will experience a welfare loss which corresponds exactly to the loss of profit from the discontinued plane production: consumers will not experience a loss, the price being the same both before and after trade. In country H, however, the increased profit from plane production reflects a social gain, which is precisely due to the fact that the price does not change. Consequently, this example shows that it may be essential for the producers in a country to enter the world market first because this may enable them to shift monopoly rents from producers in other countries.

The first-mover advantage in the world market is reinforced if not only static economies of scale are involved but also *dynamic* ones in the form of learning effects. This is the case if a large production results in continued reductions in future costs and, consequently, strengthens the competitive advantages of the firm.

3.3 OLIGOPOLY AND TRADE IN HOMOGENEOUS PRODUCTS

Intra-industry trade, i.e. a situation in which one country is both an exporter and an importer of goods from the same product category, typically occurs in the case of differentiated products. However, even in the case of *identical* products intra-industry trade may take place. Brander (1981) and Brander and Krugman (1983) have shown this for a situation with one producer in each of two countries (Figure 3.4).

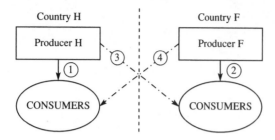

Figure 3.4 The structure of the duopoly model

Figure 3.4 divides the world into two countries, H and F, which each have one producer of the product in question. The producer in H supplies the consumers in H with the product (arrow 1), and, likewise, the producer in F supplies the consumers in F with the same product (arrow 2). Without international trade each country is subject to a monopoly situation (Section 3.2).

As we are interested in competitive rather than comparative advantages we assume that cost structure and demand conditions do not vary between the two countries (Figure 3.5). If we further assume constant marginal costs, the economies of scale (which are no longer global, however) are evident from the fact that the AC curves (which are not included in Figure 3.5) have a downward slope at the points of intersection with the demand curves. Given identical cost structures and demand patterns, prices (P_{H_0} and P_{F_0}, respectively) and quantities (q_{H_0} and q_{F_0}, respectively) are identical before trade.

In a *fully integrated* international market where demand is $D_H + D_F$ a duopoly will exist. Consequently, market equilibrium is determined by the strategic interaction between the two suppliers. Let us consider the simplest case, that of *Cournot competition*, in which the sales of individual producers are determined under the assumption that their counterpart's production is constant. In deciding whether to increase production and sales, the producer in H has to take the fact into consideration that such increases will also increase marginal revenue as compared to a situation in which this producer is the only supplier in the market. The reason is that the fall in prices following a production increase would only partly hurt the producer in H, the market share being less than 100 per cent. A change to free trade will make each of the two duopolists perceive their MR > MC and therefore make them increase production. Consequently, the market price will go down. Perhaps, but this is not necessarily the case, some consumers in H will buy their goods in F and vice versa, but net trade will be nil. In any case, such market entries will be beneficial since the increase in the number of producers will intensify competition and reduce prices.

However, in practice free trade does not lead to full market integration. The costs of transportation between markets are but one reason for this. If we assume that in the duopoly situation outlined above the firms perceive demand in each country as a separate market, then the producer in H will realize that it pays to export to market F (arrow 3 in Figure 3.4) if $P_F > MC +$ transportation costs. Compared to a situation with full market integration, the likelihood that a production increase will be profitable is now stronger: the producer will consider it entirely unlikely that the increase in sales will reduce the current marginal revenue since the producer does not at present supply the market in F and, given market segmentation, the sales increase will not cut the price in the home market. The volume of exports to market F will, at first, be precisely such that the *perceived* marginal revenue (in this case MR_{HF}) corresponds exactly to the marginal costs involved in selling to

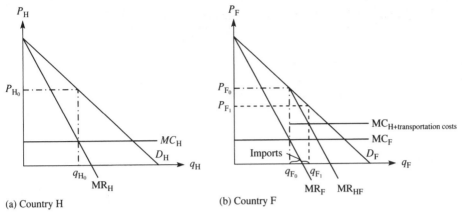

Figure 3.5 A duopoly model with intra-industry trade

this market. As regards sales to the consumers in country H, the considerations of the producer in F will be exactly parallel (arrow 4 in Figure 3.4). Intra-industry trade in identical products will result.

Of course, Cournot behaviour is not the only possible or even the most likely strategy behaviour in an oligopoly market, but more general assumptions regarding either behaviour or strategy can be shown to lead to the same conclusion (Brander and Krugman 1983).

It may be asked whether *global* efficiency accompanies this kind of intra-industry trade. Under conditions of free trade, intensified competition will result in a lower consumer price and a larger volume. This contributes to a higher level of welfare, the deadweight loss of monopoly having been reduced. The likely effect that competition in itself will be cost-reducing (lower X-inefficiency) will likewise contribute to a higher welfare level. By contrast, the costs involved in moving identical products in both directions across the border will affect the level of welfare negatively. If transportation costs are sufficiently low total welfare will increase, but high transportation costs may reduce it. Consequently, the formation of a *cartel* by two duopolists does not necessarily reduce global welfare since market sharing may save transportation costs. The European cement industry would be a case in point.

3.4 HORIZONTALLY DIFFERENTIATED PRODUCTS AND MONOPOLISTIC COMPETITION

Although intra-industry trade in identical products can be explained in terms of the strategic behaviour of oligopolists, its importance seems negligible compared to that of intra-industry trade in differentiated products. In this section we first introduce two different kinds of product differentiation—horizontal and vertical—and then explain the rationale for trade in horizontally differentiated products.

3.4.1 Kinds of product differentiation

A distinction may be made between horizontal and vertical product differentiation. *Horizontal product differentiation* (HPD) is typically the result of different consumer preferences for alternative product variants which are available at the same price. *Vertical product differentia-*

Table 3.2 Horizontal versus vertical product differentiation—an example

| | Horizontal | | | |
Vertical	Nigerian Washing Machine Company	Ghanaian Washing Machine Company	Phillips (The Netherlands)	Miele (Germany)
1. Washboard	X_1	X_2	NA	NA
2. Automatic household washing machine without spin dryer	NA	NA	Y_1	Y_2
3. Fully automatic household washing machine with spin dryer	NA	NA	Z_1	Z_2

Note: NA: not available; X, Y and Z indicate quality variants.

tion (VPD), however, results when, categorized according to quality and given the same price, the products in a range are assigned the same order of priority by all consumers. Using an example, Table 3.2 further elucidates the difference between the two kinds of product differentiation.

Four producers and three different quality levels are assumed to exist; each producer has a variant (brand) and at given prices consumers agree on the order of priority of the three quality levels. Two African producers, one in Nigeria and one in Ghana, account for quality level 1. The two products vary with respect to shape, size and wave width. These characteristics, however, are not unambiguous as regards quality, so we are faced with two horizontally differentiated product variants (X_1 and X_2). Quality variants 2 and 3 are produced by two European producers but not by the African ones. Y_1, Y_2 and Z_1, Z_2, respectively, express horizontal product differentiation. If Germany imports washing machines of quality level 2 from Holland (Phillips) and exports products of the same quality level to Holland (Miele), then this will be a case of intra-industry trade in horizontally differentiated products. Conversely, intra-industry trade in vertically differentiated products takes place if Germany exports products of quality level 3 to Holland and imports products of quality level 2 from Holland. Table 3.2 also indicates that simultaneous intra-industry trade in both vertically and horizontally differentiated products is also possible.

3.4.2 Trade in horizontally differentiated products: the core property model

Considerations relating to the causes of consumer demand for product variants should be the basis of any foreign trade model allowing for differentiated products. Two principal explanations aimed at providing models of demand for product variants have developed in foreign trade theory: (1) the core property model based on Lancaster's consumption model (1973 and 1980) and (2) the 'love for variety' model following Dixit and Stiglitz (1977). We will first consider the core property model and then deal rather briefly with the Dixit and Stiglitz model.

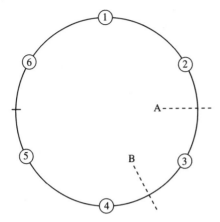

Figure 3.6   Preference structure according to the core property model

According to Lancaster, consumers differ in that each of them considers a certain mix of core properties in a product group *ideal*. In the case of a car, some consumers (the 'green' ones) attach great importance to low levels of energy consumption, exhaust gases and noise and less importance to horsepower, comfort, stylish design, etc. Other consumers attach great importance to properties like speed, comfort, etc., and little importance to the 'green' properties of a car. Clearly, any consumer will search the market for the product variant that corresponds closest to his or her ideal variant. Figure 3.6 illustrates these *demand* related conditions (Helpman 1981).

In the *circular model*, product characteristics, e.g. colour, are described on a (colour) scale symbolized by a circle. Consumer (colour) preferences are evenly distributed around the circle. Due to economies of scale it would be uneconomical to produce everybody's ideal variant, so only a few variants are offered, symbolized by the six points on the circle. Since each consumer chooses the variant that is the closest to his or her own ideal, variant number 3 will cover the market segment AB. Assuming free entry into the industry, we will have a case of *monopolistic competition*. Suppliers will obtain identical market shares and the points will spread evenly along the circle.

Let us now consider the international aspect in the case of two *identical* economies. If we assume that the producers have identical cost structures, the prices of all product variants are the same in the pre-trade situation. On the assumptions made with respect to demand and costs, Figure 3.7 illustrates the case of a 'representative' producer.

Point E_0, where the unit cost curve AC is tangent to the producer's demand curve, indicates long-run equilibrium in the pre-trade situation. The introduction of international trade does not immediately change the number of variants; as identical variants are produced in each country, their number will still be six, but the total market will now have doubled. Only one of each of two identical product variants will survive, however, since one of the producers of, for example, variant 3 will expand sales, exploit any economies of scale and force the other producer out of the market. If the lucky producer is the one from Figure 3.7, that producer will immediately face a demand volume which is *twice as large* as that of the pre-trade situation, D_{H+F}. In the short run, this larger volume of demand and the attendant marginal revenue lead to an expansion of production capacity and to profits (point S).

The profits will make it advantageous, however, to start producing new variants along the circle in Figure 3.6. These variants may be introduced either by new producers who enter the

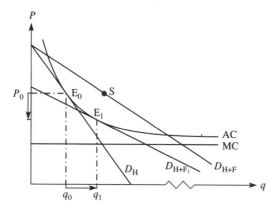

Figure 3.7 International trade under monopolistic competition

market or by producers who were at first forced out of the market or by the existing producers who may choose to extend their range of products. In the long run, the market may, for instance, offer ten variants instead of six. When the new variants hit the market they will reduce the market shares of each of the six existing surviving variants. The representative producer in Figure 3.7 will see a downward shift of D_{H+F} to D_{H+F_1}. D_{H+F_1} is less steep and, hence, more elastic than the original demand curve D_H, the increase in the number of product variants, i.e. the introduction of close substitutes, increasing price sensitivity. With the new equilibrium at E_1, prices will be lower and volumes larger. If the ten product variants are equally distributed between the two countries, they will each have five variants instead of the original six. This will lead to intra-industry trade in differentiated products.

   In the long run, the decrease in the number of product variants produced in each country will not affect the level of welfare negatively, excess profits being in any case nil. The traditional assumption that released resources may be employed for alternative use ensures this result. Further, access to a larger total supply of varieties will allow more consumers to get closer to their ideal variants and, consequently, provide them with a welfare gain. At the same time, this gain will be accompanied by lower prices caused by the improved exploitation of capacity. As mentioned previously, the increase in the number of substitution possibilities available to consumers increases producers' demand elasticities, which means that competition will be intensified. It follows that a reduction in X-inefficiency is to be expected. In sum, a number of factors result which lead to welfare gains.

   The above model is based on the assumption that the consumers in the two countries have identical preference structures. An alternative and equally extreme situation would prevail if consumer preferences along the circle in Figure 3.6 were split in two halves: one with preferences for H (1–4) and one with preferences for F (4–1). In this case, the implications of trade for both trade and welfare will be rather limited. For instance, the opening of the markets will not affect demand for variant 3, since demand for this variant only exists in country H; consequently, both price and production will remain the same. Free international trade will only affect the variants 1 and 4 at the 'ends' of the two half-circles since in these cases the tastes in the two countries overlap. National cultural conditions define the extent of overlapping tastes, in that tradition and custom may have resulted in specific national, or even regional, preferences. Beer consumption in Germany provides one example: the number of local beer brands is so large that average annual beer production per brewery amounts to 0.08m hectolitres against, for example, 0.46m hectolitres in Denmark. Given that full exploitation of the economies of scale requires an annual production of 3m hectolitres, it is evident that German beer drinkers have gone for product variation instead of low price.

3.4.3 Trade in horizontally differentiated products: 'love for variety'

Dixit and Stiglitz's (1977) model of demand for differentiated products provides the basis of an alternative approach to trade in differentiated products. On this approach, each individual likes consuming a bit of each, within a given product group, i.e. the utility value of consuming several variants is higher than that of consuming fewer. Cheese is one example of a product that can serve to illustrate the difference between the two kinds of preferences: if an individual's preferences are rather unequivocally for French brie from a certain area in France, then Lancaster's core property model is relevant; if, on the other hand, utility value depends on variation with respect to the consumption of *different* cheeses (as regards kinds of cheeses and countries of origin), then the preference structure model of Dixit and Stiglitz is relevant.

Krugman (1979, 1980, 1982) and Dixit and Norman (1980) have incorporated the latter approach to product differentiation in models that aim at explaining foreign trade between two countries that have no comparative advantages, the cost structures of the countries being identical. If it is further assumed that all consumers in the two countries have *identical consumption patterns* and that all variants offer the same utility value then, in a pre-trade situation, the two countries produce identical variants at the same prices. If the two countries are of the same 'size', the effect of trade is that all consumers are given access to twice the number of variants and in this way the consumers will gain. On this approach—and contrary to the Lancaster model with overlapping preferences—the opening of the markets does not have any effect on production levels or the number of producers in each economy: a doubling of the number of variants implies, on the one hand, that each consumer halves the consumption of each variant but, on the other hand, that the number of consumers doubles. Consequently, the demand function of each variant is unaltered, so prices and volumes will be so, too. One interesting conclusion is that the welfare gain of a small country will be larger than that of a large country, the reason being that before trade the large country produces a greater number of product variants, to which the small country subsequently gains access. As in the case of the Lancaster model, international trade will take the form of intra-industry trade, the countries involved exchanging product variants. Once again, however, it is not possible to predict which variants each country will produce and export.

In the Lancaster model, consumers' gain results from the fact that, apart from prices being lower, consumers can get closer to their ideal variants; in the Dixit and Stiglitz model, it consists in consumer access to a greater total number of variants. This is the significant difference between the two models of differentiated products. (In addition, the Dixit and Stiglitz framework eliminates the possibility provided by the Lancaster model that the preference overlap between the two countries might be moderate.) So it may reasonably be argued that the two models do not compete with each other but *supplement* each other.

As regards raw materials, semi-manufactured products and capital goods, it seems obvious that the core property model is decisive if differentiated products are actually involved. Frequent changes from one variant to another will be of no use to producers using these goods as inputs in production processes. In the case of consumer goods, however, the situation is less clear. With respect to *consumer durables*, which, as the term indicates, are acquired in limited amounts to provide useful services over a long period of time, conditions correspond to those relating to the use of capital goods in firms, so the core property model seems to be the more relevant one. In the case of *consumer non-durables* (including services), however, both preference structure models seem to provide a good description. If food and garments are involved variation may be of primary importance. The case of records may illustrate why a combination of the two preference structure models may provide the best description. Each individual consumer of music probably prefers a particular kind of music (classical music, jazz, rock, etc.) and may have a favourite composer, soloist, etc.—core properties—but the consumer may at the same time prefer to have recordings of several works by the composer and, possibly, several recordings of the same works by the composer—'love for variety'.

If we take into consideration the fact that by far the larger percentage of international trade concerns raw materials, semi-manufactured goods, capital goods and consumer durables, we have to conclude that the core property model provides the best basis for understanding actual intra-industry trade among countries.

3.5 VERTICALLY DIFFERENTIATED PRODUCTS

Products are vertically differentiated if, categorized according to quality, they are assigned the same order of priority by all consumers. In this section, we consider trade in vertically differentiated products in the light of both demand-side and supply-side conditions.

3.5.1 Demand-side conditions

Demand-side analysis is based on the assumption that demand for quality in a given product group increases with increasing per capita income. Given a certain dispersion in income distribution among the countries involved, the combined result may be intra-industry trade in various quality variants within a product group (Figure 3.8).

Based on the original contribution in Linder (1961), the assumption underlying Figure 3.8 is that a firm producing differentiated products fits its product range to its home market and gradually increases its international commitment. Consequently, its exports will focus on markets with a demand structure similar to that of the firm's home market.

Income per capita (Y/L) is measured along the horizontal axis while the *quality* and stage of technical development of the product are measured along the vertical axis. Higher levels of income will make consumers replace washboards and clothes lines with increasingly more

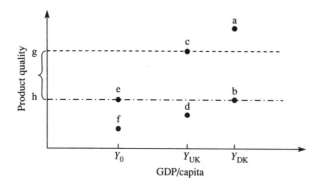

Figure 3.8 Intra-industry trade in vertically differentiated products

advanced devices for washing and drying. Let Y_{DK} be the average Danish income and let the span a–b express differences in income among Danes (and in product qualities demanded by them), the richest Danes buying product quality a and the poor ones buying quality b. If we add the corresponding points for another industrialized country, but a slightly less affluent one, such as, for example, the United Kingdom, these points will be c and d. In general, Danish exports to the United Kingdom will find no market for goods that are more advanced than c, and exporters in the United Kingdom will not be able to sell product qualities less advanced than b in Denmark. On the product quality axis the trade span is therefore g–h.

It is quite conceivable that with some countries Denmark would (almost) be unable to trade because Danish industrial products would be too advanced compared to the demand structures of these countries. In such countries average income per capita would be Y_0 or less. A heavy-handed use of the theory is not advisable, however: for instance, it is a fact that countries with rather low average incomes frequently exhibit substantial income differences and that the demand structure of the upper classes—bureaucrats or capitalists—in poor countries may be extremely advanced.

This is one suggestion of how *preference overlaps* as regards product quality may result in intra-industry trade among countries that either have very similar average income levels or in which dispersion in income distribution make preference overlaps possible. It may be asked, however, whether cost conditions in the countries involved contribute to explaining trade in vertically differentiated products.

3.5.2 Demand and supply

According to Falvey (1981), product differentiation in an industry is based on *a country's factor endowment*. Since at the same time Falvey is able to maintain *perfect competition*, assuming constant returns to scale and identical production functions, his model is a Heckscher–Ohlin-like model if product differentiation is disregarded.

Assuming that production of high-quality variants requires relatively much capital and relatively little labour and, contrariwise, that low-quality variants are labour-intensive, high-quality variants constitute a comparative advantage to capital-abundant countries while the comparative advantage of labour-abundant countries lies in the production of low-quality variants. Trade among countries with different factor endowments will be intra-industry trade, the goods traded belonging to the same product group.

The similarity between Linder's and Falvey's contributions are striking even if demand-side conditions form the basis of the former and supply-side conditions that of the latter. Falvey considers the *supply* of quality variants an increasing function of a country's capital intensity. Linder considers the *demand* for quality variants a positive function of income per employee (Y/L). Given that income (Y), slightly simplified, can be split into remuneration of labour, wL, and of capital, rK, $Y = wL + rK$, where w is the average annual wage per labour unit and r the return on capital per capital unit, then

$$Y/L = w + r\,(K/L)$$

Consequently, per capita income depends positively on the relative capital endowment of a country. However, a country with a comparative advantage in high-quality variants, i.e. one richly endowed with K, will also have a large demand for high-quality variants. This forces the pre-trade price of high-quality variants up and therefore weakens the cost advantage of the country. In a country with a comparative advantage in low-quality variants the opposite will happen. Therefore demand forces pre-trade prices towards each other and in so doing reduces the openings for trade.

In this model the welfare advantages correspond to those of the Heckscher–Ohlin model: free trade allows consumers to buy the product qualities they prefer, from the least expensive sources. The advantages differ from those of horizontal product differentiation in that they are not caused by access to the supply of a greater number of variants or by improved exploitation of economies of scale.

3.6 R&D AND INTERNATIONAL TRADE

Disregarding the discussion in Chapter 2 of Leontief's empirical investigation, we have so far assumed that only two production factors are employed in firms, labour and capital. In addition, we have assumed (with the implicit exception of the exposition of the theories of Adam Smith and David Ricardo in Chapter 2) that all countries had the same production technique, i.e. the same production function, $Q = f(K,L)$, which applies to firms in a given industry in all countries. The other assumptions of the Heckscher–Ohlin theory led to the factor price equalization theorem. Given the same real wages and return to capital, firms will use identical ratios of capital to labour (K/L).

The division of production factors into just labour and capital is too simplified, however. Moreover, experience shows that countries do not use identical ratios of factors of production and that production techniques as expressed in production functions are not identical. This is evident, for example, from the fact that the triad countries (which we shall refer to as the 'North') are centres of *innovation* while the rest (the 'South') perform the role of *imitators*. Even within the triad countries, competition is so fierce that different countries are technological leaders in different product groups. United States firms are leaders in information technology, air and space technology, etc., while Japanese firms are leaders in the technology of photo equipment, video recorders and various other consumer electronics. Even minor countries, such as Denmark, may be technological leaders in specific products, for example in insulin. Technological leadership is not necessarily everlasting since a given technology may spread to the rest of the countries and ultimately become an *international public good*. The firms in a given country will only be able to maintain their industrial leadership if they maintain their leadership in R&D activities.

Given that at any point in time technological knowledge may differ among countries and that over a period of time it may spread among them, it is necessary to include R&D in the models and to make them dynamic. Vernon (1966) is a classical contribution emphasizing technology and dynamics, while Grossman and Helpman (1991) is a more recent one. We shall discuss a number of their views on the basis of Figure 3.9, which shows national production structures.

Technological leadership within a given product group requires the firms in a country to be superior to others in respect of continuous process and product innovations. Innovations are a result of R&D activities and may be understood as independent productive activities requiring both physical and human capital. Apart from process and product innovations, the example in Figure 3.9 includes the production of two physical goods: 'high-technology products' and 'traditional products'. The former not only requires physical and human capital as well as unskilled labour but also R&D. R&D efforts are assumed to create entry barriers and profitability; the market structure is assumed to be oligopolistic. With respect to the traditional goods, which require the production factors of unskilled labour and physical capital, no entry barriers exist and it is assumed that constant returns to scale apply as well as perfect competition.

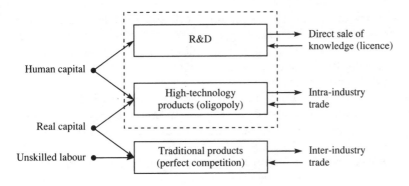

Figure 3.9 R&D and international trade
Source: Siebert (1991).

In the case of traditional goods inter-industry trade will be predominant. Countries whose endowment with unskilled labour in particular is considerable will become exporters. In high-technology industry, however, intra-industry trade will prevail. If R&D efforts are directed towards horizontal product differentiation, innovation will consist in products serving new functions and, consequently, expanding the possible range of variants, or in specializing production (see Section 3.4). By contrast, if R&D efforts are directed towards vertical product differentiation, innovation will consist in scientific breakthroughs, leading to more efficient production processes or to products of a higher quality. As explained in Section 3.5, trade in vertically differentiated products may lead to intra-industry trade.

A country's relative endowment with human capital is the pivotal factor deciding whether high-technology industry or traditional industry will account for its export strength: abundance of human capital results in a *comparative* advantage as regards R&D input but the abundance is determined by the country's previous investment in education, etc. Whether a specific firm has any *competitive* advantage in high-technology industry depends on its product or process innovations compared to those of its competitors. Both as regards a country's comparative advantage in high-technology products and a specific firm's competitive advantage, it is crucial to know whether the knowledge attained through R&D is (1) a private good, (2) a local or national public good or (3) an international public good. If it is a (temporary) *private good* secured through patents, etc., the firm (and the country) will be able to retain its advantage over a period of time, the innovation providing the firm with a first-mover advantage.

This is the case expressed in Vernon's *product cycle theory*, in which the introduction of new products and production techniques takes place in the North. As the production process becomes standardized, production is transferred to the South, where lower wages make it less costly. In this case the product variant changes over a period of time from a high-technology product to a traditional one. This technology transfer erodes the competitive advantage of the firm in the North. However, it may strengthen its advantage through further R&D activities, which may lead to further innovation in terms of new quality variants and secure continued production in the North. The result will be intra-industry trade between the North and the South.

If the result of a firm's R&D activity is a *national public good*, other firms in the industry will benefit (a positive external effect will result), as will society in general. If it is an *international public good*, however, the advantages cannot be internalized in the firm or the industry, and foreign competitors will acquire the same benefit. In this situation, the competitive advantages tied to the firm or the industry disappear but the country will still be able to maintain a comparative advantage in respect of the high-technology good and to become an exporter, since the relatively abundant endowment with human capital provides it with a cost advantage (e.g. through low salaries to engineers). In such a case we are back to Falvey's model (see Section 3.5) if we deal with vertically differentiated goods.

Between the two extremes of a private good, in which case the technological knowledge involved is either product- or process-specific, and of an international public good, in which case it concerns general scientific principles, we find the case of '*imitation*'. This involves technology transfer in the form of copying, i.e. entrepreneurs copy product designs or production processes developed by their competitors. The probability of imitation is particularly strong in the South, where legal protection of intangible rights is weak. Consequently, imitation causes the product cycle to develop a dynamic relationship between the North and the South. The innovation of the product takes place in the North. The South imitates it, which necessitates further innovation in the North so that the competitive advantages can be maintained. In the area of microprocessors this situation is well known: the first microprocessors were developed in the United States but were gradually imitated by other countries. These countries lost market shares, however, when the 286-processors were introduced, which were then imitated by the South. This led to upgrading in the North, where improved qualities were introduced in the form of 386-processors and 486-processors. Such an innovation and imitation process results in intra-industry trade in vertically differentiated products.

How should the imitation process be assessed from a welfare perspective? On the one hand, it reduces the incentive to make further R&D efforts in the North since the period for which a monopoly can be retained is cut short. On the other hand, imitation results in improved exploitation of existing knowledge and the exploitation of comparative advantages brings about a gain.

3.7 INTER-INDUSTRY VERSUS INTRA-INDUSTRY TRADE

In this chapter we have introduced a distinction between inter-industry trade and intra-industry trade. If trade between two countries is in homogeneous products and based entirely on comparative advantages, then only inter-industry trade will take place. This follows from the fact that if a country is abundantly endowed with a particular factor of production then it will export goods that require this factor intensively for their production. Conversely, it will import goods that require intensive use of its scarce production factor. This is shown in Figure 3.10(a), which illustrates trade between countries H and F as regards the goods X and Y.

If the factor endowments of the countries involved are identical, if they share the same technological knowledge and if their products are differentiated and consumer preferences overlap, it is possible that only intra-industry trade will take place (Figure 3.10(b)). Finally, trade between the two countries may involve both inter-industry and intra-industry trade (Figure 3.10(c)). This is actually the most realistic scenario. If Y is a traditional product which is homogeneous and produced under constant returns to scale and perfect competition, the country abundantly endowed with the factor used intensively for the production of Y, i.e. country F, becomes an exporter only of this product and the other country, H, becomes an importer only. In the case of the differentiated (high-technology) product X, which is capital-intensive and/or R&D intensive, intra-industry trade will prevail. Each country will specialize in its variants (e.g. in property combinations or quality) and export these to the other country.

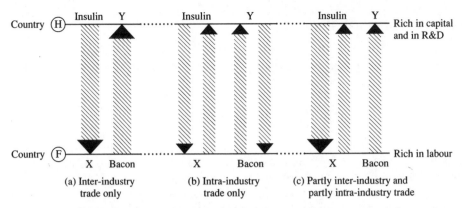

Note: The width of the arrows indicates the value of exports and imports, respectively.

Figure 3.10   Inter-industry and intra-industry trade

A range of *practical* conditions may also cause intra-industry trade to occur. In this context we shall limit ourselves to mentioning cross-border trade and seasonal variations. In the case of a number of products, high transport costs make it necessary to localize production close to the markets. These products include heavy goods such as bricks, cement and glass bottles. Consequently, producers located along a national border may have their natural market on both sides of the border, as illustrated in Figure 3.11.

The natural market of producer A in country H has been indicated by means of the circle with A in its centre. The extent of the market concerns both countries, i.e. H and F. The parallel situation applies to producer B, who is located in country F. Consequently, both countries will see exports as well as imports of the product in question. Such trade may be considerable in areas where no natural borders exist, e.g. in Central Europe.

Some goods, e.g. fruit and vegetables, are only produced during part of the year. During the height of the season, production may be so abundant that part of it is exported. Conversely, during off-seasons such goods may be imported from other parts of the world, where production is at the height of the season. On an annual basis, this is a case of intra-industry trade. Similar conditions apply, for instance, to trade in electricity among the Scandinavian countries: when the level of precipitation is high in Norway and Sweden, these countries export hydroelectricity to Denmark, while the Danish power stations which use coal for their production export electricity to Norway and Sweden in years with low precipitation levels.

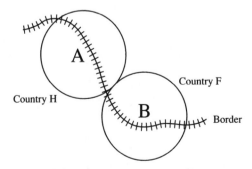

Figure 3.11   Cross-border trade as intra-industry trade

3.7.1   The degree of intra-industry trade

Whether the case illustrated in Figure 3.10(a), (b) or (c) is the most realistic one can be determined by measuring the degree of intra-industry trade by means of the so-called Grubel–Lloyd index (named after Grubel and Lloyd 1975):

$$\text{GL}_i = \left(1 - \frac{|X_i - M_i|}{X_i + M_i}\right) \times 100$$

where GL_i indicates the Grubel–Lloyd index as regards product group i, and X_i indicates the export value and M_i the import value of product group i. As can be seen, GL_i will assume the value of zero if all trade in the industry in question is unilateral (Figure 3.10.(a)), i.e. if either X_i or M_i assumes the value of zero. If all trade is balanced so that the value of exports equals the value of imports then GL_i equals 100. It follows that the closer the GL index is to 100, the higher the *degree* of intra-industry trade. In the same way as the degree of intra-industry trade can be measured in the case of a product group in terms of GL_i, it can also be measured with respect to a country's total volume of foreign trade if the individual GL_i values are weighted against the relative volume of exports and imports which they account for respectively and added up.

Typically, industrial countries with a high national income have a GL index of around 60–80 per cent (see, for instance, Culem and Lundberg 1986). This means that out of total foreign trade 60–80 per cent can be classified as intra-industry trade. Since these figures are based on foreign trade statistics, the degree of intra-industry trade depends on the level of aggregation. Calculations are typically based on three- or four-digit SITC figures. The approximately 30 per cent in the case of Japan is a marked exception. The industrialized countries have seen an historical growth in their intra-industry trade, which may be explained in terms of growing demand for product variation with growing income development. Intra-industry trade between industrialized and developing countries is relatively modest; in this case the exchange of goods tends to take the form of Heckscher–Ohlin trade. Trade in vertically differentiated products explains why some intra-industry trade does take place. By contrast, the degree of intra-

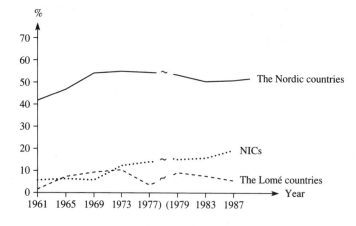

Figure 3.12   Denmark's intra-industry trade with three selected groups of countries from 1961 to 1987
Source: B. Dalum *et al.* (1991).

industry trade among industrialized countries is relatively high, particularly in the case of neighbouring industrialized countries. Figure 3.12 illustrates this with respect to the intra-industry trade between Denmark and 'the Nordic countries' (including Finland, Iceland, Norway and Sweden), Denmark and the developing countries known as 'the Lomé countries' (including a large number of developing countries in Africa, the Caribbean and the Pacific Ocean; these countries have signed special trade and cooperative agreements with the EU) and between Denmark and a number of NICs (newly industrialized countries including in this context, Brazil, Hong Kong, Korea, Singapore, Taiwan and the former Yugoslavia).

A large number of econometric analyses confirm these claims; see, for instance, Balassa (1986) and Balassa and Bauwens (1987, 1988). They show, among other things, that trade among industrialized countries may be explained in terms of comparative as well as competitive advantages. Thus the capital intensity of a country's exports is positively correlated with its relative capital abundance—physical and human. Countries in the same income bracket trade a great deal with each other: distance reduces trade and product differentiation increases intra-industry trade. They also show that intra-industry trade increases with a country's economic level of development, i.e. its GDP per capita.

APPENDIX: SURVEY OF INTERNATIONAL TRADE THEORY

Main characteristics	Major contributors	Principal characteristics of goods exchanged	What determines the direction of trade?
1. Absolute productivity of labour	Adam Smith	Labour content per product unit	Absolute production advantages
2. Relative productivity of labour	David Ricardo	Labour content per product unit	Relative production advantages
3. Factor proportions:			
(a) Homogeneous capital and labour	Hecksher Ohlin Samuelson	Capital–labour ratio (K/L)	A country's relative endowment with capital and labour: countries relatively abundantly endowed with K will export K-intensive products and import L-intensive products
(b) Human capital	Leontief	Labour qualifications ('knowledge') in production and distribution	Countries relatively abundantly endowed with well-educated labour will export knowledge-intensive products and import products for the production of which a

continued ...

Main characteristics	Major contributors	Principal characteristics of goods exchanged	What determines the direction of trade?
			relatively high volume of unskilled labour is employed
4. Economies of scale	Ohlin Helpman and Krugman	The extent of economies of scale in production and distribution	A large home market contributes to the export of goods produced under economies of scale; small home markets contribute to the export of goods produced under 'constant returns to scale'
5. Technological gap or product cycle	Vernon Grossman and Helpman	Sequential national entry into production	Early production of new goods contributes to providing an export advantage; later on, producers will have to depend on low wages
		Product differentiation	Product sophistication and early production lead to the export of differentiated goods; lack of sophistication leads to the export of standardized goods
6. Similarity of consumer preferences	Linder	Similarity between imports and exports and home market production	Trade in both directions. Trade is the most intensive between countries with identical economic structures
7. Trade within industries (intra-industry trade)	Grubel and Lloyd		
7a. Monopolistic competition			
(i) Factor proportions and vertical product differentiation	Falvey	Vertical product differentiation (i.e. consumers can assign an order of priority according to quality), where quality depends on the K/L ratio	Relative capital-abundance leads to the export of products of a high quality and vice versa

continued. . .

Main characteristics	Major contributors	Principal characteristics of goods exchanged	What determines the direction of trade?
(ii) Horizontal product differentiation	Krugman Dixit and Norman Lancaster	Horizontal product differentiation (i.e. consumers do not agree on an unambiguous order of priority among product variants) and economies of scale	The direction of trade is indeterminate
7b. Oligopoly Homogeneous goods (Cournot behaviour)	Brander Krugman	Economies of scale	Market sharing; but the import share of the home market will decrease with increasing transport costs

SUMMARY

1. From around 1980 a number of attempts have been made to supplement neoclassical trade theory, focusing on similarities between nations and on the industry or firm level, i.e. on competitive advantages.
2. Economies of scale external to the firm can make for national competitiveness in industries or clusters of firms, even if the origin of the cluster may be determined by chance.
3. Economies internal to the firm will lead to imperfect competition or monopoly, but at the same time international trade will lend to destruction of local monopolies.
4. Intra-industry trade in differentiated products will lead to increasing competition and thus be beneficial to consumers. Intra-industry trade takes place in homogeneous as well as differentiated products. In the former case it is explained in terms of oligopolists trading in segmented markets.
5. Trade in horizontally differentiated products is described in the core property model and the 'love for variety' model. Even if all consumers in the trading countries have identical consumption patterns, they will be better off with intra-industry trade due to the larger product variety.
6. Trade in vertically differentiated products is explained by Linder and Falvey. The former offers a demand-side explanation and the latter a supply-side one.
7. International trade may be influenced by technology or R&D. Technologically leading countries export R&D-intensive products but as established technology becomes an international public good, they can only sustain their competitive advantage on the basis of continued research efforts. In his product cycle theory, Vernon presented this reasoning on the basis of firm level.
8. Intra-industry trade has been presented and given a rationale. Its empirical significance is measured by the Grubel–Lloyd index, which is 60–80 per cent in high-income industrialized countries.

REFERENCES

Balassa, Bela (1986), 'Intra-industry specialization. A cross-country analysis', *European Economic Review*, **30**, 27–42.

Balassa, B. and Luc Bauwens (1987), 'Intra-industry specialisation in a multicountry and multi-industry framework', *The Economic Journal*, **97**, 923–939.

Balassa, B. and Luc Bauwens (1988), 'The determinants of intra-European trade in manufactured goods', *European Economic Review*, **32**, 1421–1437.

Brander, James A. (1981), 'Intra-industry trade in identical commodities', *Journal of International Economics*, **11**, 1–14.

Brander, J. A. and Paul Krugman (1983), 'A reciprocal dumping model of international trade', *Journal of International Economics*, **15**, 313–21.

Culem, Claudy and Lars Lundberg (1986), 'The product pattern of intra-industry trade: stability among countries and over time', *Weltwirtschaftliches Archiv*, **122**, 1.

Dalum, B., *et al.*, (1991) 'Den intra-industrielle handel i Danmark og Irland—en sammenligning' (The intra-industry trade of Denmark and Ireland—a comparison), Striffserie, K. nr. 15, Department of Economics, The Aarhus School of Business.

Dixit, A. and Victor Norman (1980), *Theory of International Trade*, Cambridge University Press, Cambridge.

Dixit, A. and J. Stiglitz (1977), 'Monopolistic competition and optimum product variety', *American Economic Review*, **67**, 297–308.

Falvey, R. E. (1981), 'Commercial policy and intra-industry trade', *Journal of International Economics*, **11**, 495–511.

Friedman, Milton (1953), *Essays in Positive Economics*, Cambridge.

Grossman, Gene M. and Elhanan Helpman (1991): *Innovation and Growth in the Global Economy*, The MIT Press, Cambridge, Massachusetts.

Grubel, Herbert Gl. and P. J. Lloyd (1975), '*Intra-Industry Trade. The Theory and Measurement of International Trade in Differentiated Products*, Macmillan Press, London.

Helpman, Elhanan (1981), 'International trade in the presence of product differentiation, economies of scale, and monopolistic competition', *Journal of International Economics*, **11**, 305–340.

Helpman, E. and Paul Krugman (1986), *Market Structure and Foreign Trade. Increasing Returns, Imperfect Competition and the International Economy*, The MIT Press, Cambridge, Massachusetts.

Krugman, P. (1979), 'Increasing returns monopolistic competition and international trade', *Journal of International Economics*, 9, 469–480.

Krugman, P. (1980), 'Scale economies, product differentiation and the pattern of trade', *American Economic Review*, 70, 950–959.

Krugman, P. (1982), 'Trade in differentiated products and political economy of trade liberalisation', in Bhagwati, J. (ed.) *Imperfect Competition and Response*, University of Chicago Press, Chicago.

Lancaster, Kelvin (1973), *Variety, Equity, and Efficiency*, Columbia University Press, New York.

Lancaster, K. (1980), 'Intra-industry trade under monopolistic competition', *Journal of International Economics*, **10**, 151–175.

Linder, S. B. (1961), *An Essay on Trade and Transformation*, Wiley, New York.

Porter, Michael E. (1990), *The Competitive Advantage of Nations*, Macmillan Press, London.

Siebert, H. (1991), 'A Schumpeterian model of growth in the world economy: some notes on a new paradigm in international economics', *Weltwirtschaftliches Archiv*, **127**(4).

Vernon, Raymond (1966), 'International trade and international investment in the product cycle', *Quarterly Journal of Economics*, **80**, 190–207.

INTERNATIONAL FACTOR MOVEMENTS

The two preceding chapters dealt with international trade in goods. Goods are produced with factors of production, and in Chapter 2 one topic is the analysis of the influence of trade on factor prices and income distribution, factors being assumed to be internationally immobile. However, apart from land, factors of production are, in fact, more or less mobile. This chapter shows that international factor movements have distributional effects in the same way as international trade has.

Assume that two countries close down their trade in goods, but accept free factor movements. This induces each factor of production to move to where remuneration is the highest: capital moves to the labour intensive country and labour to the capital-intensive one. In consequence, remuneration to each factor is levelled out until factor prices are the same in both countries.

If the countries reallow trade, factor prices having been fully equalized, this will not lead to trade in goods; at least, any trade in goods will not be the result of differences in factor endowment. If, quite realistically, we assume that movements of goods and factors cause transaction costs, it is intuitively obvious that free factor movements cause higher welfare gains than free movements of goods: factors only have to be moved once.

In accordance with the organization of Chapters 2 and 3, this chapter has two main parts. Sections 4.1 and 4.2 assume perfect competition. Section 4.1 deals with international capital movements and Section 4.2 with international flows of labour. The two factors of production are considered homogeneous units, so the exposition should be seen as an analysis of *net flows* among countries.

This view is abandoned in Sections 4.3 and 4.4, in which the analytical basis relates to the imperfect competition models presented in Chapter 3. Section 4.3 offers a survey of the diverse forms of factor movements and Section 4.4 presents one of these forms in detail, such as investments by multinational enterprises (MNEs). Since, in Sections 4.3 and 4.4, the emphasis is on individual transactions, factor movements are considered gross flows in these sections, heterogeneous entities being unable to outbalance each other.

4.1 INTERNATIONAL CAPITAL MOVEMENTS

As mentioned above, this section assumes perfect competition in the capital market. Capital movements are considered in a micro-economic perspective, the emphasis being on allocative effects. Major macro-economic consequences, as regards interest rates and exchange rates, are dealt with in later chapters.

In recent years, international capital movements have gained increasing importance, partly because capital markets have been liberalized and partly because the size of the flows passing through the markets has increased considerably. Traditionally, a distinction is made between *direct investments*, which involve some degree of control of foreign firms, and *portfolio investments*, i.e. investments in shares and other securities, but ones that do not provide a controlling interest. In terms of volume, portfolio investments prevail, but, for example, with respect to technology and management transfers among countries, direct investments are probably more significant.

This section does not attribute any importance to the distinction since welfare and distributional effects of capital movements are independent of the specific form of movements: capital imports necessarily reduce capital scarcity and thus result in lower marginal returns as regards this factor.

4.1.1 The basic model

The point of departure of our analysis of international capital movements is the neoclassical theory of marginal productivity, which is outlined in Figure 4.1. According to the theory, increases in the contribution of one factor sooner or later results in diminishing marginal productivity, other things being equal. The figure assumes this to hold for any value of capital volume (K). Thus the value of the marginal product of capital, VMP_K, which also indicates demand for K, results in a downward slope.

For any supply of capital, K_0, equilibrium in the capital market is determined by FK_0, i.e. a realized value of VMP_K. If the economic activity does not involve any risk, the return on financial claims, r, will equal VMP_K, i.e. r_0. Total capital income is defined as the return on capital to owners, which is the value of the marginal product multiplied by the amount of capital, i.e. the area of Or_0FK_0 in Figure 4.1. Total income attributable to the two production factors of capital and labour is defined by the area below AF, i.e. $OAFK_0$. AFr_0, the residual income, constitutes remuneration of labour.

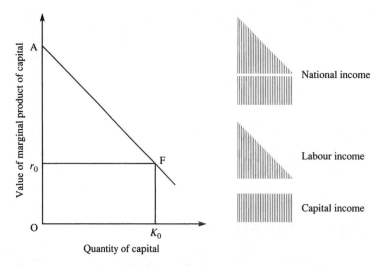

Figure 4.1 Capital market equilibrium in a closed economy

4.1.2   Welfare gains

Figure 4.2 shows that international capital movements result in welfare gains. The distance O_iO_d indicates global capital volume, which is divided between the capital-abundant countries in the industrialized world (O_iK_0) and the countries in the developing world, which are poor in capital. The value of the marginal return on capital in industrialized countries is indicated by means of the curve AN, and that of developing countries is indicated by means of BM. The two curves are identical if technology, labour supply, management systems, etc., available to both industrialized and developing countries are identical. This assumption corresponds to the neoclassical one made in Chapter 2. In the developing countries, relative scarcity of capital pushes VMP_K upwards compared to the situation in the industrialized countries, so $r_d > r_i$.

Free capital movements will induce capital to flow from industrialized countries, where return is relatively low, to developing countries. This will force the return on capital to increase in industrialized countries, where labour now has less real capital in its hands. Contrariwise, return on capital will be driven downwards in developing countries. Capital flows will not stop until the differences in returns have been equalized, i.e. not until developing countries have received the amount of capital K_0K_1 from industrialized countries. This distribution of the volume of capital represents an equilibrium where $VMP_K = r_w$ in both groups of countries.

In real life, this is a slow process, and the equilibrium is not likely to be realized at all. Massive capital transfers to developing countries would increase their indebtedness and would make investments (even) less safe than they are now. This risk increase would be counter-balanced by a risk premium, and r_i would remain lower than r_d. However, even in this case capital movements would increase global welfare, albeit to a lesser extent.

In developing countries the reallocation of capital increases production (GDP) by the area of K_1CDK_0, which offers more than full compensation for the loss of production, K_1CFK_0, in the industrialized world. The net result is a total welfare gain of CDF.

4.1.3   Redistributional effects

International capital movements cause redistribution at several levels. Firstly, if we look at the countries involved, then, as a whole, both industrialized countries and developing ones gain from capital movements. At the equilibrium with global $VMP_K = r_w$ the developing countries pay the area of K_1CEK_0 in interest rates to the industrialized countries. As this area is smaller

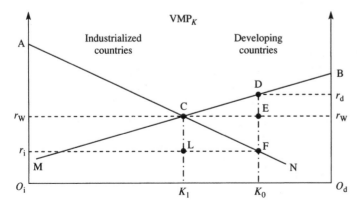

Figure 4.2   The effects of capital mobility

than the production increase in the developing countries, i.e. $K_1\text{CD}K_0$, their net gain equals the difference between the two areas, i.e. CDE. Likewise, the industrialized countries gain the area of CEF, which constitutes the difference between their interest rate gain of $K_1\text{CE}K_0$ and their production loss of $K_1\text{CF}K_0$. Both parties gain.

Secondly, consider internal distributional effects in each of the two groups of countries. In the developing countries, capitalists suffer, capital income being reduced by $\text{ED}r_dr_w$. Labour gains the area of $\text{CD}r_dr_w$, however.

The industrialized countries experience redistribution of the reverse kind. Labour loses $r_ir_w\text{CF}$, while capitalists gain $r_ir_w\text{EF}$. Thus, according to the figure, the fact that trade unions have so often fought the liberalization of capital markets is obviously in the interest of their members.

The similarities claimed above to exist between neoclassical trade theory and capital movements under perfect competition have now been spelled out. The effects are parallel. According to the Heckscher–Ohlin theory, exports of capital-intensive goods from the industrialized countries increase demand for capital. The reason is that the price of capital-intensive goods rises and, in turn, 'pulls' the value of the marginal product of capital upwards. In Figure 4.2, this translates into a rise in the AN curve.

Correspondingly, exports of labour intensive goods from the developing countries reduces demand for capital and drives BM downwards. If the distribution of the volume of capital (K_0) is maintained, return on capital will increase in the industrialized countries and decrease in the developing countries, precisely as when factor movements are possible.

4.1.4   Other effects

The analysis of the effects of capital movements is carried out under highly restrictive and even unrealistic conditions. If these are relaxed, this may result in modified or totally different effects. Below, some examples are listed:

1. A great many developing countries suffer from structural unemployment, the effects of which can only be eased by means of hard currency. In such cases capital transfers may create growth in production and demand and cause welfare gains which reach far beyond the effects indicated in Figure 4.2.
2. If, as is actually often the case, capital transfers are accompanied by technical and commercial know-how, this will push the BM curve upwards and create further welfare gains. This effect may be reinforced by dissemination effects as local trade and industry come into contact with the new techniques.
3. Capital transfers often affect competition in the recipient country. They either do so positively, in that they offer a challenge to established local monopolies or cartels, or less positively, in that they establish such a position for themselves.
4. Over an extensive period lasting until 1973, massive investments in the oil-producing countries by the large petrol companies resulted in decreasing relative oil prices. This presented the industrialized countries with considerable terms of trade gains in the form of a favourable trend in prices in relation to industrial goods and raw materials.

4.2   MIGRATION

Labour is considerably less mobile than capital, but during certain periods substantial migrations have occurred. Massive emigration from Europe to the United States (in particular)

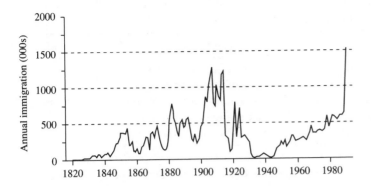

Figure 4.3   U.S. gross immigration, 1820–1991
   Sources: US Bureau of the Census, *Historical Statistics of the USA, Colonial Times to 1970*
   and *Statistical Abstracts of the USA*, 1975, 1982–3, 1992.

took place from around 1900 until the First World War. Figure 4.3 shows gross immigration into the United States since 1820. Among other things, the figure illustrates the effects of the quota system introduced after the First World War, which aimed at reducing the influx.

The flow from Southern Europe and the Middle East to the affluent Northern Europe after the Second World War constitutes another example of economically motivated migration. The immigrant countries had full employment and overheated economies, and immigration contributed to maintaining economic growth at a high level. Immigrants were tolerated because the division of labour which they became part of left them with unattractive jobs which the indigenous populations preferred not to perform. In return, real wages of immigrants were multiplied, measured by the standards of their native countries. By the time the oil crisis of 1973 reversed the migration trend and net flows started heading for the South, Western Europe was left with approximately 30m immigrant workers.

4.2.1   The migration calculus

The decisive difference between capital and labour movements is that in the latter case it is the decision-maker who is moved. Of course, this means that not only economic considerations influence the decision but that it is also affected by a number of subjective and not easily quantifiable elements. These are psychological and social advantages and disadvantages in connection with migration, which, depending on the circumstances, may be of either significant or inferior importance. In the above examples of mass emigration, the economic elements figured prominently.

Setting up a precise migration calculus, i.e. one that takes all advantages and disadvantages into consideration, is impossible. Firstly, it is impossible because any list of items to be considered would be deficient. Secondly, it is impossible because the importance of each item, e.g., in money terms, cannot be determined. In fact, whether the 'signs' of a whole range of items in the migration calculus should be positive or negative cannot be generally determined: what seems to some to be threats from their new environments may by others be perceived as opportunities. Table 4.1 lists some of the items that a migration calculus has to include.

For instance, consider taxation in the immigrant country. If taxes are low, more money is left in the pockets of the immigrants, but the social safety net stretched out under them is probably

Table 4.1 Some elements of a migration calculus

Financial conditions	Other conditions
Income loss in home country	Loss of familiar system
Removal costs	Loss of family and friends
Costs of maintaining old connections	Uncertainty relative to the new environment
Income in country of immigration	Experiencing social mobility
Transfer income in country of immigration	Experiencing a new culture

more wide-meshed. As is always the case when something seems complicated, emigrants, like others, are tempted to attribute decisive importance to a single factor; for instance, 'I want my children to have better opportunities than I had'.

4.2.2 Welfare effects

In the ideal case, which takes place between perfect market economies and is marginal relative to total labour supply, migration increases welfare. By definition, the emigrant is in a better position (having done the sum of the migration calculus). In both the country of emigration and that of immigration input and output changes by exactly the migrant's marginal productivity. Therefore only the welfare of the migrant is affected. Global welfare increases and nobody is worse off.

In fact, however, this argument has to be modified. In the case of large scale migration the effects can be examined in precisely the same way that those of capital movements were mapped out in Figure 4.2. In the case of migration, O_iO_d represents global labour supply, and the curves AN and BM indicate the value of marginal labour productivity, i.e. real wages. Migration from developing countries to industrialized countries lowers wage levels in the industrialized countries and raises them in the developing countries. Wages being a measure of labour productivity and the level of productivity being higher in industrialized countries, migration increases global welfare in the same way as capital movements.

Workers in the industrialized countries lose from this immigration. It therefore comes as no surprise that, in all industrialized countries, immigrants have to overcome considerable barriers. One of these barriers consists in politicians' fear of not being reelected if local labour perceives migration as a threat. The fact that some immigration does take place is in particular due to the heterogeneity of labour and the division of labour between immigrants and the native population, as was pointed out above.

Another significant modification relates to the public sector. In all countries, education is financed by public funds, either wholly or partly; education translates into an increase in lifetime income, higher tax payments and, consequently, an increase in the contribution to future public expenditure. It follows that emigrating, after receiving an education, often corresponds to putting those remaining in a worse position. Consequently, in imposing a special tax on well-educated emigrants or in giving export subsidies to senior citizens moving to the West, the former communist regimes in Eastern Europe behaved quite rationally.

4.2.3 Summary to Sections 4.1 and 4.2

The 'pure' theory of factor movements has been analysed in Sections 4.1 and 4.2, and the two sections reached identical conclusions, which are summarized in Table 4.2. The table gives

Table 4.2   Winners and losers of factor movements

Nature of movement	Immobile workers	Immobile capital	Mobile factor unit
Immigration	Loser	Winner	Winner
Emigration	Winner	Loser	Winner
Capital imports	Winner	Loser	Winner
Capital exports	Loser	Winner	Winner

welfare effects to the three kinds of resource owners, as seen from the points of view of the countries involved.

Apart from the case of the atomistic migrant in a perfect market economy, factor movements always create losers and winners. Those who move win each time. That is why they move.

4.3   THE VARIOUS FORMS OF FACTOR MOVEMENT

In Sections 4.3 and 4.4, we examine the heterogeneous picture with which real life presents decision-makers somewhat more closely. In Section 4.2 and quite particularly in Section 4.1, it made sense to consider *net effects* of factor movements, but this is not the case in what follows.

At a national level, value added is the result of employing basic production factors: land, labour and real capital. Labour and real capital may be subdivided in various ways, thus allowing for more factor of production concepts: technology, human capital and possibly even more refined subdivisions. From our perspective, land is not particularly interesting since, unlike any other factors, it has no cross-border mobility (although borders are sometimes mobile relative to land).

From a business perspective, which we adopt in this part of the chapter, not just the production factors mentioned above but also intermediary products enter the production function. Mobile factors therefore include the following:

- Investment goods (real capital)
- Intermediary products (real capital)
- Technology
- Human capital
- Labour

In principle, cross-border movement of production factors may take one of three *transaction forms*. As regards labour services and goods, the classical form is that of buying and selling in markets. In the case of goods, ownership is transferred, but not in the case of labour.

The other genuine form is that of factor transfers within hierarchies, as, for example, between a parent company and its subsidiary. The establishment of a subsidiary constitutes the classical case, in which the transfer of factors concerns capital, technology and human capital in the form of managerial competence. Ownership does not change as a consequence of such transactions: it remains within the group.

In connection with the internationalization of trade and industry, a number of solutions have become extremely popular which do not make use of a genuine market-based model, nor a genuinely hierarchical one. These concern licensing, franchising, subcontracting, leasing, joint ventures, etc. What these forms have in common is that they all involve a long-term contract

Table 4.3 Transaction forms in connection with factor movements

Factor	Transaction form		
	Market solution	*Long-term contracts*	*Hierarchical solution*
Consumer goods	Exports	Leasing	Horizontal integration
Intermediates	Exports	Leasing, buy-back	Vertical integration
Capital goods	Exports	Leasing, buy-back	Vertical integration
Technology	Exports	Licensing	Internalization
Human capital	Migration	Managerial contract	Stationing
Labour	Migration	Subcontracting	Stationing
Factor packages	Project exports	Joint venture	Subsidiary

which does not transfer ownership, but which, to some extent, conveys a right of use, the buyer paying for the right to exploit the competence built up by the seller.

Table 4.3 provides a survey of the three transaction forms and of their application in connection with various production factors. Apart from the production factors mentioned previously, consumer goods and 'factor packages' have been included in the table. In the case of packages, several kinds of factors are transferred as part of the implementation of a project.

As regards consumer goods, the typical form of transaction is market-based, but, in the case of certain goods, leasing takes place through contracts entered with foreign suppliers of the goods. The hierarchical form is used when an international retail chain, such as ALDI or C&A, distributes (partly) identical assortments in several countries. German heather honey arrives in Denmark and Holland on the lorries of a group and is sold from 'German' shelves.

Real capital, including investment goods and components, enters the production function of another firm. Especially in the case of business with less developed countries, transactions often take the form of buy-back agreements. This means that the recipient agrees to pay in the form of goods produced by means of the input supplied. Very often, it is a case of long-term cooperation between the firms involved. A variation on this theme is component production, e.g. to automobile factories, which is undertaken by subcontractors. If the supplying and receiving firms are members of the same group, the hierarchical solution is a case of vertical integration.

Of course, technological knowledge can be exported. However, this is particularly true of knowledge that is not quite new and does not constitute the competitive advantage of the selling firm. Consequently, much technology transfer takes place in a way that ensures that the seller retains maximal control and that other parties are excluded from it, i.e. it takes place group-internally. Often, however, technological knowledge is transferred in the form of licenses which allow the licensee, against payment, to apply the know-how acquired over a certain period, and usually in specified market areas.

Labour, be it homogeneous or human capital, is not for sale, only its services are, but, as discussed in Section 4.2, it may migrate of its own account. It may also be stationed in subsidiaries or it may be stationed in connection with the establishment of new activities or with the operation of such activities. In addition, contracting is extensively used in connection with so-called managerial contracts, which involve the undertaking by a Western firm to build up and start, for example, the marketing function of a firm in a less developed country.

Homogeneous labour may also cross borders in this fashion; this is the case of Danish craftsmen in the former GDR or Korean workers in the Saudi Arabian construction industry. In both cases, labour has been sent out by firms in its home countries, which have undertaken a task abroad.

Factor packages involve the transfer of a rather complex set of input items with a view to implementing a project. If, for example, the package concerns the construction of a turnkey dairy in China, the transaction form may be market-based. On the other hand, it might be a joint venture in which the Chinese party provides buildings, labour and contacts with customers and suppliers, and the British party contributes processing technology, managerial capacity and financing. In this case, the joint venture company is an independent firm owned jointly by the two parties.

4.4 MULTINATIONAL ENTERPRISES

This concluding section takes a closer look at the hierarchical form of transformation and at the concepts of foreign direct investments (FDIs) and multinational enterprises (MNEs), which are responsible for such investments.

The fact that precisely multinational enterprises and their activities are subjected to special treatment here is not due to any quantitative predominance they might have in respect of investments in individual nations or capital transfers among countries. As was mentioned above, portfolio investments constitute a much larger figure.

The reason for treating them here is that:

1. Multinational enterprises are responsible for a large part of investments in certain industries, in particular in growth-oriented ones.
2. Multinational enterprises are responsible for a large part of international technology and other know-how transfers and, consequently, play a pivotal role in the diffusion of technology and in economic growth.
3. Through their intra-firm trade between parent companies and subsidiaries and among subsidiaries, multinational enterprises are in charge of a considerable part of world trade in finished products and components.
4. Multinational enterprises frequently cause political controversy.

Since multinational enterprises and foreign direct investments have not really been the focus of research until the eighties, the numerical facts available and the theory relating to this subject may appear somewhat imperfect. For example, no agreement has been reached on a precise definition of what constitutes a multinational enterprise, but a minimum requirement is that production takes place in several countries.

Attempts at calculating annual investment flows or the total volume of the assets of multinational enterprises run into serious trouble. Some of the difficulties involved are the following:

1. Stated outward investments exceed stated inward investments by very large amounts, e.g. US$ 41bn in 1990 (UN 1992). Reasons for this deviation may be a number of strategic, taxation-related and other considerations.

Table 4.4 Distribution on investor countries of MNE capital value in selected years

%	1914	1938	1960	1973	1983	1989
Industrialized countries	100	100	99	97	97	97
USA	19	28	48	48	40	27
UK	46	40	16	13	17	16
FRG	11	1	1	6	7	9
France	12	10	6	4	5	5
Japan	0	3	1	5	6	11
Developing countries	0	0	1	3	3	3
Total amount US$ billion	15	26	66	210	573	1570

Sources: J. Dunning (1988) and UN (1992).

2. Payment flows among the companies in a group are not just restricted to foreign direct investments. For example, loans may be raised or extended, or 'unreasonable' transfer prices may be fixed in connection with intra-firm trade.
3. In individual subsidiaries surpluses may be recorded which are, to some extent, withheld and included in the volume of assets.
4. Principles of depreciation influence the volume of assets considerably.

Although any statistical description has to be handled with care, Table 4.4 does provide an impression of the development in the twentieth century of the distribution of capital invested by multinational enterprises. Roles have changed a bit, but the developing countries still play a moderate role as investors.

4.4.1 Motives for foreign direct investments

Business units of a multinational group form part of a network in that their ownership, overall strategy and their access to development, production, managerial and other resources are the same. In comparison with other transaction forms, i.e. market-based ones or contractual ones, their management is largely in control of resources.

Multinational enterprises operate under widely differing conditions, depending on company size, strategy, history, etc., and on the industries and geographical areas covered. It should come as no surprise that single-factor theories to explain the investment behaviour of multinational enterprises, i.e. their foreign direct investments, have found no empirical validity. Not even the intuitively convincing model presented in Figure 4.2 can be shown to hold: apparently multinational capital does not flow in accordance with the differences measured in return on capital in various markets.

In what follows, we consider only one theory, which is really an explanatory framework. This is the eclectic paradigm developed by John Dunning ('eclectic' meaning 'compounded of the ideas of others'). The theory does not aim to answer questions of the 'if–then' type, but instead it lists three necessary conditions that have to be satisfied if a foreign direct investment is to take place:

1. In order to be at all competitive in a market, the enterprise has to have some core competence, i.e. a firm-specific advantage, at its disposal. Advantages of this kind may be

based on assets such as a patent or a superior production technique, but they may also be of a managerial nature. Examples would be a particularly good management system at group level or an advanced marketing function.

In many cases, the building of experience that takes place in multinational enterprises is the foundation for creating value through efficient coordination of a ramified network of geographically separate units.

2. If a company is to be founded through a direct investment, be it through the acquisition of an existing firm or the founding of a new one, the place to be chosen has to have some localization advantages. These may be sales-oriented, e.g. in the form of customer groups with great purchasing power, or they may be input-oriented, namely if the country in question is abundant in production factors that are essential in the production of the goods supplied by the group. A firm that produces advanced cerebral scanners might, for instance, benefit from the inventive environment in Silicon Valley or around Boston.

It should be emphasized that a localization advantage may be based on a condition that is in itself negative, such as trade barriers like high customs tariffs. For many years, founding a production company has been an efficient way of gaining a foothold in Latin American markets, which, traditionally, hide behind high tariff walls.

Developments in trade policies and slumping transportation costs may have considerable effects on the international pattern of production. For example, the creation of a single, large European market has reduced the need for foreign direct investments, tariff walls having disappeared internally. (On the other hand, the incentive becomes greater because nationally discriminating procedures are expected to be abolished. The net result has been a strong European wave of foreign direct investments.)

3. The third condition that has to be satisfied is that of internalization advantages. This means that if the firm holds a competitive advantage that can advantageously be moved to another country then it has to be profitable to retain it within the enterprise rather than having other firms use it against payment (for instance, through franchising, leasing or licensed production).

If an enterprise chooses to internalize, i.e. if it prefers a foreign direct investment, the reason may be that its competence is so important for the survival of the enterprise that it does not dare to hand it over to others. However, foreign direct investments may also be the preferred choice in other situations: e.g. if the country concerned has a weak legal system so that making a fraudulent party fulfil a contract may turn out to be very difficult. The more uncertainty there is with respect to such conditions, the more likely the solution of foreign direct investments becomes.

The three aspects of the eclectic paradigm reflect partly the comparative advantages described in Chapter 2—this holds for the localization aspect—and partly the competitive advantages discussed in Chapter 3—this goes for the firm-specific advantages.

Actually, John Dunning has even made use of these three necessary conditions in defining conditions on which the three forms of transaction prevail. If localization advantages are not available, production should 'stay at home' and internationalization take place through exports. If localization advantages are available, but internalization advantages are not, then a contractual solution, e.g. licensing, is preferable. If both localization and internalization advantages are available, then a subsidiary should be established. Figure 4.4 summarizes the three situations.

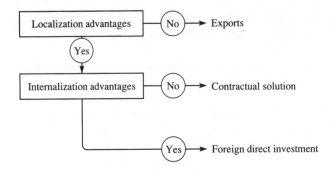

Figure 4.4 Choice of form of transaction

4.4.2 Multinational enterprises and society

Since the mid-eighties foreign direct investments have increased significantly faster than national investments and global GDP. According to the United Nations, multinational enterprises total 35 000 with approximately 150 000 subsidiaries (1990). The majority of multinational enterprises is based in the 'triad' of Western Europe, the United States and Japan. Multinational enterprises also account for an increasing share of world trade, e.g. turnover in subsidiaries now exceed total world exports. Finally, in a great number of countries multinational enterprises are the primary source of transfers of know-how, technology and training. The United Nations summarizes the situation as follows:

Transnational corporations have become the principal private actors in the world economy.

The backdrop to the explosive growth which recent years have witnessed is, in particular, the sharp change in international attitudes to multinational enterprises. Until a few years ago, international fora, especially the United Nations, held a vociferous anti-MNE mafia whose standard-bearers were the communist regimes of that time. The activities of the enterprises were seen as suspect and, consequently, a rich variety of obstacles were put in their way. Although the truth of the favourable effects of capital transfers listed in Section 4.1 was generally accepted, it was claimed that economic advantages and efficiency gains were comfortably counterbalanced by a number of unfortunate political and social effects including the following:

- The creation of monopolies and profits by multinational enterprises as a consequence of their excessive exploitation of technical and commercial supremacy relative to local competitors
- Negative balance of payments effects in host countries as a consequence of repatriation of profits—regardless of whether repatriation was direct or in the form of unreasonably high transfer prices among the companies of a group
- Multinational enterprises' retention in their own hands of any core competence and their centralization of R&D functions in their home countries so that the actual contribution to development in host countries remained moderate
- The distortion of consumption patterns towards 'Western' products appealing to the local élite, be they capitalists or bureaucrats
- Cultural imperialism resulting from the tendency of multinational enterprises to create

Table 4.5 Bargaining positions, multinational enterprise versus host country

Host country	Multinational corporation
Controls factors that multinationals want (natural resources, labour, market)	Controls benefits desired by host state (capital, employment, technology, management skill, industrialization and all the other benefits)
Legislative power	International advantages not duplicated easily (integrated production, established international distribution networks)
Power of the bureaucracy to delay and withhold	Potential parent state pressure
Police and military power	Negative host country actions will scare away other investment and international credit
Competition among multinationals for access to factors	Competition among host states for multinationals' investment
Ability to obtain advantages of multinationals from several different sources ('unbundling')	Refusal to expand investment
Nationalize foreign investment	Ultimate power to close down investment

Source: Walters and Blake (1992, p. 146).

alliances with local magnates and to employ quick-witted locals in a sort of conspiracy against local custom, values and political interests.

In practice, the critical attitude resulted in demands which host countries required multinational enterprises intending to start production in their countries to satisfy. Although the demands could assume a great many different forms, they usually included a wish for local joint venture partners, who would thus be allowed to gain insight into the know-how of a multinational enterprise and to gain certain possibilities of control. Another demand frequently made was for up-to-date technology transfers in connection with direct investments. Finally, it was common for host countries to demand the use of local input, for example, in the form of a certain minimum content of local production factors in the value added or to demand a certain volume of exports. Very often, host countries sought to play off multinational enterprises against each other and bargaining was at times quite ruthless. Table 4.5 presents a formalized outline of such a difficult bargaining position.

As indicated above, attitudes changed around 1990, and countries started competing for investments by multinational enterprises. This change is connected with the global shift away from centrally planned economies and the derived emphasis on the private sector as a growth generator. As the United Nations observes, this is where multinational enterprises are the principal actors.

SUMMARY

1. Like goods and services, factors move across borders. This gives rise to similar economic effects.

2. On the assumption of perfectly competitive markets, free capital movements result in welfare gains as capital is reallocated in accordance with marginal productivity theory. Redistributional effects cause local suppliers of scarce inputs to suffer, and vice versa. Other effects include the benefits of know-how transfer.
3. Migration of labour causes similar effects: holders of locally abundant factors gain, and so do the migrants. The decision to migrate has many effects which beg a 'migration calculus'.
4. The fact that factor markets are generally not competitive makes possible a wide variety of transaction forms: leasing, buy-back, licensing, etc. This leaves decision-makers with organizational considerations.
5. One transaction form is the purely hierarchical solution chosen by multinational corporations. A foreign direct investment results if three necessary conditions are met: firm-specific advantages, locational advantages and internalization advantages.
6. Widespread resistance to multinational corportions in the sixties to eighties has been replaced with almost unanimous acceptance as such firms have become principal private actors in the world economy

REFERENCES AND FURTHER READING

Casson, Mark (ed.) (1990), *Multinational Corporations*, Edward Elgar, Aldershot, UK.
Dunning, John H. (1988), *Explaining International Production*, Macmillan, London.
UN (1992), *World Investment Directory*, United Nations, New York.
Walters, R. S. and D. H. Blake (1992), *The Politics of Global Economic Relations*, Prentice-Hall, Englewood Cliffs, N.J.

THE THEORY OF TRADE POLICY

Although the free movement of goods increases global welfare individual countries have often intervened against free trade and obstructed it by means of tariffs and other restrictions. This was particularly the case in the 1930s, when international trade plunged. Likewise, since the mid-seventies we have seen a protectionist wave which, among other things, has taken the form of a number of voluntary export restraint agreements and of widespread use of anti-dumping measures.

This chapter concentrates on the *theoretical* aspects of trade policy, i.e. on questions such as why trade policy exists, how it may be implemented and what the effects of trade policy are. The practical aspects of trade policy, however, are dealt with in Chapter 6.

Section 5.1 deals with the aims and means of trade policy. Sections 5.2 and 5.3 look at concrete trade policy measures in markets with perfect competition, so these sections basically continue the exposition of foreign trade theories provided in Chapter 2. Finally, the recent foreign trade theories described in Chapter 3 are analysed in Section 5.4 with a view to determining whether they provide new arguments for trade policy.

5.1 AIMS AND MEANS OF TRADE POLICY

As was mentioned in Chapter 2, 3 and 4, opening the economy of a country to its external environment has both allocative and distributional consequences. In Chapter 2 this was analysed in detail under the assumption of perfect competition and within the framework of a *general* equilibrium model. Since it is easier to analyse tariffs and other trade restrictions within the framework of a *partial* equilibrium model, i.e. by looking at the market conditions of a given product in isolation, we shall begin this chapter by once again analysing the effects on efficiency and distribution that follow from free trade under perfect competition. This will allow us to answer the question of why trade policy exists.

5.1.1 The welfare gain of exports

Figure 5.1 shows the welfare effect of a country's exports. Reverting to the example used in Chapter 2, we will now consider the case of Danish bacon. The demand curve, D_H, and the supply curve, S_H, apply to domestic demand for and domestic supply of bacon, P_W is the world market price. We assume that domestic suppliers can sell all the bacon that they produce at this price.

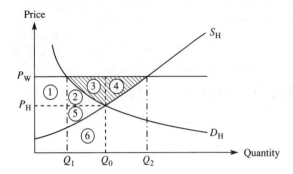

Figure 5.1 The efficiency effect of exports

Without international trade the price of P_H would form in the home market. The effects of allowing exports at the price of P_W will be a fall in the quantity demanded domestically from Q_0 to Q_1, a rise in production from Q_0 to Q_2 and an export volume of Q_1Q_2 corresponding to the sum of these quantities. In other words, this change in production and consumption may be assessed as follows: consumers are willing to pay the price of P_H for the consumption of the unit of Q_0; this unit can be sold abroad, however, at the price of P_W. Consequently, society will gain P_W-P_H if the unit is exported rather than sold domestically. It follows that the reduction in consumption of Q_1Q_0 will lead to a social gain corresponding to area 3 since the export value of this volume exceeds consumers' total utility of this volume by area 3. The reduction in consumer utility equals the area below the demand curve $(2+5+6)$, where the demand curve represents the consumers' marginal utility.

Producers are willing to supply the unit of Q_0 at P_H since this price corresponds to the marginal costs of the unit. If they export it, however, they can obtain the amount of P_W-P_H on top of their marginal costs. Therefore this amount is the social gain obtained from exporting this unit. Expanding production to Q_2 and exporting Q_0Q_2 will lead to a social gain corresponding to area 4. Consequently, the total social gain from the consumption reduction and production expansion corresponds to the area $3+4$. Compared to a situation with no foreign trade at all, this area expresses the welfare gain resulting from exports.

5.1.2 The welfare gain of imports

Figure 5.2, which may illustrate the case of the Danish cloth market, shows the corresponding analysis of the effects of imports. If domestic demand is to be covered by domestic production alone, the market price will be P_H and the volume supplied will be Q_0. If imports are allowed consumption will rise to Q_2 since the world market price of P_W will prevail. At the same time, domestic production will fall from Q_0 to Q_1. Once again, the total gain of opening the economy to foreign trade can be assessed by looking at suppliers and consumers separately. The part of imports (Q_1Q_2) that substitutes domestic production corresponds to Q_1Q_0. These imports cost $(Q_1Q_0)P_W$, i.e. area 4 or less than the costs of domestic production, which equal the area below S_H in the relevant interval, i.e. the area $2+4$. The gain equals area 2. As regards the 'new' consumption, Q_0Q_2, the willingness of the consumers to pay corresponds to area $3+5$. Consumer's surplus, which is the difference between the consumers' willingness to pay and their costs, corresponds to area 3. In sum, the total social gain equals area $2+3$.

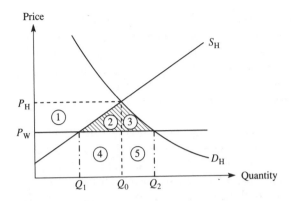

Figure 5.2 The efficiency effect of imports

5.1.3 The distributional problem

It follows that international trade has positive effects for *all* countries participating in it. Of course this does not mean that no one will be adversely affected, but it is essential that the winners will be able to compensate the losers and still be in a better position than they would have been without free trade. In the bacon and cloth examples in Chapter 2, the Danish pig industry and the English cloth industry will experience an influx of firms, and hence of factors of production. Conversely, the number of firms in the Danish cloth industry and the English pig industry will decrease. These processes will improve the earnings potential of Danish pig-breeders and the English cloth industry and they will force Danish cloth producers and English bacon producers to close down. Both labour and capital will have to move, industrially and geographically. The *lasting* advantages have some short term costs.

Among consumers, a certain redistribution also takes place. As regards cloth consumption, Danish consumers will increase their consumer's surplus by the area $1+2+3$ in Figure 5.2. With respect to bacon consumption, however, their consumer's surplus will decrease by the area $1+2$.

It is precisely the fact that free trade will put some social groups in a worse position than they would be in if trade were more restricted that often serves as an argument in favour of trade restrictions.

5.1.4 'Natural' trade restrictions

In the above examples full price equalization was assumed, home market prices being adapted to world market prices. In fact, no absolute price equalization will be achieved since selling goods in other countries always involves certain additional costs, e.g. transport costs. Therefore the world market price in Figure 5.1 has to be reduced by the additional transport costs per unit exported, which will yield the price at which producers will supply the home market. If, for instance, transport costs are DKK 100 per unit, the home market price will be reduced correspondingly. This will increase the quantity demanded and reduce production and exports.

Likewise, the transport costs of imports will increase the home market price in relation to the world market price, and this will reduce the volume imported (see Figure 5.2). So the immediate conclusion is that transport costs reduce the volume of foreign trade and prevent full international price equalization.

The two figures also show that in the case of transport costs exceeding the difference between P_H and P_W no foreign trade will take place, the price difference being insufficient to cover the costs of trade involved in exporting and importing. The industries thus protected from external competition belong to the domestic sector while the rest constitute the internationally competitive sector, i.e. the sector that faces competition from foreign suppliers.

Firms that have substantial transport costs in their production of goods belong to the protected sector. Such firms primarily supply services since services often require personal contact between the consumer and the firm and therefore involve high transport costs regardless of whether the consumer has to go to the firm or vice versa. Examples include doctor's calls, going to the hairdresser's, retail shopping, etc. Previously, goods that, compared to their price, were heavy or bulky used to be protected in this way, which is why the construction industry used to be considered part of the protected sector. With falling transport costs, however, the construction industry has become highly export-oriented. This clearly shows that an industry is not either a member of one sector or of the other but rather some industries are more protected than others. Apart from transport costs, linguistic and cultural differences may serve as natural trade barriers.

5.1.5 Goals

Three decisive factors play a role when the decision to introduce trade measures is made; these are allocation, distribution and stabilization. The conflict between the first two was pointed out above in the analysis of the results of opening the economy to the external environment: the total level of welfare in society will be higher but different social groups will not be equally affected. Without public compensation schemes, which are rarely carried out on a full scale in practice, there will be some losers. Since, in addition, international competition results in industrial reallocation of society's resources significant short-term readjustment costs may result from the process. Trade policy has similar allocative and distributional consequences but with contrary effects. Within the framework of the model, this means that if trade policy is to have a rational economic justification then the advantages gained by society from a change in income distribution have to counterbalance the losses resulting from the allocative inefficiency. Even then, it is a precondition that the distribution desired cannot be achieved by any better means than through trade policy.

Trade policy may also be used in an attempt to *stabilize* trade cycles (production, employment and balance of payments), which the economy of any country is subjected to over time. This is only rational if no better means are available for the purpose. Usually, however, fiscal, monetary and exchange rate policies will serve the purpose better.

Table 5.1 Goals of trade policy

Tax revenue	Development (infant-industry tariffs)
Employment	Balance of payments
Terms of trade (international income distribution	Efficiency
National income distribution (personal/by sectors/ functional)	Morals
	Security/self-sufficiency
Military considerations (NATO)	Health
Other foreign policy motives (UN/Serbia)	Environmental protection

Table 5.2 Trade measures

Imports	Exports
Tariffs	Export tax/duty
Anti-dumping tariffs	Variable export duties
Countervailing duty	Export subsidies
Variable import duties	Direct subsidy
Customs union	Indirect subsidy
Free trade area	Export credits guarantee scheme
Import quotas	Financial support
Import subsidies	Marketing support
Variable import subsidies	Variable export subsidies
Discriminating public procurement	Marginal export subsidy
Multiple exchange rates/monetary compensation	Multiple exchange rates/monetary compensation
Exchange restrictions	Exchange restrictions
Deposit schemes	Transport restrictions
Technical barriers to trade	Technical barriers to trade
Transport restrictions	'Voluntary' export restraint
Red tape barrier	Embargo (export prohibition)
Embargo (import prohibition)	Red tape barrier
'Voluntary' import expansion	Counter-trade conditions

The justification for trade measures typically lies in considerations of certain social groups or interest groups. As will be shown later in this chapter, trade policy may, in some special cases, improve the total level of welfare in a country.

Obviously, the formulation of allocative, distributional and stabilizing goals may receive any of a wide range of headings. Table 5.1 lists a number of such concrete goals, some of which will be commented on in this and the following chapters.

5.1.6 Means

Just as the range of trade policy goals is wide, the range of trade measures is also wide (see Table 5.2). As trade policy concerns intervention in the free movement of goods across national borders, such intervention can be categorized into two groups: intervention affecting imports and intervention affecting exports. Although measures affecting imports are used more often and are opposed more vigorously by other countries, measures affecting exports are quite significant. These include the use of various kinds of export subsidies, for example. Trade measures may also be categorized according to whether (1) they serve to regulate prices or volumes (e.g. tariffs versus quantitative import control), (2) they are implemented at the border or elsewhere (e.g. tariffs versus technical barriers to trade) and (3) they are transparent or not (e.g. tariffs versus technical barriers to trade).

5.2 TARIFFS AND IMPORT QUOTAS: TRADITIONAL MEASURES

This section deals with the two classic types of trade barriers relating to imports, i.e. tariffs and quantitative restrictions. Firstly, we examine the effects of tariffs and then those of import

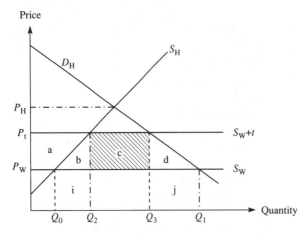

Figure 5.3   Effects of tariffs under perfect competition

quotas on a small country in which all production takes place under *perfect competition*. Differences and similarities between the two kinds of measures are explained and, finally, we discuss the differences it makes if the country is large rather than small.

5.2.1   Tariffs

A tariff is a duty imposed on an imported product. It may be a *specific* duty, i.e. a fixed duty per unit, or an *ad valorem* duty, i.e. a duty charged as a percentage of the value of the product. Historically, tariffs have been the measure used most often in foreign trade and, politically, it has often served the dual purpose of protecting domestic producers from foreign competition and being a source of revenue to the state. The effects of tariffs can be analysed on the basis of the market conditions of a single product as shown in Figure 5.3. Given a self-sufficient economy, domestic demand, D_H, and domestic supply, S_H, yield a home market price of P_H.

As a small country cannot influence the world market price, P_W, the import supply, S_W, is a horizontal curve at the price of P_W. Imports will occur when the world market price, P_W, is lower than P_H, and at this point imports will amount to Q_0Q_1, i.e. they will correspond to the volume by which domestic demand exceeds production at the world market price.

If a specific duty, t, is imposed on the product, the import supply will shift upwards by t to $S_W + t$. This will allow domestic producers to increase their prices correspondingly, but no more than this or consumers will switch to the foreign product. Therefore the home market price will increase by t to P_t, the tariff being entirely included in the price.

The *protective effect* consists in domestic production increasing from Q_0 to Q_2 as a result of the price increase. This leads to a rise in the level of employment in the industries involved, but in the case of full employment it will be to the detriment of the level of employment in other domestic industries. In addition, it will be to the detriment of the level of employment abroad, with imports falling from Q_0Q_1 to Q_2Q_3. A balance of payments gain corresponding to the sum of the areas i and j will emerge since imports still take place at the price of P_W. It is worth emphasizing that the duration of this positive balance of payments effect is limited, one reason being that the activity increase in the protected sector forces input prices up and, consequently, weakens the export opportunities of other industries. This is why import tariffs are considered to be a tax on exports.

Further, tariffs involve *redistribution* from consumers to producers. The welfare loss of consumers corresponds to their loss of consumer's surplus, which equals the areas of a + b + c + d. Domestic producers obtain a *profit increase* corresponding to the area of a. This is a result of turnover going up by the areas of a + b + i, of which variable costs increase by the areas of b + i, i.e. by the area below the supply curve.

Finally, the government obtains a tariff revenue which equals the volume of imports multiplied by the tariff rate, or by the area of c. Today, the *revenue aspect* is of minor importance to industrialized countries since tariffs constitute an insignificant part of government revenue in these countries. Previously, however, customs revenue was of major importance and even today it finances close on one-fourth of government expenditure in a great number of developing countries.

As consumers lose more than the sum of the customs revenue and the profit increase, a *social loss* ensues from a tariff of b + d. This means that the government and producers will not gain so much that they can compensate consumers for their loss and still be better off themselves. The area of b corresponds to the loss related to using expensive domestic production instead of less expensive foreign production. The area of d represents the loss of consumer's surplus not counterbalanced by 'income' elsewhere.

5.2.2 Quantitative import restrictions

Through import licences an *import quota* (IQ) restricts the imports of a certain product to a specific volume per year. This means that total supply in the market will consist of domestic supply and the quota of IQ above the world market price, P_W ($S_H + IQ$ in Figure 5.4.) Due to the limited supply the market price will rise from P_W to P_{IQ} and imports will fall from Q_0Q_1 to Q_2Q_3, i.e. by the quota of IQ. Once again, a redistribution from consumers to producers results, corresponding to the area of a.

This will lead to a gain on imports, the world market price being P_W while, in the home market, the product can be sold at the price of P_{IQ} due to the scarcity of the product. Since, usually, domestic importers obtain the import licences, the gain of the area of c will accrue to them as a *pure monopoly rent*. The distributional arbitrariness of this can be remedied, however, if the government sells the import licences in question at an auction, which will ensure that the

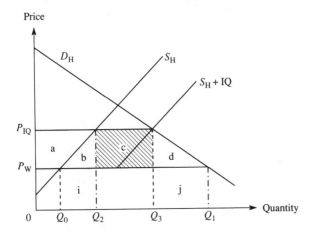

Figure 5.4 Effects of quantitative import restrictions under perfect competition

maximum revenue corresponds to the area of c. If this solution is chosen, tariffs and quantitative import restrictions will have identical effects on distribution and efficiency. If, however, foreign firms obtain the licences, then the area of c will accrue to foreign countries and therefore form part of the economic efficiency loss of the country in question. From a global point of view, it makes no difference of course whether domestic importers or foreign firms obtain the import licences.

5.2.3 Tariffs versus import quotas

The above analysis showed that if the question of who receives the import licences is disregarded, then tariffs and import quotas have *equivalent* economic effects. This equivalence only holds, however, under the *static* assumptions of the analysis, i.e. that neither domestic demand, domestic supply nor the world market price changes. In addition, the assumption of perfect competition has to be maintained.

In a dynamic world with changes in demand and supply, tariffs yield the better allocative result. This may be illustrated if we assume that the domestic supply in Figures 5.3 and 5.4 decreases as a result of, for example, wage increases in the industry involved. In the case of tariffs, the domestic price remains the same since the volume of imports will increase and replace the fall in domestic production. Given a constant import quota, the volume imported remains constant, but due to the decrease in supply the domestic price will go up. The price increase is the reason why the decrease in domestic production is limited and, seen from the point of view of domestic producers, an import quota leads to a better result. The situation of consumers deteriorates, however, as a result of the price increase: compared to the case of tariffs, domestic production increases and consumption decreases in the case of an import quota, so the efficiency loss is greater in the latter case than in the former. A further advantage of tariffs over import quotas is that tariffs have a cost-restraining effect; import quotas leave domestic producers with less inducement to restrict cost increases since costs can partly be passed on to prices. Table 5.3 sums up the effects of a decrease in supply in the case of tariffs and in the case of an import quota.

An analysis of changes in demand or in the world market price will likewise show dynamic differences between tariffs and import quotas. The overall conclusion drawn on the basis of such analyses is that tariffs are preferable for reasons of efficiency. Of course, the actual decision made depends on the political aims of the trade policy. Questions to be answered include whether the aim is that of protecting domestic producers, that of securing a certain import target or, for instance, that of ensuring constant prices.

Table 5.3 Comparison of the effects of a decrease in supply under tariffs and under an import quota

Variable	Tariffs	Quota
Domestic price	Stable	Increase
Domestic production	Marked decrease	Lighter decrease
Producer's surplus	Marked decrease	Lighter decrease
Import volume	Increase	Stable
Customs revenue or monopoly profit to importer	Increase	Increase
Allocative loss	Stable	Increase
Cost restraint (X-efficiency)	Considerable	Little

If politicians wish to reduce imports to a certain level and the actual conditions of demand and supply are unknown then of course a quantitative restriction is the safest means. As was shown above, however, quotas may cause long-term problems, for instance if domestic demand increases or domestic supply decreases. This will lead to price increases in the home market and thus increase the monopoly rent accruing to importers. In the case of tariffs, by contrast, the conditions of supply and demand in the domestic market will not affect the home market price. In sum, quotas contribute to stabilizing imports while tariffs stabilize the home market price. From an allocative point of view, however, tariffs are generally preferable.

5.2.4   The terms of trade effect

The analyses of tariffs in Figure 5.3 and of quantitative import restrictions in Figure 5.4 were based on the assumption that we were concerned with the trade policy of a small country. This was reflected in the perfect elasticity of the import supply (S_W) at the world market price P_W. Because of this, tariffs did not affect the *international terms of trade* of the country, international terms of trade being defined as the relationship between the price index of a country's exports and that of its imports. This conclusion also holds in the case of quantitative import restrictions on condition that import licences are not allotted to foreign exporters since, in this case, an increase in export prices will lead to deterioration of the terms of trade.

In the case of a large country, however, such as the United States, trade policy may affect the terms of trade favourably. If a duty is imposed on a product that is an important part of American imports, the effect on global demand will be sufficiently significant to cause the American import prices (less tariffs) to fall. Consequently, the American terms of trade will improve, which, seen in isolation, is a national advantage. This advantage is counterbalanced, however, by the allocative distortion (area b + d) expressed in Figure 5.3. It is therefore not possible to be certain in advance that the outcome will be a national advantage. This is further illustrated in Figure 5.5.

Since even in the case of individual countries the world market price is now no longer externally determined, the interaction between tariffs and world market price has to be identified (Figure 5.5(b)). The supply and demand curves in this part of the figure consist of a

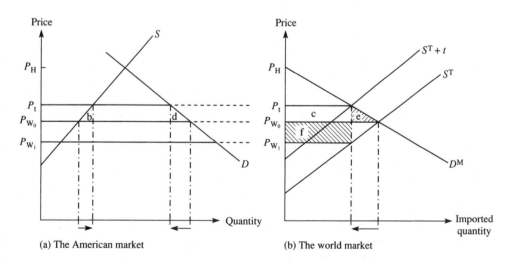

Figure 5.5   Effects of tariffs in the case of a large country

curve indicating export supply from the rest of the world (S^X) and a curve indicating American import demand (D^M). D^M results from the difference between American supply of the product in question and American demand for it (Figure 5.5(a)). If prices are below P_H, demand will exceed supply and the demand for imports will be positive. If prices are above P_H, supply will exceed demand and the difference between S and D constitutes the American export supply curve—this curve is not in Figure 5.5. Import demand and export supply curves can be similarly determined for the rest of the world.

Using Figure 5.5(b), we shall now consider the situation in which the United States is an importer (D^M) and the rest of the world an exporter (S^X). If free trade prevails, the world market price is P_{W_0}. If the United States now imposes a duty of US\$ t per unit, the export supply (inclusive of tariffs) will decrease to $S^X + t$. As a result prices in the American market will go up from P_{W_0} to P_t. Since P_t is inclusive of tariffs the import price is US\$ t lower, i.e. P_{W_1}. The difference between P_{W_0} and P_{W_1} results from the duty imposed. The figure also shows that the fall in import price depends on the elasticity of the export supply curve. The more elastic the curve is the smaller the fall in price will be. The case of the small country corresponds to a situation with an absolutely elastic export supply curve.

Let us now look at the welfare effects of tariffs on the importing country, the United States, in the above case. Had the United States been a small country, the analysis of Figure 5.3 would hold. In Figure 5.5(a), however, tariffs (of $P_t - P_{W_0}$) raise the price to P_t. The welfare loss corresponds to area b + d. In Figure 5.5(b) the area e indicates the welfare effects of this price increase, the curve D^M being the result of $D - S$. Consequently, c + e indicate the *combined* effects with respect to consumers and producers. Partly because the product in question is imported and partly because of the price increase this effect is negative. If the tariffs revenue (area c) is deducted, the net effect is e.

The United States being a large country, however, the import price will fall to P_{W_1}, as mentioned above, if a duty of t is imposed. The net welfare effect will then be as follows:

Tariffs revenue	c + f
Combined consumer and producer effect	− c − e
Net welfare effect	f − e

It is impossible to determine in advance whether f−e is positive or negative. If the duty is small the area e will approximate zero (an area of the so-called second order) and the duty will increase the welfare in the country. If, however, the duty is very heavy, the size of e will be considerable and the fall in imports will gradually reduce the tariffs revenue. Consequently, there is a tariff rate that maximizes the welfare gain of the country. This is usually referred to as the *optimum tariff rate*. Figure 5.6 illustrates the interdependence between national welfare and the tariff rates.

It would seem that a large country has a potential for welfare gains obtained through trade policy. Whether these gains can actually be realized in practice is rather questionable, however. This is primarily due to the fact that the *terms of trade gain*, which in Figure 5.5 is indicated as f, is achieved at the expense of the rest of the world. This is a case of *pure redistribution* among countries; it is therefore not wholly unthinkable that if one country takes steps to intensify its trade policy then other large countries will introduce countermeasures. The likely outcome is a commercial war leading to a reduction in the volume of trade and to the loss of all parties. In this connection, the experience of the thirties is well worth remembering.

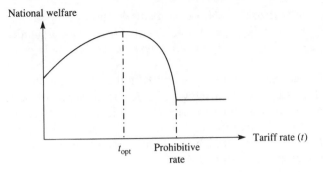

National welfare

Tariff rate (t)

t_{opt} Prohibitive
              rate

Figure 5.6   Tariff rates and national welfare in the case of a large country

5.3   OTHER TRADE POLICY INSTRUMENTS

As was shown in Table 5.2, the number of trade measures is not limited to tariffs and import quotas. In connection with the increasing protectionism which began in the mid-seventies, a wide range of other measures have been employed more and more frequently. In this section, we examine some of the most frequent measures, still assuming perfect competition as in Section 5.2.

5.3.1   Voluntary export restraint

Under a voluntary export restraint (VER) agreement an importing country and an exporting country agree that the exporting country will limit its exports of a certain product to the quota of, for example, IQ (see Figure 5.4). From the point of view of the importing country, this measure differs from a corresponding import quota in that the monopoly gain of area c now accrues to foreign exporters, resulting in deterioration of the terms of trade of the importing country. The reason for using this measure is mainly that international agreements restrict the use of import quotas considerably (see Chapter 6).

From the point of view of the exporting country, entering a VER agreement is preferable to being faced with a traditional import quota: while the latter would leave the monopoly profit to the importers in the importing country, the former will allow the exporting country to obtain this profit. In addition, the importing country will accept the resulting income loss as the price of being considered less protectionist. If, however, the import quota does not discriminate among exporters and the VER agreement is used in a discriminating fashion then it is not necessarily true that the exporting country should prefer the VER agreement to a traditional import quota. VER agreements are often used in this way and in this case an agreement, e.g. between the United States and Japan regarding Japanese car exports, increases the market shares in the United States of car exporters who are not parties to the agreement at the expense of Japan. Given that the elasticity of supply from other exporting countries is sufficiently high, accepting a non-discriminating import quota may therefore be preferable.

Apart from affecting efficiency and income distribution, VER agreements, like ordinary import quotas, also influence the quality of the products imported if the product category is *heterogeneous*, which implies that the assumption of perfect competition has not actually been satisfied (Falvey 1979). To illustrate this, let us assume that, for example, the EU and the developing countries have entered an agreement which places the latter under an obligation to restrict the volume of their exports of footwear to the EU. Let two closely substituting groups of footwear consist of A, an inexpensive low-quality group which costs GBP 10 a pair under free trade, and B, a slightly more expensive high-quality group which under free trade costs GBP 14 a pair.

Of course, exporters seek to allocate their exports between A and B so that the premium per unit (the excess of the VER-distorted domestic price over the world price) is the same for both types of footwear. If the percentage mark-up and the relative price increase is the same for both qualities, the premium will be higher on the high-quality variant in money terms (GBP). As a result, the VER quota will lead to *quality upgrading*, which has been observed in connection with several VER agreements from the eighties (Feenestra 1984).

5.3.2   Export subsidies and export taxes

A country wishing to improve its balance of payments, its employment level, etc., does not have to restrict its intervention to imports. Various kinds of export subsidies have been increasingly used in recent years despite the fact that a wide range of international agreements in principle prohibit export subsidies on industrial products. Circumventing the prohibitions is easy, however.

In Figure 5.7 the effects of an export subsidy are analysed. S^X is the export supply from domestic exporters. Correspondingly, D^M is the import demand from the rest of the world for the product in question. We assume that domestic exporters have a certain influence on price collectively, but not individually, which is why the demand curve decreases.

Prior to the introduction of the export subsidy, the annual volume of exports is X_0 at the price of P_{w_0}. If firms then receive an export subsidy of s per unit exported, the export supply curve will shift downwards by the size of the subsidy. This will cause exports to increase to X_1 and exporters to lower their prices in foreign markets to P_{w_1}. As a consequence, the terms of trade of the exporting country will deteriorate. If the producers in the exporting country had constituted only a modest part of the total world market for the product, D^M would have been horizontal and the terms of trade would have been constant.

The costs of the subsidy to the government correspond to the area ABCD or the volume multiplied by the subsidy. Out of this area FBCE represents the combined welfare gain attributable to the increase in exporters' profits and the decrease in consumer's surplus, i.e. the

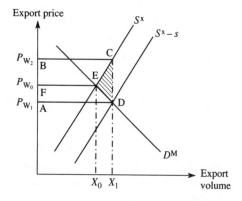

Figure 5.7   Effects of an export subsidy under perfect competition

redistribution from tax payers and consumers to producers. Likewise, AFED indicates the redistribution from domestic tax payers to foreign consumers and producers as a whole. The part of government costs that does not accrue to other groups represents the global efficiency loss; this corresponds to the area of ECD. This loss is the result of the fact that the costs of producing the additional volume of X_0X_1 (the area of X_0ECX_1) exceed the increase in the import consumer's surplus (the area of X_0EDX_1) in the importing countries. From the point of view of the exporting country, the export subsidy is really a case of 'beggar thyself' policy, the *national loss* being not just the area of ECD but also that of AFED, which represents the increase in foreign import consumer's surplus abroad.

As only exports are subsidized, domestic consumer prices will be s higher than export prices. Therefore export subsidies are more appropriate in markets with transport costs or other barriers which prevent exports from returning to the exporting country.

For this reason, most subsidies are *general* ones, i.e. they do not specifically relate to exports but to domestic production. This increases the costs to government but, in return, domestic consumers benefit in terms of lower prices from the taxes that they have paid. One example of a subsidized industry is the European shipbuilding industry: in some European countries the shipbuilding credits guarantee system has at times provided subsidies corresponding to more than 50 per cent of the price of new ships.

The positive balance of payments effect of an increase in exports is often put forward as an argument for subsidizing export industries. Figure 5.7, however, illustrates the fact that export prices have to be reduced with increasing sales. Consequently, the balance of payments effect of exporting to markets in which the price elasticity of exports is less than one will be negative.

The above analysis of export subsidies has shown that under perfect competition the welfare effect is unambiguously negative, which holds in the case of both small and large countries. Seen in this light, the extensive use of export subsidies is rather surprising, the more so as large countries with a wish to influence exports may achieve favourable terms of trade effects if they impose export taxes. Some classic examples of countries in a position to do so include South Africa, which almost has a monopoly in the international diamond market, and Saudi Arabia, which has a perceptible share in global oil exports. The size of the country is not decisive, however; instead the crucial point is whether industries in a given country have any impact on the international price of selected products. Even a small country like Denmark may influence international price formation in selected product areas including those of biscuits and hearing aids.

Figure 5.7 may also be used to analyse the effects of export taxes, an export tax (t_x) being nothing but a negative export subsidy. An export tax actually corresponds to shifting the supply curve of S^x-s to S_x. This will cause the world market price to rise from P_{W_1} to P_{W_0} and the domestic producer and consumer price to *fall* to $P_{W_0}-t_x$. As in the case of import tariffs, an export tax may, if it is not too large, increase national welfare precisely because it improves the terms of trade of the country in question. Therefore if national firms compete fiercely with each other in the global market and therefore contribute to deteriorating terms of trade, an export tax may serve to raise national welfare. Alternatively, firms may reap the would-be tax revenue if they set up joint export marketing efforts, and thus secure higher export prices.

5.3.3   Other kinds of protectionism

Protection of national producers is not restricted to the kinds dealt with above. In what follows, a brief description of some fairly important kinds of protectionist measures is provided. These include (1) discriminating public procurement, (2) technical and administrative trade barriers, (3) local content requirements and (4) counter-trade conditions.

1. In most countries, the public sector needs considerable procurement of goods and services. Even if national products are more expensive than imports, however, procurement is only rarely a border-crossing activity. As a result, international trade in a range of products that are primarily bought by the public sector is quite modest. This holds of telecommunications equipment, rolling stock, military equipment, etc. Public expenditure is increased through surcharges due to weak competition, the result of national monopolies.

2. Technical trade barriers, e.g. health and safety regulations whose primary justification lies in the interests of domestic producers rather than the health and safety of the population, are used extensively. If such regulations are drawn up in cooperation with domestic producers, then the products of these producers immediately satisfy the requirements, but foreign producers will have to change their specifications to be allowed to enter the market involved. This may force these producers to make minor batches specifically for the country in question, which of course increases the costs of production and thus weakens the competitiveness of foreign producers. The regulations may also include marketing and packaging. Germany used to have regulations prohibiting the marketing of beer as beer if it contained anything but natural ingredients (the 'Reinheitsgebot' Act[*]). Similarly, Denmark is known for its bottle recycling system, which prohibits the sale of canned beer and soft drinks and which other countries look on as a case of protectionism rather than one of environmental protection.

    Another kind of barrier targeting imports consists in administrative harassment in connection with customs clearance. The techniques are legion. They include unnecessarily complicated registration involving numerous documents to be filled in, possibly in the local language, which may be difficult for many firms even if the language is a widely known one such as French or Spanish. Another variety consists in delaying customs clearance, which is what happened in France a few years ago in the case of video recorder imports. Customs clearance was moved to a small customs office with just a few employees and situated far away from the principal market. This technique ensures that customs clearance will be slow and inflicts additional transport and insurance costs on foreign producers. Yet another technique consists in requiring importers to deposit an amount corresponding to the value of the goods imported in the central bank of the country in question for a certain period of time. This has been used, for example, in Italy and comes very close to the imposition of a tariff, the loss of interest on the deposit being fully comparable to the effects of a tariff.

3. A number of developing countries serve extensively as assembly plants assembling components produced in the industrialized countries. In an attempt to have a larger part of the added value produced locally, some of these developing countries allow components to be imported at a reduced tariff if the import share of components does not exceed a certain level. This kind of regulation obviously yields protection to local component producers in the same way as a quota does. As regards local assembly plants, however, it amounts to a cost increase, which weakens their competitiveness. Typically, producers of finished products will then demand compensating protection. Discriminating procurement is one extreme example of a 'local content' requirement whereas 'Buy British' campaigns are a watered-down version.

---

[*] In 1987, the European Court of Justice decided that Germany should repeal the act with respect to beer produced in other countries.

4   A barrier to free international exchange of goods which has gained ground rapidly in recent years consists in so-called *counter-trade transactions*. They originally stem from East–West trade, which involved supplying Western exporters with goods instead of paying them in a convertible currency and leaving it to them to sell the goods in the West. Transactions of this kind are on the decline in Eastern Europe but have spread to a great number of developing countries, which consider counter-trade deals their only possibility of financing imports, foreign exchange being in short supply in these countries. Major international banks have special offices for this kind of trade, and a number of firms have been established, in particular in Austria and Germany, which actually specialize in business of this kind.

5.4   TRADE POLICY: COMPETITIVE ADVANTAGES

The conclusion from our analysis above of the welfare effects of trade policy was the following: in the case of small countries, trade measures result in a welfare loss; in the case of large countries not subjected to retaliation, a welfare gain might be obtained in the form of a terms of trade gain. These conclusions are based on the assumption of perfect competition and on the assumption that no *domestic* disturbances such as externalities exist.

Reality, however, often differs from this scenario. Both positive and negative externalities exist and, as was mentioned in Chapter 3, a very large part of international trade flows, particularly among industrialized countries, must be considered to concern markets without perfect competition. Consequently, imperfect competition caused by economies of scale and product differentiation has to be included, and the question that we want to answer is whether such market conditions change the conclusions pertaining to the effects of trade policy.

5.4.1   External benefits: the infant-industry argument

Even if we retain the assumption of perfect competition the existence of positive or negative externalities may force us to adjust the conclusion reached. Figure 5.8 gives an example of this. In a free trade situation and given a world market price of P_W, the small country in question imports Q_0Q_1. It is possible, however, that due to a positive external effect S_{Pr}, the supply curve shown, does not simultaneously represent the marginal social costs. Production may, for instance, result in experience that generally improves society's production possibilities and thus creates advantages that individual firms will not take into consideration in their production decisions. If marginal social costs are S_{So} rather than S_{Pr}, then the optimum production volume

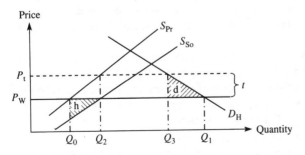

Figure 5.8   Welfare gain through tariffs under positive externality

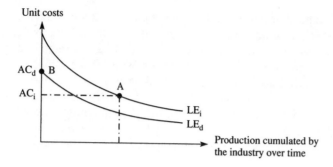

Figure 5.9 Learning curve and infant-industry protection

will be Q_2 rather than Q_0. Obviously, a tariff of t will precisely make it possible to produce this volume, which will eliminate the loss of h. By the same token, a tariff causes distortion in consumption, and a welfare loss of area d. For this reason a tariff is not the best way of correcting positive externalities in production. In this situation, a production subsidy would be preferable as it has no influence on home market price, and thus the consumption structure.

One of the most important sources of positive externalities is the accumulation of knowledge over time taking place in firms. The improvements of products and production techniques which result from the experience gained can be copied by other firms and thus be of benefit to them (see Chapter 3). As a result of the knowledge gained by the industry over time, production costs in individual firms will fall (see the learning curve in Figure 5.9). As costs decrease with the production cumulated over time, this phenomenon is known as an example of *dynamic economies of scale*.

Figure 5.9 represents the learning curves of existing producers in an industrialized country (LE_i) and of potential producers in a developing country (LE_d). Point A represents unit costs, price and cumulated production at a given point in time. Point A merely represents a brief instant since cumulation of production continues all the time and thus forces the equilibrium point down the LE_i curve. The developing country possesses a comparative advantage with respect to production, however, which is reflected in the position of its potential learning curve below that of the industrialized country. Nevertheless, individual potential producers in the developing country will have no incentive to enter the market, their costs, i.e. point B, being above the world market price. Protectionism in the developing country may be justified in such a situation since a tariff of at least AC_d–AC_i will permit the country to establish a domestic industry. If the home market is sufficiently large it may be possible over time to gain production experience in this way, which may then result in unit costs becoming lower than in the industrialized country.

> This externality effect is the core of the so-called *infant-industry argument* for protection. Developing countries in particular make use of the argument, claiming that they will have comparative or competitive advantages in certain industries if these industries are provided with some protection for a *limited period of time* so as to allow them to gain a foothold in the market. During this period the industries will acquire sufficient production competence and knowledge to be able to handle international competition.

Of course the problem is to single out the infants who need such a learning period. Fairly often, firms that exist under favourable tariff regulations do not obtain the necessary competitiveness behind the tariff walls and, as a result, the tariff regulations tend to become permanent.

Apart from the learning effects, infant industry protection is valid in the case of a true *market imperfection* which prevents private markets from developing the industry in question themselves at a sufficient pace. Due to poor financial infrastructures the growth of newly established firms will often be limited by their own savings. Consequently, necessary long-term investments aimed at establishing competitive advantages are difficult to make, even though they are profitable. Other arguments in this connection relate to *labour market imperfections*, e.g. in the form of wage rigidity which leads to unemployment. In such cases the costs of additional employment accruing to society will be below wage levels.

The problem of using trade policy in situations with internal market imperfections is that better means are usually available for the correction of such imperfections. In the case of imperfect capital markets the best means will be the establishment of improved financial institutions; alternatively, the second best means will be the granting of capital subsidies to new firms. If the imperfection relates to the labour market, wage subsidies are a better means than trade policy, the general rule being that the best means is the one that targets the market imperfection directly.

Industrialized countries argue in the same way when they advocate *old-age protection* of an industry which has lost its competitiveness to developing countries. The protection is to last until the production factors involved can be moved to other and more competitive industries. This kind of protection, like the former, tends to become permanent.

5.4.2 Strategic trade policy

This is an innovation in the theory of trade policy. It dates back to the beginning of the eighties when Brander and Spencer (1981, 1983) emphasized the national strategic aspects of trade policy as a means of creating national advantages at the expense of other countries. As mentioned in Chapter 3, the concept of strategy is related to imperfect competition and to the concept of competitive advantages. Based on the idea that firms may increase their profits through strategic behaviour, e.g. through excess investments which scare away potential newcomers, the point of Brander and Spencer's view of trade policy is that a country may introduce export subsidies or tariffs to provide the firms of other countries with an incentive to reduce their production, thus leaving larger market shares and profits to domestic producers. In what follows, we attempt to provide a better understanding of this complex of problems by considering the simplest case possible, which really continues the case of global economies of scale discussed in Chapter 3.

The next generation of jumbo jets will be our example. Traditionally, the industry has been dominated by three American firms, Boeing, McDonnell Douglas and Lockheed, and one European consortium, Airbus. It is unlikely that all four firms will be able to make a profit in this sub-market. Let us assume that, technically, only Airbus and Boeing are capable of developing the new type of aircraft and that the market will allow only one producer to produce at a profit. If each producer adopts a strategy either of production or of no production then the choice of decisions that they face may be expressed as in Table 5.4 (compare Krugman 1987).

If both firms decide on production, they will both suffer a loss of five. If only one of them starts producing, this firm will have a gain of 100, and if none of them starts production, then of course neither will suffer a loss or a gain. If the Americans set out to work on it and their prospect of gaining a 'first mover's advantage' looks entirely convincing, then the Europeans will not dare follow and run the risk of being 'latecomers'; the result appears from the bottom

Table 5.4   *Ex-ante* pay-off matrix

		Boeing	
		Production	No production
Airbus	Production	$(-5, -5)$	$(100, 0)$
	No production	$(0, 100)$	$(0, 0)$

Note: The first number in each cell indicates the gain of Airbus, the second that of Boeing.

Table 5.5   Pay-off matrix after Airbus subsidy

		Boeing	
		Production	No production
Airbus	Production	$(5, -5)$	$(110, 0)$
	No production	$(0, 100)$	$(0, 0)$

Note: The first number in each cell indicates the gain of Airbus, the second that of Boeing.

leftmost cell (0, 100), showing a clear American gain. The European countries behind the Airbus consortium may of course influence this result, e.g. by placing US$ 10 bn at the disposal of Airbus *before* Boeing actually plans its aircraft development and spends resources on it. In such a case the gain matrix corresponds to that shown in Table 5.5.

In the latter case Boeing knows that regardless of whether they go ahead with the project, Airbus will start developing the new aircraft. Going ahead would automatically involve a loss, so the result will be that the market is left to Airbus alone. Interestingly, the 'small' subsidy of US$ 10 bn increases the profits made by Airbus to 110; i.e. exclusive of the subsidy, the result is a profit increase, which, according to our analysis, did not apply to the case of export subsidies under perfect competition (compare Figure 5.7). The reason is that the signal from the European countries that they will subsidize Airbus makes Boeing withdraw from the market, leaving Airbus a monopoly and a monopoly profit. Considerations of this kind have given rise to the new concept of *strategic trade policy*, which covers the attempt by governments to secure future growth markets for their own firms through trade and industrial policy.

The above model is independent of whether the market has room for only one producer, i.e. of the assumption of a global monopoly. Strategic trade policy has been developed for oligopolist markets. Specifically, it is a prerequisite of strategic trade policy that national tariffs, export subsidies or other measures can contribute to making it *credible* that national producers will expand production so that foreign competitors are led to reduce theirs. Such shifts in competition change market shares, the result being that profits may be transferred from foreign producers to the benefit of national ones. This *rent shifting* is precisely the point of strategic trade policy.

It follows that strategic trade policy is only of relevance in markets in which monopoly profits are feasible, which requires a low number of producers and, consequently, significant barriers to entry. For this reason, the importance of this new trade policy is *limited*: in practice, most markets have more than a few producers and, in the long run, markets with *free access* (monopolistic competition) will not provide excess profits, so there will be no rent to transfer from one country to another. In addition, implementing strategic trade policy involves running the risk of *retaliation*. Actually, retaliation is likely since strategic trade policy is a 'beggar thy neighbour' policy in that the welfare gain of one country is acquired at the expense of another country. If the governments of both countries intervene, profits (exclusive of subsidies) will tend to disappear. A better solution would then be for the countries to cooperate with a view to liberalizing trade. Finally, it is probably worth mentioning that if the use of strategic trade policy is to be successful the information requirements of the regulating authority will be absolutely gigantic. This is all the more true as the proper choice of instrument (tariffs, subsidies, etc.) depends strongly on actual circumstances (strategic behaviour of producers, etc.).

5.4.3 Monopolistic competition and trade policy

If we look at a market with monopolistic competition and Lancaster preferences, see Chapter 3, Section 3.4, we can further illustrate that the range of effects of trade policy is quite wide. Figure 5.10 shows the case of a representative producer of a differentiated product in the home market of a small economy. The producer produces for the home market only, but the country imports variants from abroad. E_0 indicates the initial equilibrium with production of q_0 and the price of P_0. The country now imposes a unilateral tariff on all variants imported so that consumers face higher prices on all imported variants. If imported and domestically produced variants are close substitutes, then the demand curve will shift in the short run from D_0 to D_1 as a result of the tariff. D_1 is to the right of D_0 because the tariff will make domestic variants relatively more attractive, which, in addition, makes D_1 less elastic since domestic producers will gain more influence on the market.

In the long run, however, the accompanying profits will attract more domestic producers to the industry until competition has eliminated these profits. The increase in the number of producers will increase the number of variants (substitutes), which in turn increases competition and the elasticity of demand of each individual domestic producer. It is not possible, however, to determine *a priori* whether the resulting D curve will be more or less elastic than the original curve and thus whether the final point of equilibrium corresponds to a higher or lower price than the original one. Figure 5.10 shows the case in which the final demand curve, D_2, is more elastic than the original curve. In this case, the price of domestic variants has decreased as a result of the tariff. Thus the welfare effect may in fact be that the sum of the resulting customs revenue and the gain of consumers of domestic variants exceeds the loss of those consuming

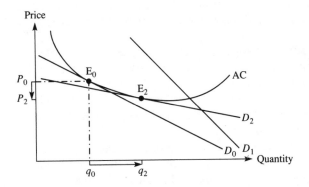

Figure 5.10 Tariffs under monopolistic competition

foreign variants. The message delivered by the analysis, however, is that although, theoretically, a national gain through protective measures is feasible, this outcome is not at all certain, and the ability of authorities to calculate the sign of the result in advance is doubtful at best.

5.4.4 Anything new under the sun?

Others have claimed that the decisive new contribution to the theory of trade policy is the insight that for individual countries free trade is not always the best option (see Krugman 1987). Both the terms of trade argument and the externality argument are, however, old and well-known examples where, on a purely theoretical analysis, deviation from free trade may be advantageous.

However, it is evident of both the new and the old arguments against free trade that it does not follow from their theoretical validity that they will work out in practice. For this reason, the new trade theorists have clearly emphasized that as a rule of thumb free trade is the best policy to pursue (see Baldwin 1992). Their argument runs as follows: firstly, the new contributions to trade policy carry no unambiguous messages; secondly, the information requirements are immense; and, thirdly, trade policy is one of the areas most strongly influenced by interest groups. Therefore a government that allows deviations from free trade will immediately become the target of lobbyism and political pressures whose interests rarely coincide with those of society at large. In addition, deviations from free trade may easily result in *economic nationalism*, including retaliation against other countries for their trade policies.

SUMMARY

1. The welfare gain from exports and imports of a good relates to trading nations, whereas individual groups such as customers or suppliers may be hurt.
2. In some industries transport or transaction costs make for a trade restriction, thus protecting domestic suppliers. Other industries are inherently open to international competition and constitute the internationally competitive sector.
3. A wide range of goals may divert nations from the path towards globally efficient free trade. Most of the goals are related to national income distribution.
4. Tariff is the best-known traditional measure that has protective and redistributional effects, fairly equivalent to those of import quotas—although quotas have even more disruptive allocative effects.
5. A large country imposing a tariff may cause a change in its terms of trade. This may change the general conclusion and give the large country—not the world—a welfare gain from the tariff. In this case there will be an optimum tariff rate
6. From the mid-seventies onwards a number of new trade policy instruments have been devised, including VERs, export subsidies and taxes and technical barriers, which all have negative welfare effects on the international community.
7. In theory, trade policy may have positive welfare effects, e.g. if external benefits are reaped. This is the backbone of the arguments for infant-industry protection. In the case of internal economies of scale (strategic) trade policy can help shift the rent to national companies.
8. It is not entirely certain that free trade is always the best option for all nations, but a robust rule of thumb would be to stick to it.

REFERENCES AND FURTHER READING

Baldwin, R. E. (1992), 'Are economists' traditional trade policy views still valid?', *Journal of Economic Literature*, June, **XXX** (2), 804–829.

Brander, J. A. and B. J. Spencer (1981), 'Tariffs and the extraction of foreign monopoly rents under potential entry', *Canadian Journal of Economics*, **14**, 371–389.

Brander, J. A. and B. J. Spencer (1983), 'International R&D rivalry and industrial strategy'. *Review of Economic Studies*, October **50** (4), 707–722.

Corden, W. M. (1974), *Trade Policy and Economic Welfare*, Clarendon Press, Oxford.

Falvey, R. E. (1979), 'The composition of trade within import-restricted product categories', *Journal of Political Economy*, **87**, 1105–1114.

Feenestra, R. (1984), 'Voluntary export restraint in U.S. autos, 1980–81: quality, employment, and welfare effects', in R. Baldwin and A. Krueger (eds), *The Structure and Evolution of Recent U.S. Trade Policy*, University of Chicago Press, pp. 298–325.

Helpman, E. and P. R. Krugman (1989), *Trade Policy and Market Structure*, The MIT Press, Cambridge, Massachusetts.

Krugman, P. R. (1987), 'Is free trade passé?', *Journal of Economic Perspectives*, **1**, 131–144.

Vousden, N. (1990), *The Economics of Trade Protection*, Cambridge University Press, Cambridge.

CHAPTER
SIX

THE INTERNATIONAL TRADE SYSTEM

In Chapter 5 we considered trade policy from a theoretical point of view. The conclusion reached was that with few exceptions free trade is preferable to restricted trade. In the present chapter, we examine the relationship between this conclusion and the real world. It is not at all obvious what precisely the relationship is as the world has seen successive waves of free trade and protectionism: the protectionism of the thirties was succeeded by a wave of liberalization until 1973 when another protectionist wave set in.

Section 6.1 deals with the multilateral trade system of the GATT framework. Section 6.2 focuses on the discriminating trade liberalization in the form of customs unions and free trade areas which has taken place in Europe since the Second World War. Finally, the neoprotectionism and regionalism of the past twenty years are analysed in Section 6.3.

6.1 MULTILATERALISM

Although the analysis provided in Chapter 5 did not show that free trade is always and indisputably preferable to restricted trade, this doctrine still carries considerable force as the principal doctrine of international trade both globally and in the case of individual countries. It seems reasonable to question why individual countries do not choose to liberalize their foreign trade unilaterally by removing import quotas, reducing tariffs to nought, etc. As shown in Figures 5.1 and 5.2, *unilateral liberalization* of this kind will raise the welfare level of a country. If the influx of imports increases, domestic producers will reduce their prices and production output. At the same time, the increase in exports implies a transfer of released factors of production to areas in which efficiency is higher and therefore society's real income will increase.

Nevertheless, most countries have found it unacceptable to pursue unilateral liberalization of foreign trade, typically, for the simple reason that they think of imports as 'bad' and exports as 'good'. Besides, the pressure from capital owners and workers in protected industries not to liberalize is typically much more intense than the pressure to liberalize exerted, for example, by consumers envisaging lower prices. The reason is that the former expect a marked fall in real income (in the short run) while the real income of the latter, i.e. of consumers, will not change significantly, protected products constituting but a small part of their total consumption. In addition, consumers are rarely well organized for lobbying purposes.

84

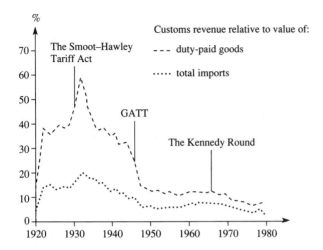

Figure 6.1   The United States Tariff Wall, 1920–80
Sources: Dobson (1976); Office of US Trade Representative (1980).

Consequently, *multilateral liberalization*, which means that a large number of countries agrees to reduce their protection at the same time, stands a better chance of succeeding precisely because in such a situation exports may be expected to increase with imports. Resistance from industries competing with imports will be countered by support from exporting industries, which will expect to profit directly from improved access to foreign markets. Further, multilateral trade liberalization may contribute to expanding world trade significantly, thus raising the welfare level of these countries even more. In this connection, it is worth remembering that adjustment problems are easier to solve under considerable economic growth than at any other time.

It is precisely in this connection that postwar international organizations like OECD and GATT are examined in the following. Evidence of the need for these organizations and of their success is provided in Figure 6.1, which shows the United States tariff wall from 1920 to 1980. In the context of the global economic crisis of the thirties, most countries imposed ever higher tariffs and introduced a variety of other barriers to trade. In the United States the strongly protectionist Smoot–Hawley Tariff Act was passed, which soon resulted in retaliation from other countries. This development in trade policy and the unsuccessful monetary policies pursued in the United States and Europe are considered the decisive factors leading to the depression of the thirties. The policy of the thirties has been called 'beggar thy neighbour' policy since it reduces any neighbours to beggary: each country attempts to win at the expense of others. This is the reason why in the postwar era Western countries have generally agreed to strive for a higher degree of free trade; Figure 6.1 shows that they have been fairly successful.

6.1.1   OECD—Organization for Economic Cooperation and Development

Immediately after the Second World War, the United States offered the European countries considerable economic aid, which was later called the *Marshall Aid* after the then US Secretary of State. The United States demanded that in return for this aid the countries involved should phase out the volume restrictions on their trade with each other. In addition, the currencies of these countries had to be made convertible, which means that a currency can be freely exchanged for other currencies. This was not the case at the time because ever since the beginning of the thirties the countries had attempted, two by two, to balance their trade by means of various exchange controls.

The aid and the American demands all formed part of the Marshall Aid Plan, which was administered by the OEEC, a precursor of the OECD. The OECD was established in 1961 and its membership was extended to include not just European countries but also the United States, Japan and Canada. Today, the most important functions of the OECD are those of analysing the economic development in member states and of proposing economic policies. In addition, the OECD tries to coordinate the economic policies of member states and of their policies in respect of developing countries. Likewise, members cooperate through the OECD to solve both environmental problems and energy problems.

6.1.2   GATT—General Agreement on Tariffs and Trade

Originally, the plan had been formed that trade liberalization should be administered through a large, effective organization called the International Trade Organization (ITO). The US Senate and the governments of some other countries, however, were not willing to accept the highly ambitious plans for this organization. Instead, the GATT agreement, which was signed by 23 countries in 1947, came to provide the framework of postwar trade liberalization. Today, GATT has more than 100 members.

The basic principles of GATT are those of non-discrimination, reciprocity and transparency:

1. *Non-discrimination* is ensured, *inter alia*, through the *principle of most favoured nation* by which tariff reductions agreed by two or more members are automatically extended to include all GATT members. This ensures that trade development among GATT countries is based on comparative and competitive advantages.
2. In order to prevent mercantilist governments from acting as free-riders, the *principle of reciprocity* was introduced. According to this 'quid-pro-quo' principle, a country has to open its own market when, due to tariff reductions in other countries, it gains increased access to the markets of these countries. Apparently, this principle is based on the belief that countries typically regard their own trade barriers as an advantage only to be abandoned if something is received in return.
3. In order to ensure that trade measures employed are *transparent*, the GATT countries have agreed on a prohibition against direct control of exports and imports. As was shown in Chapter 5, tariffs and import quotas are generally non-equivalent: as a price regulator tariffs are more in accordance with efficient allocation of resources than quantitative restrictions would be.

Only rarely will such a set of ideal principles be accepted in practice without exceptions. Accordingly, the GATT system allows a number of *exceptions* to the three basic principles. Some important exceptions to the non-discrimination principle are those of (1) acceptance of regional trade agreements such as free trade areas or customs unions* and (2) acceptance of the

---

* This presupposes that certain requirements have been satisfied, see Article 24 of the GATT Treaty. In practice the trade agreement has to include all goods, and all internal tariffs have to be removed from these goods. In a customs union, which includes a common external tariff wall, the new external tariff wall is not allowed to be any higher than the average wall resulting from individual countries' tariff rates prior to the establishment of the customs union.

tariff preferences (GSP[*]) which industrialized countries have given to developing countries. In addition, they include (3) the use of countervailing tariffs aimed at matching foreign subsidies and (4) the use of anti-dumping tariffs aimed at firms which dump their products in the market of a foreign country. Likewise, the principle of reciprocity does not fully apply to developing countries, and there are some exceptions to the prohibition against quantitative import restrictions. A country that suddenly encounters a balance of payments problem may, for example, be allowed to make temporary use of import quotas. In addition, the development of GATT has resulted in agricultural products largely being outside the scope of GATT regulation and world trade in textiles and clothing being regulated by a special agreement, the Multi-Fibre Agreement (MFA), the negotiation of which is not governed by the usual GATT regulations.

In spite of these exceptions, GATT has served as a catalyst for considerable reductions in trade restrictions. This result has mainly been achieved through a series of tariff reduction negotiations; the names of these rounds and the years in which they took place as well as their significance appear in Table 6.1.

Table 6.1 GATT rounds

Year	Round	Number of countries	Value of trade affected	Average tariff reduction (%)	Subsequent tariffs (%)
1947	Geneva	23	US$ 10bn	35	NA
1949	Annecy	33	NA		NA
1950	Torquay	34	NA		NA
1956	Geneva	22	US$ 2.5bn		NA
1960–61	Dillon	45	US$ 4.9bn		NA
1964–67	Kennedy	48	US$ 40bn	35	8.7
1973–79	Tokyo	99	US$ 300bn	34	4.7
1986–93	Uruguay	118	NA	40[†]	NA

† Expected.
Source: Jackson (1991) and GATT (1993).

As a result of the rounds concluded, import quotas have largely disappeared in industrialized countries and tariff rates have been reduced considerably, except in the case of agricultural and other particularly sensitive products, e.g. textiles. The tariff rates agreed upon at the Tokyo round reflect the rates applicable until the end of the Uruguay round (Table 6.2).

---

[*] GSP is an abbreviation of Generalized System of Preferences. GSP refers to an interational agreement which was signed in 1971 under the auspices of GATT, and under which a number of industrialized countries give temporary and non-reciprocal tariff preference to a number of developing countries.

Table 6.2   Tariff rates[†] after the Tokyo round, selected countries (%)

Country	All industrial products	Raw materials	Semi-manufactured products	Finished industrial products
USA	4.4	0.2	3.0	5.7
Japan	2.8	0.5	4.6	6.0
EU	4.7	0.2	4.2	6.9
Total[‡]	4.7	0.3	4.0	6.5

[†] Weighted averages
[‡] Average of the nine most important industrialized countries (including the EU as one country).
Source: Kelly *et al.* (1988).

6.1.3   Effective tariffs

The low level of protection indicated in Table 6.2 does not in any way reflect the real level. Firstly, there are other kinds of protection than tariffs, and many of these have been applied increasingly since the mid-seventies (see Section 6.3). Secondly, the fact that typically tariffs on finished products are much higher than tariffs on raw materials and semi-manufactured products may cause the real level of protection on a product to be much higher than that expressed by the nominal tariff rate since raw materials and semi-manufactured products may enter the production of the finished product. This case has been illustrated in Figure 6.2.

In the example shown, a sweater costs NLG 100 under free trade: raw materials and semi-manufactured products, i.e. wool and buttons, cost NLG 60 while the value added to each unit produced amounts to NLG 40. In the case of a tariff rate of 20 per cent on the finished product and a rate of 10 per cent on raw materials and semi-manufactured products, the value added

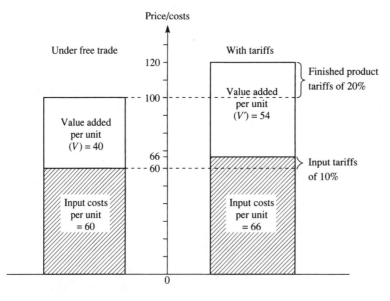

Figure 6.2   Calculation of effective tariffs

will increase to 54, as shown on the right-hand side of the figure. It is this increase in the value added which is of importance for the calculation of the real or effective level of protection of domestic industries in the country in question. Effective (tariff) protection, t_e, is defined as the difference between value added per unit in domestic prices (V') and value added per unit in world market prices (V), or

$$t_e = \frac{V' - V}{V} = \frac{54 - 40}{40} \times 100\% = 35\%$$

If, in the example, there had been no duty on inputs, effective tariff protection would have amounted to 50 per cent. Therefore the real degree of protection of a domestic industry increases, firstly, with the share of raw materials and semi-manufactured products entering domestic production and, secondly, with the difference between finished product tariffs and raw materials tariffs. Table 6.2 shows that industrialized countries have adopted the policy of having relatively low tariff rates on raw materials and semi-manufactured products, which has increased the real protection of their finished products quite considerably in spite of the low nominal tariff rates. Table 6.3 illustrates this.

As the three countries do not impose a tariff on ox hides, the protection of their tanyards amounts to more than three times the finished product tariff on leather. The raw materials share required for leather articles is much smaller than that required by the tanyards, which is why the effective tariff on leather articles exceeds the nominal one by only 50 per cent. Among the products listed in the table, the highest level of protection is that obtained by the Japanese dairy industry in the case of butter: the effective tariff is nine times the finished product tariff.

It follows that a fall in average nominal tariffs does not necessarily indicate a corresponding liberalization of trade. If, for example, countries lower tariffs on raw materials and semi-manufactured products, effective tariffs will fall less—they may even rise. If, however, tariffs on raw materials have already been abandoned, the fall in nominal tariffs expresses a higher degree of liberalization. The development of the GATT rounds until 1980 actually reflected precisely such a situation, i.e. one in which the fall in effective protection did not correspond to that in nominal protection.

Table 6.3 Nominal and effective tariff rates in selected countries and industries

	USA		Japan		EU	
	Nominal	Effective	Nominal	Effective	Nominal	Effective
Ox hides	0.0	—	0.0	—	0.0	—
Leather	17.8	57.4	6.2	20.2	7.0	21.4
Leather articles	22.4	32.5	10.5	15.8	7.1	10.3
Milk and cream	6.5	—	0.0	—	16.0	—
Cheese	11.5	34.5	35.3	175.6	23.0	58.8
Butter	10.3	46.7	45.0	418.5	21.0	76.6
Raw cotton	6.1	—	0.0	—	0.0	—
Cotton yarn	8.3	12.0	8.1	25.8	7.0	22.8
Cotton fabric	15.6	30.7	7.2	34.9	13.6	29.7

Source: Yeats (1974).

6.2 DISCRIMINATING TRADE LIBERALIZATION

As mentioned above, exceptions may be made to the basic GATT principle of non-discrimination. One of these exceptions is the formation of free trade areas or customs unions on condition that no third country is affected negatively by this; no attempt has ever been made, however, to monitor the effects. One reason why GATT accepted regional trade agreements was that internal trade liberalization among participating countries was considered another step towards global trade liberalization.

6.2.1 Forms of integration

Discriminating trade liberalization among a number of countries may assume one of several fundamentally different forms. A group of countries may unilaterally reduce their trade restrictions in respect of another group of countries without demanding anything in return. The GSP agreements between developing and industrialized countries, mentioned previously, represent precisely this form of integration. These agreements have not led to extensive economic integration among the countries in question, the reason being, among other things, that particularly sensitive products are generally excepted. Various more far-reaching forms of economic integration have been listed in Table 6.4.

6.2.2 Free trade areas

A free trade area consists of a group of countries among which trade takes place freely, i.e. without tariffs or quantitative restrictions, the so-called *visible trade restrictions*, but in which each country retains its individual tariffs and quantitative import restrictions against countries outside the free trade area. In order to prevent differences in external barriers from causing goods from third countries to flow through the country with the lowest barriers (this is known as trade deflection), a free trade area has to apply *rules of origin*. This means that goods from one country inside the free trade area will only be allowed to enter another country in the free trade area free of duty if the goods have received a certificate of origin. Such a certificate will only be given if the goods have largely been produced inside the free trade area, i.e. if raw materials and semi-manufactured products from third countries have been extensively processed in the area. The rule may be that a certain percentage of the value added to the goods, typically

Table 6.4 Degrees of economic integration

	No visible trade restrictions	Common external trade restrictions	No hidden trade restrictions	Free mobility of factors of production	Common currency	Common economic policy
Free trade area	X					
Customs union	X	X				
Internal commodity market	X	X	X			
Common market	X	X	X	X		
Monetary union	X	X	X	X	X	
Economic union	X	X	X	X	X	X

50 per cent, has to originate in the free trade area. As such rules are difficult to handle in practice, customs clearing often becomes a very complicated and time-consuming process.

One important free trade area until 1995 was EFTA, which stands for the European Free Trade Association. EFTA was established in 1960 by the United Kingdom, Denmark, Sweden, Norway, Switzerland, Austria and Portugal. Iceland became a member in 1970 and Finland did not become a full member until 1986. By contrast, the United Kingdom and Denmark left EFTA in 1972, Portugal left it in 1985 and Austria, Finland and Sweden left in 1994 in order to participate in the closer cooperation of the EC. EFTA was established because in 1958 the EFTA countries were not willing to participate in the more extensive EC cooperation since this was of a supranational character. EFTA cooperation only involves industrial products so it is a weak form of economic integration. Important free trade areas include the North American Free Trade Area (NAFTA), signed in 1993, which includes Canada, the United States and Mexico, and that of the New Zealand–Australia Free Trade Agreement from 1965.

6.2.3   Customs unions

As opposed to the countries in a free trade area, the members of a customs union have a common external trade policy as regards visible trade restrictions, i.e. a common external tariff wall and common external import restrictions. Because of this common foreign trade policy, a customs union represents a higher degree of economic integration. Previously, it was a conviction that the formation of a customs union and a free trade area would increase world welfare, trade restrictions being removed. As was shown by Jacob Viner in 1950, however, this result was by no means certain since such *discriminating trade agreements* have both positive and negative trade effects. This is illustrated in Figure 6.3 as regards a customs union, but the analysis may largely be applied to free trade areas as well (a theoretical treatment is given by Robson 1987).

S_H and D_H indicate domestic supply and demand in a small country admitted to a customs union, for example the EU. Prior to membership, the country imports the product from third-party countries at the price of P_W, which the horizontal supply curve of S_W represents. At a tariff of t per unit, the home market price is P_t and the volume of imports Q_1Q_2. As the product has been imported from third-party countries, the price of the product in the EU has to be higher than the world market price; P_{EU} and the perfectly elastic supply curve of S_{EU} represents this situation. The EU membership will cause the home market price to fall to P_{EU} with the

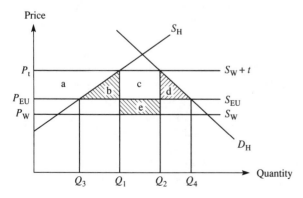

Figure 6.3   Effects of establishing a customs union

phasing out of the internal tariff. This leads to a fall in domestic production from Q_1 to Q_3 while consumption rises from Q_2 to Q_4; thus imports go up from Q_1Q_2 to Q_3Q_4.

The positive effect of customs union membership, which is known as the *trade-creating effect*, is precisely due to the increase in the country's total volume of imports. In welfare terms, this effect corresponds to areas b and d. The area of b is a social gain, the import increase of Q_3Q_1 corresponding to a production decrease and, consequently, a cost reduction which exceeds the import expenditure by area b. Likewise, the import increase of Q_2Q_4 corresponds to a consumption increase whose utility gain exceeds the import expenditure by area d. The trade-creating effect involves a range of *redistributional effects*. The fall in price from P_H to P_W results in a total increase in consumer's surplus of area a + b + c + d: area a corresponds to the loss to domestic producers while area c corresponds to the loss of tariff revenue, i.e. to the redistribution from tax payers to consumers.

The negative effect of customs union membership, which is known as the *trade-diverting* effect, is the result of the inexpensive imports of Q_1Q_2 from third-party countries being replaced by more expensive production from member countries. The additional cost per imported unit amounts to $P_{EU}-P_W$ and the total loss is that of area e. Taken together area e + c constitutes the total loss of customs revenue. In sum, the net welfare effect of a customs union can be calculated as follows:

Trade creation	b + d
− Trade diversion	−e
Net gain	b + d − e

It is therefore not possible to determine whether participation in a customs union is an advantage, i.e. whether the net gain is positive. A number of factors, however, are decisive. Firstly, *price elasticity* of both supply and demand is of importance: the higher the levels of elasticity, the higher the trade-creating effect. Secondly, the difference between the price level in H (P_t) and that in the EU (P_{EU}) plays a role. This difference is partly the result of unit costs and partly of tariffs in H; the larger the difference, the higher the trade-creating effect will be. At the same time, the tariff rate influences the volume of imports from third-party countries, i.e. it contributes to trade diversion. Thirdly, the difference between production costs in the EU and in third-party countries ($P_{EU}-P_W$) is also of importance: the larger the difference, the higher the trade-diverting effect (area e). In addition, the size and number of member countries will influence the net result. Clearly, if the customs union included the entire world, only trade creation would result; the more numerous and the larger the participating countries, the more probable it is that the producers who have the lowest costs will be inside the customs union, which will eliminate trade diversion.

The trade-creating effect illustrated in Figure 6.3 is the result of the countries in the EU specializing according to their comparative advantages within the union. Low-cost producers expand their production at the expense of the home country, but because they are inefficient, compared to third countries, all member countries are protected by a tariff. In order to ensure that total trade creation following from the formation of the union is considerable, the industrial structure of member countries has to be highly *competing* (as opposed to complementary) in the sense that the range of products produced by protected high-cost industries has to be large. If, by contrast, industrial overlap within high-cost industries is modest, the possibility of considerable trade creation through reallocation of factors of production will be correspondingly modest.

On the basis of the above static and partial analysis which assumes perfect competition, we have to conclude that the effects of a customs union are uncertain. This holds in the case of both individual countries and the customs union as a whole. This result should come as no surprise, given that completely free trade under the assumptions made corresponds to 'first best'. Only a customs union which is sufficiently large to be able to influence international terms of trade has the possibility of obtaining a welfare gain by building an optimum external tariff wall. Thus politicians ought not to opt for a customs union as a roundabout way of reaching the goal: the solution of free trade is immediately available. Consequently, the arguments for a customs union have to be sought elsewhere—primarily, at a purely political level.

Apart from purely political considerations, *imperfect competition* and *dynamic* factors may result in more beneficial effects of a customs union than indicated above. Firstly, a customs union may have beneficial effects on competitiveness, protected national markets often leading to cost inefficiency. Secondly, the probability of better exploitation of economies of scale is higher in a large market. This and the improved access to product variants may increase the level of welfare (see Chapter 3). Specialization among customs union members is in fact typically characterized by increased intra-industry trade rather than inter-industry trade. Consequently, it seems reasonable to expect that resistance against participation in a customs union will be moderate, for economic reasons, the restructuring of the economies being moderate in the case of intra-industry specialization.

6.2.4   EU: European Union

As in the case of free trade areas, history presents various examples of customs unions. The classical example is the 'Zollverein', which was formed in 1834 and became the basis of the unification of Germany. However, the most important customs union ever is still the EU. Table 6.5 presents an outline of EU history.

Table 6.5   Outline of the development of the European Union

European Coal and Steel Community (ECSC). Agreement signed in Paris	1951
European Economic Community (EEC). Agreement signed in Rome	1957
European Atomic Energy Community (EURATOM). Agreement signed in Rome	1957
Amalgamation Treaty. Agreement signed	1965
Common tariff wall	1968
Common Agricultural Policy	1968
Werner Report adopted	1971
Free trade agreement with EFTA, signed	1972
First enlargement with the entry of the United Kingdom, Denmark and Ireland	1973
European Monetary System (EMS)	1979
Second enlargement with the entry of Greece	1981
White Paper	1985
Third enlargement with the entry of Portugal and Spain	1986
Single European Act	1987
Delors Report	1989
European Economic Area, signed	1991
The Maastricht Treaty, signed	1992
The Single Market, effective from	1993
EC rebaptized as EU	1993
Fourth enlargement with the entry of Austria, Finland and Sweden	1995

The signing in 1951 by France, the Federal Republic of Germany, Belgium, Luxembourg, Italy and Holland of the treaty on the European Coal and Steel Community marked the beginning of the EU. The overall objective of this community was a *political* one, viz. that of ensuring peace in Europe by placing both French and German steel industries under the control of a supranational body. Later, the six countries extended their cooperation through the establishment of EURATOM and the EEC, which both became effective in 1958. The three treaties still exist as independent treaties,[*] but the EU institutions governing the three treaties merged into the Commission, the Council of Ministers, the Court of Justice and the European Parliament, which took effect in their new capacity in 1967.

The EU is first and foremost a customs union: tariffs and quantitative restrictions on trade among member countries are banned and after a period of transition a common external tariff wall was set up. As a result, all external trade policies are common business. However, going by the integration scale shown in Table 6.4, some of the features of more wide-ranging forms of integration also characterize the EU. From its inception, the EU was intended to become an internal commodity market and a common market.

6.2.5   The Single Market

The difference between an internal commodity market and a customs union is that the former allows neither visible nor invisible barriers, i.e. non-tariff barriers, to trade that restricts the free movement of goods. Non-tariff barriers include physical, technical and fiscal barriers to trade. Physical barriers are customs posts at frontier crossings. Technical barriers, which were mentioned in Chapter 5, include specific national requirements relating to product design, but they also include discriminating public procurement. Fiscal barriers may result from differences in national tax rates.

A *common market* or a single market is not only a single market for goods but also a market that allows the free movement of labour and capital. This means that employees are free to apply for a job in any other EU country without special permits and that no restrictions are imposed on the movement of capital.

While the customs union was established fairly rapidly, the formation of a single commodity market and a common market has been a much slower process—for several reasons. One of them was the international recession of the mid-seventies which caused the countries to become more preoccupied with their own national problems. Another reason has been the requirement that EU decisions have to be unanimous: this has made legislation on common product standards more difficult and slowed down the legislative process. Yet a third reason lies in Article 36 of the Treaty of Rome, by which an EU member country may introduce technical trade restrictions against other member countries if the aim is to ensure public safety or health. It is a condition, however, that the trade barrier serves a legitimate purpose and that consideration of the free movement of goods does not outweigh the consideration of the purpose, e.g. health or environmental purposes, served by the trade barrier. This slowness created frustration with EU cooperation. In an attempt to revitalize the process, the 'idea' of a Single Market was conceived in the mid-eighties, when a white paper was published (1985) with 300 different proposals for directives aiming at removing essential physical, technical and fiscal barriers to the free movement of goods, labour and capital, and thus leading the way to a genuine common market within the nineties.

---

[*] However, with the adoption of the Maastricht Treaty, the three treaties became integrated into one.

The formal foundation of the Single Market was laid when the EEC treaty was changed with the adoption of the Single European Act, which took effect in 1987. This introduced votes by qualified majority in areas that concerned the Single Market. As in the case of customs unions, the establishment of a single commodity market leads to both trade creation and trade diversion, so the welfare effects are uncertain in this case as well.

Once again, Figure 6.3 may help to clarify this. The common external tariff wall (t) is now—due to non-tariff barriers—assumed to protect partner countries inadequately, so the home country imports the volume of Q_1Q_2 from third-party countries at the price of P_W, which includes non-tariff barriers involved in exporting to the EU. The home market price will be P_t. If the removal of technical, physical and fiscal barriers *discriminates* in such a way that producers in other EU countries will experience cost reductions, then their export costs will decrease, e.g. to S_{EU}, while the supply curve for the rest of the world remains at S_W. Imports, which will now be Q_3Q_4, have shifted from the rest of the world to the other EU countries since they are now able to supply the product at a lower price. As in the customs union analysis, the welfare effect can be divided into a trade-creating effect of area b + d and a trade-diverting effect of area e. It is therefore not possible in this case either to determine unequivocally whether the net welfare effect is positive or negative. This somewhat paradoxical result follows from the fact that despite the external tariff wall non-tariff barriers may block trade within the customs union.

However, the result is highly sensitive to the assumption that the creation of an internal commodity market is an instance of *discriminating* trade liberalization. In connection with the creation of the single market within the EU, this holds of the physical barriers. In the case of technical barriers, however, it is in no way certain that these have a discriminating effect. Product standardization in the EU, where meeting certain product specifications gives access to all EU markets, apply to both EU firms and firms from third-party countries. If barriers are exclusively removed in this fashion then the single market is a case of general trade liberalization.

The establishment of a single commodity market may have a wide range of other positive effects. Generally, production costs must be assumed to fall, partly as a result of fiercer competition and partly as a result of the deregulation of trade and production. At the same time, the possibilities of exploiting economies of scale improve and the increase in market integration does not allow the same scope for price discrimination.

The free movement of goods which results from a single commodity market does not necessarily lead to full factor price equalization, regardless of any expectations that the factor price equalization theorem might give rise to (see Chapter 2). The reasons for this include transport costs, economies of scale and non-traded goods. Consequently, supplementing a single commodity market with the free movement of factors of production, i.e. with the establishment of a common market, may hold some advantages. The welfare advantages following from this were dealt with in Sections 4.1 and 4.2 of Chapter 4.

Capital mobility among EU member countries was fairly moderate until the beginning of the eighties, when no more than approximately half the member countries had removed exchange regulations on all capital transactions. In connection with the implementation of the Single Market fully liberalized capital movements became a key issue: this liberalization was to ensure the welfare gains mentioned above, but it was also supposed to lead to the economic and monetary union which was to be formulated in the Maastricht Treaty (see Chapter 14).

Labour mobility in the EU is still very moderate despite the removal of most formal barriers and the significant real earnings differences, particularly between the northern and southern EU countries. This may be explained in terms of the high level of unemployment which has prevailed since the first oil crisis and, more generally, by the language and cultural barriers among the countries. In an attempt to stimulate labour mobility, the realization of the Single Market involves the removal of the last formal barriers to mobility. Mutual recognition of training and education in all member countries is one step in this process. Although the free movement of labour and capital is one of the aims of the EU, massive factor movements within the EU are not intended since they might lead to depopulation and deindustrialization of certain regions. One means of countervailing such a trend involves the transfer of income from the wealthy EU countries (in the north) to the less wealthy ones (in the south) through various regional measures.

Various economists as well as the EU Commission have attempted to estimate the economic effects of the EU. Thus Bela Balassa (1975) estimated the statistical welfare effects of the original customs union of the EU to amount to no more than 0.15 per cent of the GDP of the six member countries. An investigation by Petith (1987) estimates the terms of trade gain to exceed the advantage of trade creation, the former being estimated at one-third to one per cent of GDP. These are probably both underestimates as none of them take advantages obtained through economies of scale or increased competition into consideration. Such effects are included in the Commission's estimate of the effects of the establishment of the Single Market, (see Emerson *et al.* 1988), where the effects are estimated at 4.3–6.4 per cent of GDP. However, this rather optimistic estimate has been criticized by others, who have claimed that it is idealistic among other things because actual cost differences among EU countries in the mid-eighties were minimal as a result of preceding EU cooperation.

6.2.6 Economic and monetary cooperation

On the integration ladder the rung of the common market is followed by those of the monetary union and the economic union. Apart from a common market, a *monetary union* includes entirely fixed exchange rates among member countries, e.g. in terms of a common currency. This eliminates exchange rate uncertainty in connection with economic transactions among member countries, and it leads to reduced exchange transaction costs and thus to cost-saving. Both aspects contribute to efficiency gains.

Until 1979, monetary matters were of little importance to EC cooperation. It is true that the Werner plan (1970) included the creation of a monetary union before 1980 but with economic development in the seventies, i.e. with oil crisis, floating exchange rates after the collapse of the US$ in 1973, etc., events overtook the plan. The establishment of the European Monetary System (EMS) in 1979 laid some of the foundations of a monetary union in that the participating EC countries formed a system of fixed but adjustable exchange rates (see Chapter 8). The Maastricht Treaty brings monetary relations in focus as it plans for the establishment of a genuine monetary union with one common currency (see Chapter 14).

Table 6.4 defines an *economic union* as a monetary union in which member countries coordinate their economic policy. While a monetary union harmonizes monetary policy, integration in an economic union particularly presupposes a certain degree of harmonization of fiscal policy. Apart from coordination of macro-economic policy, however, an economic union also presupposes coordination of industrial policy. Thus it is a precondition for a smoothly working common market that the framework within which industry and agriculture operate does not differ among member countries. In the EU, this aim is expressed in the common agricultural policy, the common fisheries policy, common programmes for industrial development, common legislation on competition, etc.

Today, in the mid-nineties, the EU may reasonably be characterized as a fully fledged customs union with essential features of a single commodity and factor market and with detailed plans for a fully fledged economic and monetary union.

6.3 TRADE POLICY TRENDS

6.3.1 1947–1973: successful trade liberalization

As was mentioned in Section 6.1, GATT has been rather successful, since 1947, in reducing trade barriers. As regards tariffs, its success has been unequivocally positive, the average nominal tariff level having been reduced from approximately 40 per cent to approximately 5 per cent on industrial products but somewhat less in terms of effective tariffs.

The period from 1947 to 1973 was characterized by fairly stable economic conditions with production and foreign trade growing noticeably: for instance, over the period from 1963 to 1973 annual growth in production was 5.2 per cent and that in foreign trade was 8.9 per cent, which means that the income elasticity in foreign trade was 1.7 (see Table 6.6). The trade liberalization formally directed by GATT but in fact by the United States is usually considered the crucial cause of these trends.

International *political* theory assumes that a leading power, the *hegemon*, can stimulate a stable pattern of cooperation among countries (see Bhagwati and Irwin 1987). After the Second World War, the hegemon has been the United States, which has been an example to other countries with its free trade-oriented policy: in the fifties and sixties the United States lifted its quantitative import restrictions faster than any other country and it was also the main initiator of the tariff-reduction rounds.

6.3.2 Neoprotectionism: 1973–?

Despite continued significant trade liberalization under the auspices of GATT during the Tokyo round (1973–1979), countervailing trends, which were seen as a neoprotectionist wave, emerged in the mid-seventies and have persisted ever since. The reasons for this neoprotectionism are various but they include the international recession which followed in the wake of both the first and the second oil crisis (see Table 6.6 again, which shows the reduced growth over the period of 1973–1985). At the same time, the increase in competition from newly industrializing countries created severe adjustment problems in the industrialized countries. In order to alleviate both employment and balance of payments problems, a great many industrialized countries saw it as a reasonable solution to restrict imports and attempt to stimulate exports through protectionist measures. Over the same period, the less developed countries (LDCs) were debt-ridden and therefore resorted to protectionism as a way out of their difficulties.

Table 6.6 Growth in world production and exports, per cent per annum, for selected periods

	1953–63	1963–73	1973–79	1979–85	1985–90
1. World trade	6.5	8.9	4.7	2.1	6.1
2. World GDP	3.7	5.2	3.1	2.1	3.4
3. Foreign trade income elasticity[†]	1.8	1.7	1.5	1.0	1.8

[†] Equals growth in world trade/growth in world GDP.
Source: Boltho and Alsopp (1987) and GATT (1992).

Even the United States, the hegemon, has seen an increase in protectionist trends. This is partly the result of the deterioration in the global position of the United States: its share of global GDP has fallen from approximately 40 per cent in 1950 to approximately 22 per cent in 1993. According to the hegemony theory, this may lead to turbulent conditions in the international system of trade and exchange rates; thus the international exchange rate system fragmented after 1973, when the major currencies were allowed to float (see Chapter 8). In addition, the increase in American protectionism partly results from the American balance of payments deficit, which followed in the wake of the increase in the value of the US$ at the beginning of the eighties.

As a result of this development, non-tariff barriers have been spreading and their number is increasing (see Chapter 5, Section 5.3) throughout the industrialized world, affecting almost 50 per cent of world trade (see the World Bank 1991). According to estimates, the effect of these barriers is twice the average tariff of 5 per cent, i.e. approximately 10 per cent. Of course, this development is contrary to the mission of GATT, whose purpose it is to freeze or reduce trade barriers, leaving tariffs as the only legitimate means. In addition, many of the non-tariff barriers violate the non-discriminating principle of the GATT Treaty. The violations include the voluntary export restraint agreements which have been spreading, for example, within the car, footwear and electronics industries.

The use of non-tariff barriers is strongly concentrated in terms of products. Agricultural products play a highly significant role, but textile and clothing (the Multi-fibre Agreement) and iron and steel are also seriously affected. Table 6.7 provides an overview of major neoprotectionist trade instruments, their conformity with GATT rules, i.e. their legitimacy, and the products and countries affected.

Until the Uruguay round, agriculture has been exempt from the GATT agreement and this sector is indeed the most protected one of all. However, agricultural policy assumes all kinds of different forms in different countries. The Common Agricultural Policy may serve as an example: internally, the EU price level is high as a result of minimum prices and variable import duties, and surplus production is sold in the world market with export subsidies.

Next to agriculture, the textile and clothing industry is the most protected one in the industrialized countries. The Multi-fibre Agreement of 1974 provides the framework for this protection. It is under this agreement that the industrialized countries use import quotas to protect their production against competition from the more efficient LDCs.

Under GATT rules intervention against so-called *unfair trade practices* may be legitimate. This would be the case if a country subsidizes its production and consequently gains market shares. Other countries would then be entitled to make use of *countervailing duties*. Similarly, a country is entitled to make use of tariffs if its firms suffer from the dumping of goods by producers in other countries. It is a case of *dumping* if a product is sold in a foreign market at a price that is lower than that in the home market. This may be the result of geographical price discrimination with no intention of obtaining a monopoly status in the market, but of course it may be the result of a strategic move with a view to conquering the market by selling at prices that do not cover production costs. A crucial problem relating to intervention against dumping is the difficulty involved in distinguishing harmless cases from harmful ones; therefore anti-dumping protection actually makes abuse and protectionism possible.

The most recent form of neoprotectionism involves 'voluntary expansion of a country's imports'. Traditionally, quantitative restrictions on foreign trade have aimed at reducing imports, but the new phenomenon covers a situation in which an agreement is reached that a country will increase its imports of certain products by given quantities.

Table 6.7   Neo-protectionism, products and instruments

Instrument	GATT legitimacy	Products	Countries actively involved	Countries affected
Voluntary export restraint (VER) agreements	Not yet determined conclusively ('grey' area)	Cars, electronics, iron and steel, textile, clothing, footwear, etc.	EU, USA	Japan, Eastern and Central Europe, NICs
Multi-fibre Agreement (MFA)	Temporary suspension of GATT rules	Textile and clothing	Industrialized countries	LDCs
Anti-dumping	Legitimate on certain conditions	Chemicals, iron and steel, clothing, electronics, etc.	EU, USA, Canada, Australia, Mexico	LDCs, Japan NICs, Eastern and Central Europe
Countervailing duty	Legitimate on certain conditions	Steel, etc.	USA	A large number of industrialized countries and LDCs
Export subsidies	General prohibition; agricultural products not covered by the GATT agreement being excepted	Ships, steel, agricultural products	EU, USA, EFTA, Japan, other industrialized countries	LDCs exporting agricultural products
Voluntary import expansion agreements	Not yet determined conclusively	Wide range of products	USA	Japan

Note: The table presents the situation holding until the end of the Uruguay round.

This idea, which is of American origin, and the more extensive use of anti-dumping measures and countervailing duties by the United States are clear signs of a change in the American attitude to free trade. This reorientation has been termed *aggressive unilateralism* (see Bhagwati 1990) as it differs from the unilateralism of the fifties and sixties, when the United States set an example and liberalized unilaterally, in that *unilateral concessions* are now demanded from other countries by the United States. The tools invoked by the Americans are two sections,

'Section 301' and 'Super 301', in United States trade legislation. Under 'Section 301' the President is entitled to retaliate if in the opinion of the United States foreign conditions of trade make it possible for specific products to offer unfair competition. By contrast, 'Super 301' may be used against certain countries if in the opinion of the United States they make use of 'unfair' trade practices, in a wide sense of the term. Such countries will be put on a surveillance list and will have to reach an agreement with the United States Department of Commerce within a certain time limit if they are to avoid retaliation. The 'structural impediments initiative', which is an agreement between the United States and Japan and which concerns the opening of the Japanese market to American firms, is a result of the United States having used the threat of 'Super 301'. The clash with GATT principles is evident.

Likewise, the external trade policy of the EU provides for measures against 'unfair' trade practices. These measures are primarily anti-dumping ones, which the EU uses extensively.

It would seem then that under the influence of neoprotectionism the idea of the GATT system, which was the creation of a trade system with *fixed rules*, has instead assumed the form of what might be called *managed trade*, or results-oriented trade, whose goals are quantitative ones and not a fixed framework in which trade is driven by market forces.

The costs of neoprotectionism have been calculated in a large number of analyses, both ones that investigate a specific case of intervention and more general ones. One analysis estimates that, in the case of car exports, VER agreements between the United States and Japan cost American consumers somewhere between US\$ 93 000 and US\$ 250 000 for each job saved. More comprehensive investigations show that the gains of 'moving towards free trade' are between one and six per cent of GDP (see the World Bank 1991).

6.3.3   Does regionalism pave the way to multilateralism?

Regionalism, i.e. discriminating regional trading blocs and other kinds of narrow regional, economic and political integration, has been a marked feature of economic development in the postwar era. The first wave involved the formation of the EU and EFTA. The second wave emerged during the mid-eighties. In North America, this involved the free trade agreement between the United States and Canada, and later the formation of NAFTA. In Europe, it involved the creation of the Single Market within the EU and the European Economic Area, which extends the Single Market to most of the EFTA countries. In addition, the EU has opened up to Eastern and Central Europe through a number of cooperation agreements. Further, the Maastricht agreement will increase integration in depth within the EU in the next few years as an increasing number of areas will be included in EU internal cooperation. At the same time, the EU will be enlarged if the remaining EFTA countries and Eastern and Central European countries enter the EU (as full members). In the Far East, a *de facto* trading bloc led by Japan seems to be emerging.

The first wave of regional trade agreements was definitely seen as a step along the path to *multilateralism*, but the increase in the number of trading blocs has led to considerable disagreement over whether regionalism actually paves the way to multilateralism.

On the face of it, it would appear that reaching international agreements is much easier if, for example, three blocs are involved rather than 100 independent GATT countries—among other things the free rider problem increases with the number of negotiating parties. This has provided GATT with the nickname 'General Agreement to Talk and Talk' (Bhagwati 1992). In a situation in which the dominant role of the United States has more or less disappeared, it seems particularly appropriate to divide the role of leader among three blocs. This position is further strengthened by the fact that regional trade agreements typically involve a higher degree of integration, in terms of product standardization, harmonization of taxes, free trade in services, etc., than that known from multilateral GATT agreements. As mentioned previously, product standardization within the EU is non-discriminating and thus a case of general liberalization. This makes member countries in a regional bloc more competitive and more extrovert, which in turn may reduce protectionist pressure. In addition, the political dimension involved in regional agreements may contribute to increased political stability. The EU is usually quoted as an example of this as EU cooperation is assumed to have contributed to peace in Europe.

Of course, the number of blocs formed and the countries actually inside these blocs are of crucial importance to the discussion. The advantage of the triad blocs is that the countries inside each bloc are natural trading partners, which results in minimal trade diversion. The danger of trading blocs is that they become introvert and pursue 'beggar thy neighbour' policies as in the thirties. This possibility is precisely the one that is envisaged by those who see the formation of the Single Market within the EU as the beginning of a European fortress.

In sum, although regional trading blocs discriminate by definition, it does not follow that their trade effect on third countries and on the global trade system is negative. In this connection, the Uruguay round, which started in 1986, should be understood as an important attempt to bring the international trading system back on the multilateral track in that it expands the GATT system to include all sectors in the world economy (textile, agricultural products and a wide range of services) and all kinds of trade barriers, even the ones in the grey areas, such as VER agreements.

As a part of the new trade agreement, a new organization, the World Trade Organization (WTO), has been established. The WTO Treaty was signed on 15 April 1994 and provides a framework that includes both the GATT Treaty and the agreements reached during the Uruguay round. In order to ensure that the organization will be efficient and that protraction and obstruction of the decision-making process becomes minimal, decisions under the Treaty will be made by simple majority. Thus the WTO seems to have been given the role that was originally intended for the ITO

SUMMARY

1. Internal pressure group resistance keeps nations from attempts to liberalize trade unilaterally, and as a consequence trade liberalization tends to be a multilateral cause left to international organizations such as the OECD, GATT, etc.
2. Nominal and effective levels of tariff protection may differ. Effective tariff rates distinguish between value added in domestic and world market prices and thus reflect the effective level of protection.
3. Economic integration in free trade areas, customs unions, etc., represents discriminating forms of trade liberalization.
4. Customs unions, such as the EU, produce calculable trade-creating and trade-diverting effects, and in addition incalculable dynamic effects on member economies.
5. The EU goes further than a mere customs union and attempts to realize a common (single) market for goods and factors. The European single market is a large-scale experiment to stimulate mobility in the union.
6. The postwar period may be subdivided into two eras, successful liberalization (before 1973) and increasing neoprotectionism (after 1973). The latter period has seen the rise of a multitude of non-tariff barriers to trade, such as VERs, export subsidies, etc.

7. Regionalism has become a most important feature in international trade. The question is whether the trade blocks will facilitate the way towards global trade liberalization—or the reverse?

REFERENCES AND FURTHER READING

Balassa, B. (1975), 'Trade creation and diversion in the European Common Market', in B. Balassa (ed.), *European Economic Integration*, North-Holland, Amsterdam, pp. 79–120.

Bhagwati, J. (1990), 'Departures from multilateralism: regionalism and aggressive unilateralism', *The Economic Journal*, **100**, 1304–1327.

Bhagwati, J. (1992), 'The threats to the world trading system', *The World Economy*, **15**, 4.

Bhagwati, J. and D. Irwin (1987), 'The return to the reciprocitarians: US trade policy today', *The World Economy*, **10**, 109–130.

Boltho, A. and C. Alsopp (1987), 'The assessment: trade and trade policy', *Oxford Review of Economic Policy*, **3**, 1.

Commission of the European Communities (1985), 'Completing the internal market', White Paper from the EC Commission to the EC Council, COM (85), Brussels.

Dobson, John M. (1976), *Two Centuries of Tariffs*, Washington DC.

Emerson, M. *et al.* (1988), *The Economics of 1992. The EC Commission's Assessment of the Economic Effects of Completing the Internal Market*, Oxford University Press.

GATT (1992), *GATT activities 1991. An Annual Review of the Work of GATT*. Geneva.

GATT (1993), *Focus GATT newsletter*, December.

Jackson, J. H. (1991), *The World Trading System. Law and Policy of International Economic Relations*, The MIT Press, Cambridge, Massachusetts.

Kelly, M. *et. al.* (1988), '*Issues and development in international trade policy*', Occasional Paper 63, IMF.

Lloyd, P. J. (1992), 'Regionalisation and world trade', *OECD Economic Studies*, **18**, Spring.

Nielsen, J. U.-M., H. Heinrich and J. D. Hansen (1992) *An Economic Analysis of the EC*, McGraw-Hill, London.

Office of US Trade Representative (1980), 24th Annual Report of the President on the Trade Agreements Program 1979, Washington DC.

Petith, H. (1977), 'European integration and the terms of trade', *Economic Journal*, **87**, 262–272.

Robson, P. (1987), *The Economics of International Integration*, 3rd edn, Unwin Hyman, London.

The World Bank (1991), *World Development Report 1991. The Challenge of Development*. Oxford University Press, Oxford.

Viner, J. (1950), *The Customs Union Issue*, New York.

Yeats, A. J. (1974), 'Effective tariff protection in the United States, the European Economic Community and Japan', *Quarterly Review of Economics and Business*, **14**(2), 41–50.

SEVEN

BALANCE OF PAYMENTS AND INTERNATIONAL INDEBTEDNESS

The preceding chapters have dealt with open economies from a micro-economic angle, focusing on resource allocation and distribution. An alternative approach is that of viewing economies from a macro-economic angle, which focuses on *aggregate* units such as total national production, consumption and investment, rate of inflation, etc. Adopting the macro-economic approach necessitates the availability of national accounts which record the activities of firms and industries and which sum them up into aggregate units. The import and export transactions of each firm have to be recorded, aggregate figures giving total national imports and exports for example in 1995 or in a given quarter of a year.

In this chapter we will consider the macro-economic side of international relations. Thus the chapter centres on the relationships expressed in the balance of payments and the balance of international indebtedness of a country and on the economic interpretation of the two.

A nation's *balance of payments* account provides an aggregate statement of the value of all the economic transactions taking place between that nation and all other countries in the course of a year. The *balance of international indebtedness* or the external wealth account of a country expresses its aggregate assets and liabilities, i.e. its international indebtedness. It has always been a topical issue in politico-economic debates whether a given country had a payments surplus or deficit and whether it had net assets abroad or net liabilities. This interest dates back to the age of mercantilism: mercantilists conceived of a nation's reserves of precious metals as a measure of its welfare. Therefore an increase in the level of welfare could only be achieved through a payments surplus. In fact, mercantilism has left its mark on modern usage. A 'favourable balance of payments trend' is commonly thought of as a trend towards a surplus increase.

In Section 7.1 we will consider the implications of adopting a macro-economic approach instead of a micro-economic one. In Section 7.2 we will consider the composition of a balance of payments and of a balance of international indebtedness as well as the part accounts that they include. Subsequently, in Section 7.3, we turn to the transfer problem, which has attracted a great deal of attention. The crux of the problem is whether a financial transaction between two countries will result in a flow of real resources, i.e. whether it will create trade between the two countries. In Section 7.4 we consider international capital flows. In particular, we will be concerned with what they consist of, whether they exhibit systematic patterns, and—in Section 7.5—with whether external debt can generally be said to be a problem to each individual country.

7.1 DISEQUILIBRIUM IN THE MODEL OF INTERNATIONAL TRADE

Figure 2.4 presented an analysis of the possible welfare gains provided by international trade. Assuming full employment, i.e. production at a point on the production possibility curve, we showed that trade in goods offers the possibility of a gain: it allows countries to place themselves at a consumption point in which the composition of goods is more favourable than that obtained prior to trade. This line of arguing should be recognizable in Figure 7.1. In this figure X and Y are the imported product and the exported product, respectively, M′ is the production point and M″ is the consumption point. In order to reach the point M″ from M′, the volume of $X_1 X_0$ is imported and the volume of $Y_0 Y_1$, is exported, trade taking place at current world market prices, p_W.

7.1.1 External disequilibrium

Now that we are on the threshold of macro-economics, we will extend the exposition in two ways. Firstly, we will broaden our angle so as to include total national resource utilization, i.e. both consumption and investments by both the public and private sectors, and not just goods for consumption. Secondly, the figure may be used to illustrate the case of foreign trade disequilibrium. Let us imagine that consumption and investment only bind the volumes of Y_2 and X_2 of the two kinds of goods, e.g. on account of a lump sum tax. The resources released will then be used for the production of consumption and investment goods for exports. At the world market prices given, this will result in a trade surplus because point M′ is still the optimum production point.

Out of the total resource endowment, some part will be put at the disposal of other countries, namely the part that is not needed for consumption and investment, i.e. the volumes of $X_1 X_2$ and $Y_1 Y_2$. The trade surplus corresponds to the distance between the two price curves through M″ and B, respectively. In terms of product Y, this corresponds to $Y_3 Y_4$, and in terms of total production, the trade surplus may be expressed as $Y_3 Y_4 / Y_3$. The trade surplus is outbalanced by external lending. This is known as capital exports. Likewise, a country that can borrow internationally may obtain consumption possibilities beyond M″. In both cases, it is important to notice that a trade surplus or deficit is exactly outbalanced by a financial item.

If capital movement, e.g. loans, results in subsequent changes in trade, this is known as a case of real transfer. This particular issue will be dealt with in a later section.

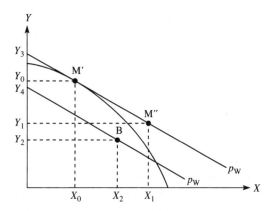

Figure 7.1 Trade in equilibrium and in disequilibrium

7.2   THE BALANCE OF PAYMENTS

International relations with other countries consist of a wide range of different transactions. One kind of transaction consists of trade in *goods*. In this connection, imports partly include raw materials and capital goods for business and partly consumer goods. Likewise, countries export a large number of goods. As will be seen from Table 7.1, Denmark's international trade in goods showed a surplus of DKK 43bn in 1992, i.e. a surplus on the *trade balance*, which provided the country with net currency receipts. In what follows, we will use the Danish balance of payments account as an example.

Table 7.1   The balance of payments of Denmark, 1992 (DKK bn)

		Foreign currency receipts	*Foreign currency expenditure*	*Net foreign currency receipts*
1	Trade	244	201	43
2	Carriage by sea	30	28	2
3	Travel	23	23	0
4	Other goods and services	36	16	20
1–4	Goods and services balance	333	268	65
5	Interest, dividend, etc	93	127	− 34
6	EU transfers	11	8	3
7	Unilateral transfers	2	8	− 6
1–7	Current account balance	439	411	28
8	Public and private capital movements, errors and omissions			− 29
9	Decrease in currency reserves	1		1
8–9	Capital account			− 28
1–9	Total			0

Source: Danmarks Statistik: (1993), Nationalregnskab, offentlige finanser og betalingsbalance

Another kind of transaction consists of trade in services. These include transport and insurance services as well as travel, among other things. As a whole, goods and services yielded a surplus of DKK 65bn on the Danish balance of goods and services in 1992.

A country with external indebtedness has relied on foreign factors of production and has of course to pay for the factor services rendered. The line showing interest, dividend, etc., is a result of this. Along with EU transfers and unilateral transfers such as development aid, the sum of these items was DKK − 37bn in 1992. As a whole, these are known as transfer items.

Together, goods, services and transfers constitute the current account balance. 1992 saw a surplus of DKK 28bn on this account. The common reference to a balance of payments surplus or deficit, known from politico-economic discussion, is precisely a reference to the current account of the balance of payments.

Finally, international dealings may be in the form of transactions involving securities, e.g.

shares and bonds, and money, i.e. bank deposits. International trade in money and securities results in capital movements, which are recorded on the capital account of the balance of payments. If a Danish government bond is sold to Switzerland, this will not be recorded as export of a security but as capital import. This is because Denmark, in this case, receives a share of Swiss saving, i.e. Denmark imports capital. Consequently, borrowing abroad results in currency receipts.

Likewise, from a Danish point of view it is a case of capital export when Danish firms and public authorities extend loans to other countries, e.g. through the purchase of shares in foreign companies. It should be emphasized that exports and imports of capital goods, such as trucks, lathes, etc., are recorded on the balance of trade as movements of goods: they are not capital movements even though real capital is involved.

7.2.1 Current account versus capital account

If, as in Denmark in 1992, the current account of the balance of payments shows a surplus, then the capital account must at the same time show a corresponding deficit, i.e. it must show a change in currency reserves and in international lending. In 1992, the balance of payments was in equilibrium because loans extended to other countries and/or international debt reduction by Danish authorities and private persons amounted to DKK 29bn while currency reserves were reduced by only DKK 1bn.

Currency reserves consist of the liquid claims of the central bank on other countries minus the foreign liabilities of the bank. The currency reserves include the gold reserves of the bank, its reserve position with respect to the IMF, special drawing rights (SDR) with the IMF and the EU (member countries only) and other claims on other countries, obtained through international borrowing.

Formally, the current account surplus (CA), public and private net borrowing abroad (B) and the increase in currency reserves (ΔL) are related as expressed in

$$CA + B = L \qquad [1]$$

This follows from the fact that the increase in currency reserves may be considered a currency expenditure since an increase in liquid claims on other countries is obtained by means of foreign currency. This means that when public and private net borrowing differs from the current account surplus, then the result is a change in currency reserves.

The relationship between current items and capital items may additionally be illustrated by means of the principles of double-entry book-keeping (Table 7.2). Of course exports increase foreign currency receipts, i.e. currency receipts are placed to the credit of the current account (4), while the capital account is debited with the increase in currency reserves (9). If exporters extend a credit of three months, item (4) on the current account will still be credited on the dispatch of the goods, but item (8) on the capital account will be debited since the credit extended involves an increase in the claims of the private sector on other countries. Three months later when payment is made, these claims are reduced, so item (11) will be credited while item (9) will be debited since currency reserves will increase.

If the government raises a loan abroad, item (11) will be credited while item (9) will be debited since receipts from borrowing increase currency reserves. These examples should make it clear that borrowing does not in itself increase external debt, currency reserves increasing correspondingly. The underlying deficit on the current account drains currency reserves, however, and therefore necessitates external borrowing. If we consider imports, this becomes

Table 7.2   Balance of payments: double-entry book-keeping

	Currency expenditure (debit)	*Currency receipts (credit)*
Trade in goods	(1)	(4)
Services	(2)	(5)
Transfers	(3)	(6)
Current account	(13)	(14)
	Increase in assets	*Increase in liabilities*
Direct investment	(7)	(10)
Lending	(8)	(11)
Change in currency reserves	(9)	(12)
Capital account	(15)	(16)

immediately obvious. If imports are paid in cash, item (1) will be debited while the decrease in currency reserves will be placed to the credit of item (12).

Likewise, the sale of a domestic firm to another country does not influence external debt. The purchase by foreigners of a controlling share of a domestic firm is considered a case of *direct investment* and is placed to the credit of item (10). As receipts from the sale are placed to the debit of currency reserves, i.e. item (9), however, the capital of the nation remains unaffected relative to other countries.

Compared to the accounts of a firm, the current account corresponds to the profit and loss account, while the capital account corresponds to a balance sheet showing the financing of transactions over the period. In accounting terms, the total of the current items (14) − (13) sets off the total of the capital items (15) − (16). Therefore a current account surplus over a given period reduces the indebtedness of the nation as a 'firm' over the period considered. Conversely, a deficit will increase its indebtedness.

Figure 7.2 presents a survey of the way in which subtotals on the balance of payments are related. Taken as a whole, a balance of payments is always in equilibrium, any difference between current items and net borrowing abroad being outbalanced by a change in currency reserves, which form part of the capital items.

7.2.2   Autonomous and accommodating items

As a whole, a balance of payments is always in equilibrium, therefore any disequilibrium will be in one of the subtotals shown in Figure 7.2 or in some other subtotal. A categorization frequently used is based on the *motives* for the transactions; in this connection a distinction is made between autonomous and accommodating items.

The crucial characteristic of *autonomous* items is that they result from 'independent business

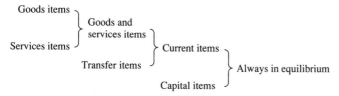

Figure 7.2   Balance of payments subtotals

motives'. Clear-cut examples of autonomous items include exports and imports, tourism and interest payments. On the assumption that private sector capital imports and exports are autonomous and that public borrowing and lending are not based on independent business motives, equation (2) results. The equation is based on formula (1) and divides B into private (B_p) and public (B_g) capital movements.

$$CA + B_p = \Delta L - B_g \tag{2}$$

This groups autonomous items on the left-hand side of the equation sign and [2] *accommodating* items on the right-hand side. If a country has *floating* exchange rates, the autonomous items will automatically be in equilibrium as the authorities do not intervene and, as a result, the right-hand side is zero. Under *fixed* exchange rates, if we except the case of pure coincidence, the autonomous items will not equal zero and, consequently, they will cause foreign exchange to flow into or out of the country. If the exchange rate of the country is fixed, the public authorities are under an obligation to secure the rate of exchange. This is done by controlling currency flows in precisely such a way that the rate of exchange is maintained. As will be seen from the following chapter, public authorities have to compensate for any disequilibrium caused by the autonomous items. For this purpose, two tools are at their disposal: they may either have the public sector raising loans abroad or extending loans to other countries, or they may change currency reserves.

If, in a situation with a deficit on the autonomous items, currency reserves are judged to be abundant, the government may choose to reduce currency reserves instead of having recourse to public borrowing. In other situations, it may be more appropriate to maintain currency reserves and to accommodate the deficit on the autonomous items through public borrowing.

From time to time, the extent to which the autonomous items are actually autonomous becomes the subject of debate. The debate focuses in particular on private capital movements, which governments to some extent influence through their monetary policies. If borrowing conditions are made more favourable, e.g. if the domestic interest rate is lowered, then members of the private sector may choose to raise loans in the home country instead of doing so abroad.

In spite of the difficulties involved in making a sharp distinction between autonomous and accommodating items, formula (2) is a useful tool for exchange market analyses (see Chapter 8 and subsequent chapters). Table 7.3 shows the relationships holding in the case of Denmark

Table 7.3 Balance of payments and external borrowing, Denmark, 1986–92 (DKK bn)

Year	Balance of payments surplus (CA)	External net borrowing		Increase in currency reserves (ΔL)
		Private sector (B_p)	Public sector (B_g)	
1986	− 34.5	− 16.3	36.7	− 14.1
1987	− 19.0	33.5	20.9	35.2
1988	− 8.9	23.5	− 5.9	8.7
1989	− 8.2	− 15.7	− 3.8	− 27.7
1990	8.2	5.1	8.4	21.6
1991	14.2	− 7.0	− 27.9	− 20.8
1992	29.0	− 40.4	10.2	− 1.1

Source: Statens låntagning og gæld, various years.

during the period from 1986 to 1992. The first two columns indicate autonomous items while the other two indicate accommodating items. As appears from the table, the fluctuations in the three variables, B_p, B_g and ΔL, have been quite marked.

7.2.3   Balance of indebtedness

The capital account of the balance of payments shows the change in a country's indebtedness towards other countries. A country's total claims on and liabilities to other countries at a given point in time are stated in the national *balance of indebtedness*. However, the current account total, and hence capital items, are not the sole factors determining the change in position with respect to other countries. This change may also be influenced by changes in rates, in particular exchange rates, affecting the assets and liabilities that form part of the balance. Therefore the following holds:

Current account surplus + exchange rate gains on net liabilities
= decrease in external net liabilities

Table 7.4 shows that the net external liabilities of Denmark amounted to DKK 218bn at the end of 1993. The claims of the Danish central bank amounted to DKK 75bn, net liabilities of the public sector were DKK 501bn and net claims of the private sector including financial institutions were DKK 208bn. This figure consists of net claims held by financial institutions and of assets and liabilities which approximately outbalance each other in the rest of the private sector

The private sector items consist of three major kinds of obligations: direct investments, portfolio investments and business loans and credits. Direct investments include capital transfers in connection with the establishment of subsidiaries across borders, which may either involve purchase or new establishment.

Currency reserves, or the international liquidity of Denmark, amounted to DKK 75bn at the end of 1993. As mentioned previously, currency reserves serve as a kind of 'buffer' during periods of imbalance between exchange receipts and expenditure. Adjusting the size of the

Table 7.4   Balance of indebtedness, Denmark, end-year 1983–93 (DKK bn)

Year	Central bank of Denmark	Public sector	Private sector	Total
1983	−41	153	73	193
1984	−40	165	99	224
1985	−53	172	125	243
1986	−36	200	99	262
1987	−64	236	104	276
1988	−76	249	121	293
1989	−45	232	103	290
1990	−63	261	84	282
1991	−45	281	29	264
1992	−45	343	−57	241
1993	−75	501	−208	218

Note: A minus indicates net claims on other countries.
Source: Danmarks Nationalbank, Årsberetning 1993.

buffer allows the government to avoid unintended exchange rate adjustments and other politico-economic measures.

Holding considerable currency reserves is of course associated with costs since reserves mainly consist of short-term claims on other countries. Consequently, the costs correspond to the difference between the interest rate at which loans have been extended and the return on short-term investments. Typically, the difference will be less than 1 per cent a year, so the costs of the Danish currency reserves are around DKK 0.5bn annually.

7.3   THE TRANSFER PROBLEM

The preceding section focused on the current items of the balance of payments and their interaction with other part accounts. This section centres on the effects which capital items have on current items. In particular, we will consider the extent to which and the mechanisms by which capital imports 'attract' real resources in the form of goods and thus influence the balance of goods and services.

After the First World War, theoretical economists were intensely fascinated by the issue of whether the massive German reparation payments in 'transferring' goods and services from Germany would give a great impetus to the economies of the victors. This discussion concerned unilateral transfers which are a part of the current account (see Table 7.2). Reparation payments arguably caused an equivalent deficit on the goods and services items of the victorious nations. They thus obtained access to additional real resources for a *given* current account position (Keynes, 1929; Ohlin, 1929)

If, alternatively, an industrialized country (A) *lends* to a developing country (B), what is the possibility of a real resource transfer?

On the assumption that the capital was transferred by the private sector, the problem may be analysed by means of formula (2), which states that, in the case of given capital movements and currency reserves, an increase in private capital import necessarily results in the transfer of goods, i.e. CA will be reduced in the borrowing country.

Whether or not the conclusion materializes depends upon the economic policy in the countries. If country B adds the receipts to its currency reserves, then ΔL increases by the receipts from the loan and no real effects will occur. The two countries will merely have claims of identical sizes on each other.

However, if the public authorities in country B choose to let the loan affect money supply, then economic activity will increase by the derived effect on the balance of goods and services, with imports increasing as a result of increased economic activity. The closer the country is to full capacity utilization, the sooner and more forceful the impact on imports will be.

In this case, therefore, a real economic effect occurs which may be described by means of the following well-known national accounts identity:

$$Y = C + I + G + (X - M) \qquad [3]$$

where Y, C, I and G are gross domestic product, private consumption, private investment and public purchases of goods and services. $X - M$ is the surplus on the goods and services account. Given that income which is not consumed $(Y - C)$ is either saved (S) or paid as taxes (T), the following equation results:

$$Y - C = S + T = I + G + X - M \qquad [4]$$

If we rearrange the elements in this equation, the result is the following relation:

$$(S - I) + (T - G) = (X - M) \qquad [5]$$

which states that the sum of private $(S-I)$ and public $(T-G)$ sector savings surplus corresponds precisely to the current account (CA) surplus. If we disregard interest and dividend, the savings surplus corresponds to the surplus on the goods and services accounts $(X-M)$.

Thus capital flows among countries serve the purpose of financing any imbalance between saving and investment in each country. The balancing act is performed by means of transfers of real resources $(X-M)$ between the countries involved.

7.4 INTERNATIONAL CAPITAL MOVEMENTS

The preceding chapter concluded that capital movements among countries may generally be considered as transfers of resources from countries with a savings surplus to countries with a savings deficit. This section provides a theoretical and an empirical profile of international capital movements.

7.4.1 A stylized profile

Countries undergoing an industrializing process, which involves investments in infrastructure, capital stock, technology and management systems, must of necessity be borrowers. Contrari-wise, 'mature' economies act as lenders to developing countries. On the basis of the experience gathered by the World Bank since the Second World War, Figure 7.3 shows such a stylized course of development.

1 *'The young debtor'.* During this stage, which is characteristic, for example, of a developing country with considerable investment needs, a deficit on the goods and services balance (B) will make possible a corresponding increase in the domestic absorption of goods and services and, hence, in the investment level. This presupposes, of course, that the domestic

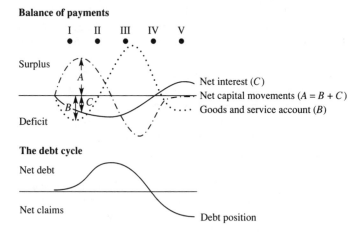

Figure 7.3 Balance of payments and external debt, course of development
Source: The World Bank (1985).

rate of saving remains unaltered. As external debt increases, the country incurs net interest expenditure in relation to other countries (C) so that its current account deficit will be $B + C$. This is outbalanced by equivalent net capital imports (A), which correspond to the increase in foreign debt.

2   *'The mature debtor'*. As capital stock is developed and the country becomes competitive within new industries, it is not unlikely that it will increase its volume of exports substantially. As a result the deficit on the goods and services account will be reduced and gradually become a surplus. Consequently, the increase in debts will also be reduced, as will interest payments.

3   *'Debt reduction'*. During this stage the surplus on the goods and services account will exceed interest payments, i.e. a current account surplus persists throughout the stage. This causes the country to become a capital exporter while debt decreases (and disappears).

4   *'The young creditor'*. The goods and services account declines but is still positive. Interest payments change into net revenue. In sum, the current account surplus declines and the country establishes itself in a creditor position.

5   *'The mature creditor'*. The deficit on the goods and services account continues and the claims on other countries result in corresponding net interest receipts, so the current account will be in equilibrium; net foreign assets will stabilize.

7.4.2   Capital movements in recent years

No country precisely follows the stylized course of development outlined above of course. The past 20 years have seen various examples which illustrate this. In this connection, the two oil crises are worth mentioning.

The immediate effect of the tripling of oil prices in 1973–74 was quite naturally increased rates of inflation, deterioration of balances of payments and slumping economic activity in the oil-importing countries. While the first two results called for contractionary measures, the slump in economic activity called for an expansionary economic policy. This was a very real dilemma.

As is well known, the dilemma was not solved, but countries had to make a choice. The industrialized countries largely chose to pursue a contractionary economic policy, i.e. they gave priority to the fight against inflation and balance of payments problems, while developing countries largely chose the expansionary solution. In addition, all oil-importing countries introduced various energy-saving measures, which, however, did not provide any genuine defence against OPEC.

The sudden and strong increase in the export receipts of the oil-producing countries, which appears in Figure 7.4, could not immediately be translated into efficient demand because of the economic stage of the oil countries and the relatively small size of their populations. Consequently, a savings surplus emerged in the form of large current account surpluses, which by definition were outbalanced by substantial capital export. Through the international banking system, these surpluses found their way to the debtor countries; this was the so-called *recycling* of petrodollars.

The graph also shows that within a few years the OPEC countries succeeded in increasing their absorption ability to such an extent that as a whole the current accounts of the group were almost in equilibrium. Even the severe price increases during the second oil crisis in 1979–81 did not succeed in keeping current accounts above zero for very long.

One conspicuous feature of the figure is that adding the curve vertically yields quite considerable negative 'balances'. The fact that the Eastern bloc countries, which were rather

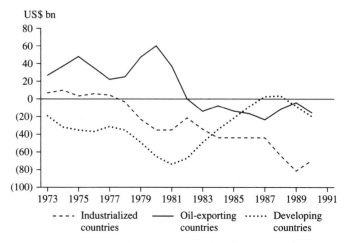

Note: The figures are sliding averages, i.e. the figure for each year is an average
of that year and the two years surrounding it.

Figure 7.4   Current accounts, 1973–90 (US$ bn)
       Sources: IMF Annual Reports for 1983, 1987 and 1992 and own calculations.

unimportant in this respect, are not included in the statistics does not account for this: a quite
substantial item of 'errors and omissions' is the underlying reason.

The most frequently used explanation attributes this to the national accounting procedures
and 'erroneous' entries of the various countries in connection with overseas interest receipts. If
interest payments, e.g. among companies in the same group, are not reported, the resulting
picture will be a distorted one. A further explanation emphasized by the IMF is that a large part
of the world's merchant navy sails under the flags of 'banana republics' which do not report
'carriage by sea' to the Fund.

As mentioned previously, the industrialized countries chose to pursue tight economic policies
after the first oil crisis, and, taken as a whole, their foreign trade was largely in equilibrium in
the seventies. The savings surplus in the OPEC countries (hence the idle capital) passed through
the large banks in the West, where the OPEC countries had their claims as deposits, to the oil-
less developing countries, which through the period of 1973 to 1983 accumulated a balance of
payments deficit of around US$ 500bn, which was primarily financed through loans in Western
banks. As this capital transfer was not primarily spent on investments, payment of interest on
the loans raised became a major burden to the developing countries. In the eighties a large
number of developing countries could not meet the business and repayment conditions agreed
to, so an international debt crisis resulted.

Among the industrialized countries, substantial capital transfers have also taken place. In the
eighties these transfers were primarily from Japan and West Germany to the United States.
However, these massive transfers were not motivated by industrialization either, but were due
to a partial imbalance in trade among these countries. To a large extent, the imbalance was the
result of the tight monetary policy pursued by the United States at the beginning of the eighties,
which resulted in an historically high value of the US$. A further reason for the imbalance was
the savings ratio in the United States, which was considerably lower than the ratios in the two
other economically leading countries. Finally, the savings deficits of the US federal government
have been very large.

German unification in 1990 and the resulting investments in the reconstruction of the new federal states have made the German surplus disappear. The Japanese surplus, however, is larger than ever.

7.5   IS INTERNATIONAL INDEBTEDNESS A PROBLEM?

It would be nonsensical to claim that foreign indebtedness generally presents a problem. The theoretical model in Figure 4.2 showed that both a borrower and a lender may benefit from international capital movements, i.e. from indebtedness. The argument was repeated in Figure 7.3: a country will pass through a cycle of development and in the process its financial position changes from that of a borrower to that of a lender. The theoretical ideal of all agents benefiting from the transactions was probably reflected in the real world during the period prior to the First World War. Capital moved from the industrialized centre to the countries investing in industrial and infrastructural development, i.e. to places in which its marginal productivity was undoubtedly considerably higher. Figure 7.5 reproduces the *raison d'être* of borrowing used for productive purposes.

This period, however, is likely to have been unique. In later periods the effects of international indebtedness have been less positive and in the eighties the 'debt crisis' of a number of primarily Latin American LDCs generated much concern: indebtedness had risen to a level that appeared to prevent adequate debt servicing.

It seems reasonable to ask how this could have happened. In some cases, e.g. that of Chile, the deficit was spent on consumption and did not increase productive capacity for the purpose of servicing the debt. In other cases, e.g. that of Brazil, the deficit was in fact invested in capital equipment but a combination of inflexible borrowing conditions and sky-rocketing international interest rates made these investments unprofitable: capital costs surpassed the marginal productivity of imported capital. Many LDCs were hit by this situation and resorted to contractionary economic policies. The decrease in income was in several cases larger than the immediate increase resulting from borrowing: international indebtedness resulted in losses—to lenders, too, in several cases.

In the late eighties, as in the nineties, interest rates dropped and less was heard of the debt crisis. In addition, renegotiation of terms of borrowing helped ease the burden in some cases. Yet, in the mid-nineties, the most indebted nation is the United States, which also happens to be one of the most capital-intensive nations.

The obvious conclusion is that foreign indebtedness presents no problem in itself but may turn out to be highly problematic if lenders and borrowers do not behave rationally or if

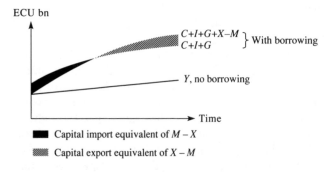

Figure 7.5   Borrowing for productive purposes

conditions change quite unpredictably. Thus long-term borrowing aiming at industrial or infrastructural development has to be based on long-term calculations.

It is difficult, however, to determine whether decision-makers have actually behaved rationally. At a given level of production, a payments deficit will allow the deficit country to ncrease its absorption of goods and services. It is impossible to determine whether the deficit translates into increased investments or into consumption through reduced domestic savings. Equation (5) cannot be subjected to a causality analysis.

Leaving the overall discussion of international indebtedness, we will turn to two rather technical questions: (1) whether limits exist to the size of a debt and (2) whether it is possible to run a sustained deficit on the goods and services account.

7.5.1   Limits to foreign debt?

How much a country may borrow internationally and the terms of a loan are determined by the creditworthiness of the country concerned. Institutions such as Standard & Poor assess the ability of nations to meet their obligations and to service their debt. The assessment and credit-ranking are based on both political and economic factors. Political stability plays an important part, as do economic key figures such as

- International liquidity relative to imports
- Interest payments relative to exports
- Exports relative to GDP
- Foreign debt (D) relative to GDP (Y)

The last expression in this list defines the *debt burden*:

$$b = \frac{D}{Y}$$

Towards the end of 1993 the Danish debt burden was approximately 30 per cent, which leaves the country well below top rankings. The creditworthiness of a large number of LDCs is considerably lower, however, because they face a far more severe debt burden.

If a country reaches the 'ceiling' and b cannot increase any further, the balance of payments deficit may still continue. By definition $\Delta D = b \times \Delta Y$, so if GDP increases by 6 per cent per annum, international debt may increase by the same percentage, leaving b unchanged. If we disregard the possibility of exchange rate changes, this growth rate of D implies a current account deficit amounting to 6 per cent of the nation's net debt.

7.5.2   Is a sustained deficit possible?

It is rather questionable, however, whether a nation can run a sustained deficit on its goods and services account, $X - M$, without causing its debt burden to increase. The reason for this is that part of its current account deficit is spent on interest payment. Thus the change in indebtedness is

$$\Delta D = i \times D - (X - M)$$

where i is the nominal interest rate involved in the debt service, including exchange rate changes but excluding other income transfers.

Given an unchanged debt burden, the debt may increase by

$$\Delta D = b \times \Delta Y = b \times g \times Y$$

where g is the nominal growth rate of GDP. Combining the two expressions of ΔD, we obtain the following expression of the relation between the deficit on the goods and services account and GDP:

$$\frac{M - X}{Y} = bg - i\left(\frac{D}{Y}\right) = b(g - i)$$

Only if the growth rate in GDP is above the average interest rate involved in the debt service will a sustained deficit $(M - X)$ be consistent with an unchanged debt burden. Adjusting g and i for inflation, we obtain the condition that the real growth rate has to exceed the (international) real interest rate.

By contrast, in periods such as those of the early eighties when i exceeded g, a substantial trade surplus is needed just to prevent the debt burden from increasing. This was what paved the way to the debt crisis.

SUMMARY

1. A nation's balance of payments features its external transactions as a flow, e.g. over one year, and the balance of international indebtedness expresses its assets and liabilities at a given point in time, i.e. as a stock.
2. The balance of payments is composed of a number of balances, each of which may be positive, negative or zero. This is also valid for the current account balance, but its total is precisely counterbalanced by the capital account, leaving the total of the balance of payments at zero.
3. Depending on the motives of transaction, a distinction is made between autonomous and accommodating items. Non-intervention under floating exchange rates results in equilibrium in autonomous items, but under fixed rates they will not automatically equal zero.
4. The transfer problem deals with spill-over from capital items on current items. The actual effects depend on the policy chosen by authorities.
5. Nations, on their path of economic development, move through phases of indebtedness— from young debtor to mature creditor.
6. Violent changes in oil prices and interest rates created a debt crisis for a number of LDC debtor countries in the seventies and eighties. In recent years the pressure has lifted.
7. A nation may run a balance of payments deficit over extended periods, increasing its debt, but observing a maximum debt burden. However, a sustained goods and services deficit is only possible if the growth rate is above the average interest rate of the debt service.

REFERENCES AND FURTHER READING

IMF, *Balance of Payments Yearbook*.
Johnson, H. G. (1956), 'The transfer problem and exchange stability', *Journal of Political Economy*, June.
Keynes, J. M. (1929), 'The German transfer problem', *Economic Journal*, March.
Meade, J. (1951), *The Balance of Payments*, Oxford University Press, Oxford.
Ohlin, B. (1929), 'The reparation problem', *Economic Journal*, June.
The World Bank (1985), *World Development Report 1985*, Oxford University Press, New York.

EIGHT

THE FOREIGN EXCHANGE MARKET

In this chapter we will be concerned with foreign exchange. Today the world counts some hundred different national currencies since for political as well as economic reasons countries prefer to have their own currencies.

The price of foreign exchange is expressed in terms of exchange rates. Except in the United Kingdom, where exchange rates are based on the value of £ sterling, a given exchange rate states the amount payable in the national currency for 100 units of the foreign currency. The *foreign exchange market*, which in terms of turnover is the world's biggest market, consists of all the economic agents willing to exchange different currencies, i.e. willing to supply and demand them.

This chapter will deal with the role of foreign exchange, and by implication national currencies, in the international economy. Firstly, the structure and functioning of the exchange market is considered. Then Section 8.2 focuses on price formation in the foreign exchange spot market, i.e. the part of the exchange market in which delivery is immediate. Institutional conditions in the exchange market vary rather much, so Section 8.3 describes various exchange rate systems. Finally, Section 8.4 discusses the measurement of and the causes underlying long-term exchange rate trends. The topic of the following chapter will be the foreign exchange forward market, in which delivery takes place some time, typically somewhere between three days and three years, after the deal has been closed.

8.1 MARKET DESCRIPTION

A market is usually defined in terms of its geographical extent, the number of buyers and sellers and the nature of the product.

8.1.1 Extent and structure

Geographically, the foreign exchange market is indeterminate, foreign exchange transactions taking place all over the world. Exchange bureaux in international airports, the numerous foreign exchange departments of commercial banks and other exchange dealers are all part of the exchange market (see Figure 8.1). However, because individual agents make use of modern technology and thus keep abreast of exchange rate trends in other parts of the world, in particular in the large centres of London, Frankfurt, New York and Tokyo, then it makes sense to speak of 'the foreign exchange market'. This market (practically) never closes. When the market closes in New York, for example, trade continues in Tokyo and later in Singapore; and when they close, London takes over, etc.

As can be seen from Figure 8.1, the structure of the exchange market is pyramidal with a number of vertical links. More than 90 per cent of the total volume of trade in the exchange market is due to transactions between principal banks and other foreign exchange dealers. In such cases, transactions are restricted to particular foreign exchange departments located in or close to one of the financial centres. These transactions always involve large sums of money and it is precisely through the offers to buy and sell made by the agents that the market rate is formed. The rate is published by principal banks and major dailies.

Few lines connect the row at the bottom of the figure, exporters, etc., with the next link in the pyramid, simply because the exchange market is so efficient that it rarely pays to obtain information on exchange rates from various sides. The costs to banks of foreign exchange transactions with exporters and importers, tourists, etc., are mainly covered by a spread between the rates at which the banks buy and sell foreign exchange. However, a basic charge may be added in the case of minor transactions or the selling of foreign exchange to tourists. The difference between buying and selling rates typically depends on the volume of transactions with the customer concerned. If the volume is large, as is often the case when the customer is another bank, a branch or an exchange bureau, then costs will be low and the offer of the principal bank will be close to the market rate. However, if the customer is a tourist then the difference between buying and selling rates may be considerable, e.g. 5 per cent, since tourists typically exchange only small amounts at a time.

Central banks may influence the market rate directly through intervention on the exchange market, but they can also do so indirectly if they intervene on money markets. This will be shown in the following chapters.

8.1.2   The nature of the product

Chapters 2 and 3 described international trade theory without paying attention to the fact that countries have different currencies. The introduction of an exchange market does not change this insight into the nature of trade, but it is a further step towards a more realistic description of international transactions. Figure 8.2 shows how the exchange market contributes to oiling the wheels of international trade and at the same time ensures that economic agents in individual countries can retain their liquidity in the domestic currency.

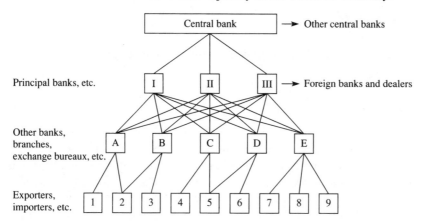

Figure 8.1   The structure of the exchange market

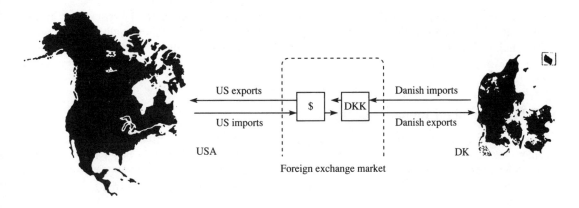

Figure 8.2   The function of the exchange market

In the exchange market, transactions involve the buying of money issued by one country for money from another. The money may be in notes or coins but transactions primarily involve bank deposits which are transferred among countries. Money is like any other product subjected to supply and demand. As a product, money satisfies the conditions for being a standard commodity exceptionally well.

8.1.3   Functions

The principal functions of the exchange market are evident from the description above. Firstly, the market serves as a *mediator of purchasing power* from one currency area to another. The exchange market makes it possible to exchange liquidity in one's own currency for goods or services located in a far-away country, and it makes it possible for exporters to sell goods to customers in a foreign currency area while being paid in currency units that are current coin in their own country. Of course American exporters prefer to be paid in US$ since their costs, i.e. wages, taxes, etc., have to be paid in this currency. Similarly, importers of American goods prefer to pay in their own currency.

Secondly, exchange markets make it possible to provide *credit facilities* in a foreign currency since payment of goods or services may be postponed until a later date. In addition, firms and institutions borrow on the exchange market and governments with a liquidity need also make use of it.

Finally, the exchange market may be used for *reducing exchange risks* since foreign currency may be bought or sold in the forward market, which will be studied in Chapter 9. The advantage of this option is that recipients of future earnings in a foreign currency will know exactly what these amount to in their own currency, or that debtors will know precisely how much they will have to pay in their own currency in order to meet a future obligation in a foreign currency.

8.2   THE SPOT MARKET

Given that currencies are largely similar to other goods, it seems a natural assumption that an ordinary supply and demand analysis will provide a relevant description of the exchange market. This viewpoint is only further strengthened by the fact that (1) currencies are a commodity of quite exceptional homogeneity—a distinction between 'high-quality dollars' and 'low-quality dollars' seems inconceivable—and (2) individual suppliers and buyers of foreign exchange are insignificant in relation to the market.

8.2.1   Demand for foreign exchange

A glance at the balance of payments (see Chapter 7) reveals several motives for the demand for foreign exchange: importers of foreign goods demand foreign exchange in order to be able to pay their suppliers; carriage by foreign vessels, tourism, etc., also entail demand for foreign exchange; and firms demand foreign exchange in connection with credits extended, overseas investments, etc.

Let us take the case of a Danish importer who has entered a contract for the purchase, in Germany, of a consignment of goods. If the account is to be settled in DEM, the importer will have to buy DEM for DKK from his bank. Therefore he demands DEM. Conversely, if the contract had specified DKK, the German exporter would have had to sell DKK in the exchange market in order to obtain DEM. Both cases would involve demand for DEM—and a simultaneous supply of DKK. The currency specified in the contract is therefore of no consequence to the exchange market.

Let us assume that 1 DEM is worth 4 DKK, the Danish rate of exchange being 400. A certain volume of demand for DEM will follow from individual buyers' wishes to buy. If the value of DKK relative to DEM *depreciates** and if as a result 1 DEM is worth 5 DKK, then German goods will cost more DKK than previously and the demand for them will decrease in Denmark. Consequently, demand for DEM from Danish importers will go down. Similarly, some tourists will prefer to visit the Danish provinces rather than to go sightseeing in Munich, so their demand for DEM will also fall.

Of course, the reverse may happen, too: DKK may appreciate relative to DEM, which will cause an increase in demand for DEM. Consequently, there is every reason to believe that a demand curve for DEM will assume the traditional shape by which an increase in price results in a decrease in the quantity demanded. Figure 8.3 illustrates such a traditional demand curve.

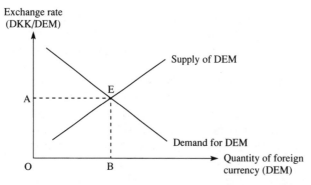

Figure 8.3   Demand and supply of a foreign currency (DEM)

---

* If the value of a currency falls or rises due to market forces, this is termed *depreciation* and *appreciation*, respectively, but if, in a fixed exchange rate system, the value changes due to a political decision to change it then the corresponding terms are those of *devaluation* and *revaluation*.

The vertical axis states the Danish exchange rate for DEM and the horizontal axis states the quantity of DEM demanded per time unit (e.g. per day).

8.2.2   Supply of foreign exchange

We will treat this topic like that of demand for foreign exchange. Supply of DEM may be *motivated* in Danish exports to Germany, the decision of German tourists to spend their holidays in Denmark, German investments in Danish firms or the purchase of other Danish assets.

The supply curve in Figure 8.3 has the usual slope of supply curves, which corresponds to a situation in which a higher exchange rate results in the supply of a larger volume of DEM. Some of the results of a higher exchange rate will be that German tourists will find it less expensive to go to Denmark, that purchasing Danish goods will become more attractive and that more goods will be carried by Danish ships.

However, it is not certain that the supply curve will assume its traditional appearance. In particular, the supply of foreign exchange due to exports may cause an atypical slope. This is the case if exports of goods and services face inelastic demand. In such a situation a lower price in a foreign currency will not be able to bring about an increase in demand which can compensate for the decrease in price. In the long term exports of goods are typically characterized by elastic demand, so for this reason we will exclusively be concerned with foreign exchange supply curves with a positive slope in this chapter, but the issue is considered in more detail in Chapter 11.

8.2.3   Market equilibrium

Market forces, if left alone, will bring about the equilibrium illustrated in Figure 8.3, which shows that the day's average exchange rate is OA, that turnover per day is DEM OB and that, measured in DKK, this turnover corresponds to the area of OAEB. In Chapter 7, formula (1) expressed equilibrium on the balance of payments as follows:

$$CA + B = \Delta L \qquad [1]$$

where CA is current account surplus, B is net external borrowing and ΔL is the increase in international liquidity. Given that balance of payments items measure flows in the foreign exchange market, condition (1) is satisfied with respect to the foreign exchange market.

A system of genuinely floating exchange rates, i.e. one in which this equilibrium is brought about, prevents central banks from intervening on the foreign exchange market. Thus international liquidity may be considered a constant, which means that the change in international liquidity, ΔL, equals zero. Given floating exchange rates,

$$CA + B = 0 \qquad [2]$$

Very often public net external borrowing is based on considerations of exchange rate stability or stability in international liquidity. In the case of freely floating exchange rates, governments will abstain from such borrowing, so that $B_g = 0$ and the following condition holds:

$$CA + B_p = 0 \qquad [3]$$

This formulation says that only transactions with the external environment by the private sector affect the foreign exchange market and, consequently, exchange rates. It follows that equilibrium in the foreign exchange market is affected both by current items (exports, imports, interest, etc.) and by private capital items (external borrowing, repayment of foreign debt, etc.). It is worth mentioning that, as a result, exchange market equilibrium only rarely implies current account equilibrium. A current account surplus will be matched by a deficit on the private capital items, yielding net capital export, and a current account deficit will be matched by a surplus on the private capital items, thus yielding net external borrowing.

The illustration in Figure 8.3 is based on the assumption of *ceteris paribus*, so, if any conditions change, supply of and/or demand for foreign exchange may be affected. If domestic conditions lead to a *cyclical upturn* the resulting increase in real income will lead to increased imports and consequently to an increase in the demand for foreign exchange. The equilibrium rate of exchange will rise. By contrast, if foreign real income increases this will result in an increase in domestic exports; therefore exporters will supply a larger volume of foreign exchange, which will cause the supply curve to shift to the right and make the equilibrium rate of exchange go down. If the cyclical upturn occurs both domestically and abroad, then imports as well as exports will increase. Consequently, the effect on exchange rates is uncertain but likely to be moderate.

If the *rate of inflation* in Germany increases, then French exports will be in a stronger position due to the cost advantage that they gain as a result, and the supply of DEM will increase, thus leading to a fall in the equilibrium rate. In addition, the equilibrium rate will be affected by imports because French products will replace more expensive foreign ones and consequently demand for foreign exchange will decrease. Conversely, French francs (FRF) will depreciate if the French rate of inflation is higher than the German one.

Our third example is that of a domestic *increase in the rate of interest*, which will stimulate capital imports. In this case the capital items will lead to an increase in the supply of foreign exchange and consequently to a decrease in the equilibrium rate. In Chapter 9 the influence of capital movements on exchange rates will be dealt with in greater detail.

8.2.4 Arbitrage

In the preceding sections we showed how exchange rates are formed in the case of market equilibrium, and in addition we touched upon the organization of the foreign exchange market, including its geographical distribution. If the currency of a country is traded against a total number of $n-1$ other currencies, then this will result in $n-1$ exchange rates. Among themselves these countries face $n(n-1)/2$ exchange rates. Therefore, in the case of the 20 currencies traded most often, the number of exchange rates amounts to 190. In what follows, we will show why unequivocal exchange rates between pairs of currencies exist throughout the world at any given time despite such numbers.

Let us assume that in Frankfurt one DEM can be bought for US$ 0.40, while the rate in New York is 0.42. Then it will pay to buy DEM in Frankfurt and to sell them simultaneously in New York. The effect of this will be that the rate goes down in New York and up in Frankfurt until such transactions are no longer worth while.

The activity that ensures exchange rate identity and thus unites the exchange market is known as *exchange* or *currency arbitrage*. Without this activity it would make no sense to speak of the exchange market for a currency; one would have to speak of several exchange markets for each currency, e.g. one in London, one in Zurich, etc.

Apart from the fact that exchange rates have to be the same in all geographical areas, they also have to be mutually consistent. This is illustrated in Table 8.1, which provides a set of exchange rates valid at some given moment in New York, Frankfurt and Copenhagen. An

Table 8.1   Three-point arbitrage

| | Market | | |
Exchange rate	New York	Frankfurt	Copenhagen
US$ per DEM	0.40	0.40	—
US$ per DKK	0.10	—	0.10
DKK per DEM	—	4.20	4.20

exchange dealer will only need a moment's consideration to be able to see that three simultaneous transactions will yield a profit:

(1) buying DKK 4.2m against DEM 1m;
(2) buying US$ 420 000 against DKK 4.2m; and
(3) buying DEM 1.05m against US$ 420 000.

This *three-point arbitrage* yields an immediate gain of DEM 50 000. This figure is unrealistically high but even relatively much smaller gains represent a high return on the effort made, given that they are acquired on the basis of a few seconds' work. In this connection, it is worth noting that the amounts involved in a single transaction in the exchange market are very large. The transactions involved in our example of three-point arbitrage will contribute to a drop in the rate of DKK against DEM (1) and the rate of US$ against DKK (2), and to a rise in the rate of US$ against DEM (3).

The point of arbitrage is to sell a product at a higher price than it has been bought at, which will bring demand and supply into harmony and eventually, i.e. when price differences have been neutralized, the market will offer no opportunities for arbitrage. The efficiency of exchange arbitrage is the result of various conditions. Firstly, transaction costs (from the use of telexes) are low and the product traded in does not entail any storage or transport costs. Secondly, the product is a standard commodity; in the case of products with quality differences, arbitrage would not have been able to create such evident harmony and to merge all parts of the globe into one market.

8.2.5   US$ at the centre

As mentioned above, the majority of transactions take place among foreign exchange dealers, i.e. in the so-called *interbank market*. For the purposes of these exchange transactions, it is convenient to make use of a *vehicle currency*, i.e. a single accounting unit. Because of the importance of the United States in the global economy this part has been assigned to the US$.

Let us consider a Belgian importer who wishes to buy Italian lira (ITL) from his exchange dealer for a major amount. As the market for Belgian francs (BEF) and ITL is insignificant, the importer's bankers will buy US$ in the interbank market by means of BEF and then buy ITL for US$. Consequently, the rate of ITL that the Belgian importer will have to pay depends on the interbank market US$ rates against (1) ITL (ITL/US$) and (2) BEF (BEF/US$), given

$$\frac{\text{BEF}}{\text{ITL}} = \frac{\text{BEF/US\$}}{\text{ITL/US\$}} \qquad [4]$$

Even if an independent market for BEF and ITL existed, equation (4) would be fulfilled through three-point arbitrage.

8.2.6 Fixed exchange rates

In economic history, systems of freely floating exchange rates have not been widely used. On the contrary, national authorities have intervened so often that the exchange market is the most thoroughly regulated market. This is due to the importance of exchange rates to the economic performance of nations, which we will discuss in Chapter 11, and to the belief of national authorities that they can fix the rate of exchange more 'correctly' than the market is able to.

The kind of government control of the foreign exchange market used most often is that of the *fixed-rate system*. Under this system, the domestic currency is given a parity value, also known as a central rate, relative to some other currency, or to a basket of currencies or to gold, and it is allowed to vary around its parity value within a predetermined band. Figure 8.4(a) illustrates the way in which an exchange rate may fluctuate around its parity value but has to remain within its upper and lower intervention limits.

Figure 8.4(b) shows a situation in which, at a given demand schedule, supply of a currency has dropped from S to S'. This has resulted in an equilibrium rate above the upper intervention limit which the central bank has committed itself to observing. Consequently, maintaining the agreed rate of exchange results in a daily deficit corresponding to AB, which has to be covered by the foreign exchange reserves of the country in question.

If the disequilibrium persists, the exchange rate may be defended as long as the national economy allows foreign exchange reserves to be watered down with public foreign borrowing and as long as this is considered politically desirable. If foreign borrowing does not take place, then sooner or later foreign exchange reserves will be depleted. Formula (2) in Chapter 7, which concerns the autonomous items, yields this relation, viz.

$$CA + B_p = \Delta L - B_g \tag{5}$$

If we assume that foreign exchange supply and demand are due to current items and private

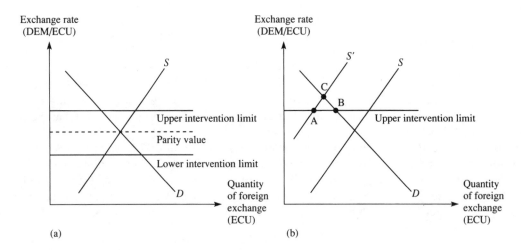

(a)   (b)

Figure 8.4 Fixed exchange rates

capital items, then the foreign exchange deficit (AB) is matched by a corresponding surplus on the remaining capital items ($\Delta L - B_g$). If the government does not raise foreign loans ($B_g = 0$), then the deficit of AB will result in a corresponding drop in foreign exchange reserves. Consequently, a system of fixed exchange rates calls for foreign exchange reserves of an appropriate size. In a system of freely floating exchange rates, such reserves are unnecessary. The reason why countries with floating exchange rates hold foreign exchange reserves, nevertheless, is that they do not want to be in a position that prevents them from intervening on the exchange market at some future time.

If foreign exchange reserves continue to drop, the government will have to make use of other means: in the medium term, traditional economic policy in terms of monetary and fiscal measures may suffice, but in the long term structural changes or cost-dampening measures (in the form of incomes policy) will have to be introduced. Finally, the central rate may have to be realigned, which in this case will result in a devaluation, i.e. an exchange rate increase, of the currency.

8.3   EXCHANGE RATE SYSTEMS

In principle, as mentioned above, countries may choose between a fixed or a floating exchange rate system. In fact, however, various intermediate solutions are possible, as can be seen from Table 8.2. The table shows that fixed exchange rate systems are still widespread but that approximately 30 per cent of all countries have opted for floating exchange rate systems.

A number of countries with a dominant role in world trade, e.g. Japan and the United States, have opted for individually floating exchange rates. This typically means that national authorities allow exchange rates to fluctuate in accordance with market conditions but nevertheless intervene from time to time in order to exert influence on the rate at which exchange rate adjustments take place, but not in order to neutralize them. Countries with managed floating only differ from those with independently floating rates in that they intervene more often. The difference between these two systems is a minor one.

Most countries still have fixed exchange rates and the majority of these countries have pegged their currencies to the US$. Fluctuation margins are usually no more than 1 per cent on either side of the parity value. In Europe, a fixed exchange rate system has been established under the auspices of the EU, namely the 'European Monetary System', or EMS, whose member currencies fluctuate jointly against other currencies. Before turning to a more detailed description of the EMS, we will give a brief outline of the historical development.

Table 8.2   Exchange rate systems, 31 March 1994

System	Number of countries
Independent floating	55
Managed floating	32
Joint floating	13
Rates pegged to US$ or other currencies	46
Stabilization of trade-weighted exchange rate or similar system	29
Total	175

Source: IMF Annual Report, 1994.

8.3.1 Gold standard

From around 1879 until 1914, the international foreign exchange system was characterized by the so-called *gold standard*. During this period gold was the basis on which national money supply was determined, and, consequently, central banks were obliged to buy and sell gold at a fixed price, which means that indirectly the official exchange rate had been fixed against other currencies. For example, the gold value of one £ sterling was 4.87 times that of one US$, thus the official exchange rate of £ sterling against US$ was 4.87 US$/£ sterling.

Although central banks did not intervene directly on the exchange markets, market rates could not deviate very much from the official rate. The reason for this was the so-called *gold arbitrage*. If the market rate of £ sterling increased, for example, to 4.92 US$/£ sterling, then a gold dealer would be able to perform the following profitable transactions:

(1) buy gold from the United States central bank at US$ 4.87;
(2) ship the gold to the UK;
(3) sell the gold to the Bank of England at £ sterling 1.00; and
(4) sell £ sterling 1.00 against US$ 4.92 in the exchange market.

If transport and insurance costs amount to US$ 0.03 then the dealer has made a profit of US$ 0.02. These transactions will increase the supply of £ sterling (item 4) and therefore the exchange rate of £ sterling will gradually fall to a level at which gold arbitrage is no longer profitable. At this point the market rate will deviate from the official rate by an amount determined by the costs of transport and insurance.

This clearly shows that the gold standard is a fixed exchange rate system as long as all countries maintain the gold content in their coins. Given that this was the case during the period up to 1914, this is the historical time that most closely adhered to a system of fixed exchange rates.

After the First World War, an attempt was made to continue the gold standard but it was not successful. The war and the immediate postwar era had created such economic differences among nations, for example as regards price levels, that the old exchange rate system had become unrealistic. The crisis in the thirties led to the final collapse of the gold standard. Like other economic areas, the foreign exchange area was characterized by the chaotic conditions of the thirties: using competitive devaluations and exchange controls, the countries affected by the crisis attempted to export unemployment to each other.

8.3.2 The IMF system

At the Bretton Woods Conference in 1944, even before the end of the Second World War, the foundations of the exchange rate system of the first postwar era were laid. The agreement reached had two cornerstones: the establishment of a system with fixed but adjustable exchange rates and the setting up of certain credit facilities for each member country with the International Monetary Fund, the IMF, which administered the new exchange rate system.

Any country that was a member of the IMF would notify the IMF of a par value defined in terms of gold. Given that the United States undertook to exchange one ounce of gold against US$ 35, it was in fact a dollar standard rather than a gold standard. Each country then committed itself to maintain the market rate within a margin of 1 per cent on either side of the par value.

If a country encountered a balance of payments disequilibrium of a permanent nature, a so-called *fundamental disequilibrium*, it could be permitted to realign its par value. The number of realignments was rather limited, however, over the 20-year period during which the system worked. This was in part due to political unwillingness to change par values, the result being that trade restrictions and exchange controls were extensively used. Most West European currencies were not convertible, i.e. freely negotiable, until 1958.

Through the sixties currency speculation intensified. Foreign exchange crises became more frequent and more serious. Because devaluation is usually interpreted as a sign of weakness, deficit countries hesitated to devalue, and surplus countries piled up foreign exchange reserves. On top of this, the Vietnam War gave the United States a balance of payments deficit. The resulting situation was not one that had been taken into account when the system was designed. The US$ had to be devalued but the United States was in no position to do so itself: all the other countries had to revalue their currencies.

Having made various minor, untenable revisions of the IMF system, leading Western countries decided in 1973 to float their currencies against the US$. In Europe the fixed exchange rate system was continued in the form of the so-called 'snake'. Thus the IMF system has been of great importance to European cooperation in the foreign exchange area: the system provided the basis on which this cooperation was designed.

8.3.3 The European Monetary System (EMS)

At the collapse of the IMF system at the beginning of the seventies, a fixed exchange rate system was established in Europe and was strengthened considerably when the European Monetary System was established in 1979 under the auspices of the EU. Cooperation intensified during the eighties and at the beginning of the nineties all EU member countries participated in the EMS with the exception of Greece.

The core of the exchange rate system is the ECU, the European Currency Unit, which is the common currency of the EU. It is defined as the sum of fixed amounts of each member country's currency. Each EMS member currency is registered at a central rate against the ECU. On this basis bilateral exchange rates between EMS member countries are calculated, and finally the intervention limits of 2.25 per cent on either side of the central rates are determined. Consequently, market rates cannot deviate by more than ± 2.25 per cent from bilateral central rates.

For example, if the FRF comes under pressure relative to the DEM, then, in France, DEM will jump towards its upper intervention limit and in Germany FRF will, at the same time, drop towards its lower intervention limit. When these intervention limits are reached, the central banks in the two countries have to intervene on the exchange market and keep the two currencies within their limits. For this reason it is important that the central banks in the EMS can draw on each other almost without limits, since this allows them to acquire the foreign exchange needed to counter speculative pressure. Therefore the EMS includes ultra-short-term credit facilities, among other things, which permits participating central banks to obtain unlimited credits for a period of up to 75 days following the month in which they have intervened on the exchange market or respectively obliges them to grant these credits to intervening central banks.

During the exchange crisis in 1992–93 currency speculation took place on a considerable scale. This was in part due to the lack of political willingness to coordinate the monetary policies of the participating countries. Italy and the United Kingdom chose to leave the EMS while the intervention limits to be observed by the remaining participants were extended to ± 15 per cent, except in the case of Germany and the Netherlands, which chose to maintain

Table 8.3   EMS currency adjustments since the beginning of the system in 1979

| | Adjustment percentages | | | | | | | | | |
Effective from	DEM	FRF	NLG	BEF	ITL	IEP	ESP	£ sterling	PTE	DKK
24 Sep 1979	+5.0	+3.0	+3.0	+3.0	+3.0	+3.0	•	•	•	—
30 Nov 1979	+5.0	+5.0	+5.0	+5.0	+5.0	+5.0	•	•	•	—
23 Mar 1981	—	—	—	—	−6.0	—	•	•	•	—
5 Oct 1981	+5.5	−3.0	+5.5	—	−3.0	—	•	•	•	—
22 Feb 1982	—	—	—	−8.5	—	—	•	•	•	−3.0
14 June 1982	+4.25	−5.75	+4.25	—	−2.75	—	•	•	•	—
21 Mar 1983	+5.5	−2.5	+3.5	+1.5	−2.5	−3.5	•	•	•	+2.5
22 July 1985	+2.0	+2.0	+2.0	+2.0	−6.0	+2.0	•	•	•	+2.0
7 Apr 1986	+3.0	−3.0	+3.0	+1.0	—	—	•	•	•	+1.0
4 Aug 1986	—	—	—	—	—	−8.0	•	•	•	—
12 Jan 1987	+3.0	—	+3.0	+2.0	—	—	•	•	•	—
8 Jan 1990	—	—	—	—	—	—	—	•	•	—
14 Sep 1992	+3.5	+3.5	+3.5	+3.5	−3.5	+3.5	+3.5	+3.5	+3.5	+3.5
17 Sep 1992	—	—	—	—	•	—	−5.0	•	—	—
23 Nov 1992	—	—	—	—	•	—	−6.0	•	−6.0	—
1 Feb 1993	—	—	—	—	•	−10.0	—	•	—	—
14 May 1993	—	—	—	—	•	—	−8.0	•	−6.5	—
2 Aug 1993†	—	—	—	—	•	—	—	•	—	—

† Margins of intervention were extended to ±15 per cent. DEM and NFL continued to observe the narrow band.
Source: Danmarks Nationalbank, Årsberetning (1993).

the original narrow band. In fact, this amounted to a suspension of the fixed exchange rate system.

EMS participation does not exclude devaluations or revaluations if the participating countries agree on them. For example, the DKK has been devalued within the EMS by approximately 35 per cent against the DEM through consecutive adjustments over the period lasting until 12 January 1987 (see Table 8.3). The adjustments were generally frequent in the beginning of this period, while the latter part of the period saw no adjustments, a situation which lasted until the exchange crisis in 1992–93.

By means of the Maastricht Treaty from 1992, the EU countries have indicated that they wish to reinforce EMS cooperation and that they wish to work towards a genuine Economic and Monetary Union, EMU. Denmark and the United Kingdom, however, have chosen not to participate in Stage 3 of the monetary union, which the other members have accepted. It is the intention of the participating countries to set up the EMU by the turn of the century. If they succeed, a joint European central bank will guarantee entirely fixed 'exchange rates' among the participating currencies, eventually by means of a single common currency. The non-participating countries may decide to peg their currencies to this new European currency if the EMS is dissolved, but no final decision has yet been made. In Chapter 14 we will discuss the economic aspects of the establishment of a monetary union in more detail.

8.3.4   International trade and exchange rate uncertainty

A country's choice of exchange rate system greatly affects the range of economic policies it can choose to pursue in order to influence the level of unemployment, the rate of inflation and its balance of payments; we will revert to this in Chapters 10 to 14. At present we will briefly discuss the effects on international trade as this subject is often the focal point of the debate on the advantages and disadvantages of the various systems.

The claim is often made that under a system of floating exchange rates, exchange rate fluctuations increase uncertainty with respect to the return on the international buying and selling undertaken by firms. Consequently, if firms are averse to risk they will give priority to domestic customers and suppliers, which will restrain the international division of labour. Interviews of business management have revealed that this attitude is widespread.

It is of course an empirical issue whether exchange rate fluctuations reduce the volume of trade. Generally, the empirical investigations made have not revealed any relationship between exchange rate variability and trade volume with respect to individual countries (see, for example, EC Commission 1990 and Saviades 1992).

The fact that exchange rate uncertainty does not play a significant role as regards trade volume under floating exchange rates is perhaps due to the various ways in which firms may cover this risk. One of the options available to them is the forward market, which will be dealt with in Chapter 9.

8.3.5   Speculation

Instability in the exchange market is often connected with currency speculation. Under fixed exchange rate systems the effects of speculation may be very destabilizing to the fixed-rate policies of central banks. By contrast it is very unclear how currency speculation affects exchange rate trends under a system of floating exchange rates.

While exchange rate arbitrage consists of simultaneous operations in geographically separate places, a *temporal dimension* characterizes speculation. Speculation is generally defined as buying or selling motivated by expectations of changes in future exchange rates.

Speculation is reflected in *open positions*. This means that debts and outstanding accounts in a given currency at a given future point in time do not cancel each other out. If a person has an outstanding account of US$ 1.7m to be settled in three months, then this is an open position if viewed separately. If, however, the 1.7m are intended to cover a debt of precisely this size, then the position is a *closed* one.

It is rather popular to consider speculators as a special group of people whose more or less obscure intentions are to capitalize on the work of honest people. In fact, by definition almost everyone who operates in the exchange market automatically becomes a speculator: because of changes in exchange rates any outstanding account and any obligation in a foreign currency provides firms with an opportunity of making a profit or incurring a loss.

Of course, this situation is merely one end of a scale at whose other end we find conscious and 'genuine' speculation. If Thyssen expects an increase in the exchange rate of US$, the company is unlikely to sell a US$ bill of exchange to its German bankers before maturity; to the extent that other agents in the exchange market share the expectations of Thyssen this will affect the exchange rate because expectations result in changes in the supply and demand curves. This is illustrated in Figure 8.5, which distinguishes between 'normal' supply and demand caused by ordinary business activity and speculative supply and demand.

The fall in supply of US$ from German exporters is but one effect of these expectations.

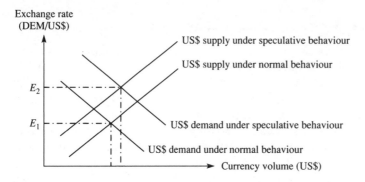

Figure 8.5   Speculation in the spot market

Conversely, American firms and individuals will sell amounts outstanding in DEM and thus increase their demand for US$, as will German importers. As a result the exchange rate will go up, i.e. expectations (partly) fulfil themselves, which is quite common in the case of speculation.

The effects of currency speculation depend on whether the exchange rate system has fixed or floating rates of exchange. If expectations arise in a fixed exchange rate system, e.g. DEM cannot maintain its international value, then a situation will occur that corresponds to that depicted in Figure 8.4: step by step Germany's foreign exchange reserves will be drained and if expectations are not reversed or if the drain is not restricted by other means, the parity rate will have to be adjusted. Under this system, speculation profits will be the result of a political decision to realign exchange rates, i.e. they will be realized overnight. As it is unlikely that the currency under attack will be adjusted in a direction opposite to the one represented by the majority of expectations, speculation is 'free' in the sense that it involves no exchange rate risks. Hence speculative waves may assume considerable importance in a system of fixed exchange rates.

In a floating exchange rate system, where exchange rates are determined by supply and demand, the situation is different. Some economists, e.g. Milton Friedman (1953), argue that speculation stabilizes exchange rate trends. The argument appears from Figure 8.6, in which the fully drawn curve shows the exchange rate trend that will occur if, hypothetically, speculation does not exist. Add to this the fact that speculation consists in buying at low exchange rates and selling at high ones: the arrows indicate the smoothing effect of such stabilizing speculation.

This might be a realistic description if speculators based their expectations as to the long-term trend of exchange rates on *fundamental* economic conditions in the economies, such as competitiveness, economic growth, etc. In addition, stabilizing speculation will be profitable, whereas speculators who cannot read long-term exchange rate trends and, consequently, pursue reversed buying and selling patterns will lose money and therefore their speculation will cease at some point.

On the basis of experience from the period after 1973, during which the major currencies floated, other economists believe that speculation may be destabilizing if it persists and that for this reason it may intensify fluctuations. The argument rests on the fact that speculators have no particular knowledge as to long-term exchange rate trends; on the contrary, they allow themselves to become influenced by all sorts of arbitrary news items, political as well as economic ones, and to be guided by trends already evident in the market. This means that if an exchange rate is decreasing then speculators often assume that it will continue, and vice versa.

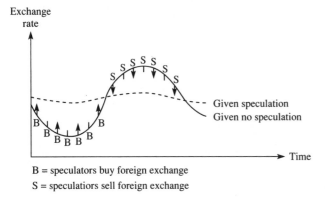

B = speculators buy foreign exchange
S = speculatiors sell foreign exchange

Figure 8.6   Stabilizing speculation under a system of floating exchange rates

8.4   LONG-TERM DETERMINATION OF EXCHANGE RATES

As described above, foreign exchange supply and demand depend on both the current account, in particular on exports and imports, and on the capital account of the balance of payments. It may be appropriate, however, to examine which of these influence exchange rate trends the most—exports and imports or capital movements?

The answer depends decisively on the length of time considered. Exchange flows due to the capital account of the balance of payments react much faster than exchange flows resulting from exports and imports. This follows partly from the lack of 'production time' involved in capital movements (the buying and selling of securities) and partly from the fact that transaction costs are very low. As a reaction to changes in international interest rates, a Japanese pension fund can sell its American shares and bonds with lightning rapidity. Thus in the short term capital movements and not exports and imports determine exchange rates; of course, this presupposes that exchange rates are changeable.

In Chapter 9 we will consider the significance of capital movements in greater detail. In this section we will focus on exchange rate trends which in the long term ensure equilibrium in the trade in goods and services. The so-called purchasing power parity theory plays a central part in this connection. However, before turning to this, we will briefly consider the concept of effective exchange rates.

8.4.1   Effective exchange rates

Above, we discussed how imports and exports and capital movements determine bilateral exchange rates, i.e. the exchange rate between two national currencies. However, more than 200 countries exist today and almost as many currencies, so the question may reasonably be posed as to what one should consider to be a country's exchange rate. In the same way as the calculation of a price index allows us to refer to the price level of a group of products, a calculation based on weighted bilateral exchange rates allows us to refer to an *effective exchange rate*. The weighting of individual currencies in the overall index depends on the importance of each currency to the balance of payments or to the competitiveness of the country in question. The calculation of the weighting takes export and import shares into consideration and usually

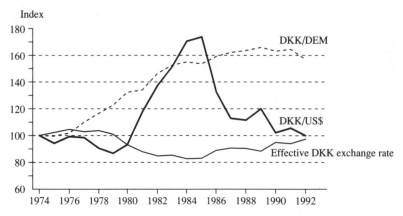

Note: The effective exchange rate is normally defined by means of reciprocal exchange rates.
A decrease indicates a weakened DKK as it implies fewer foreign currency units to the DKK.

Figure 8.7 Development of two bilateral exchange rates and of the effective exchange rate of DKK
Sources: OECD *Economic Outlook* and own calculations.

involves double-weighting. This is necessary since French exports to, for example, the United Kingdom compete with Japanese and German goods in the British market; double-weighting ensures that the share of French exports to the United Kingdom is weighted against the French share of total British imports.

In calculating effective exchange rates, OECD makes use of such double-weighting, and, not surprisingly, Figure 8.7 shows that the development of the effective exchange rate of DKK has been much more stable than that of the bilateral exchange rates; these are exemplified in the figure by means of the US$ and the DEM.

The figure also illustrates that the average exchange rate has been the subject of considerable fluctuations in spite of the fact that Denmark participated in a fixed exchange rate system over the period considered; thus the effective exchange rate of DKK fell by approximately 20 per cent from 1976 to 1984 but rose correspondingly from 1984 to 1992. Some of the fluctuations are of course due to conscious realignments within the European exchange cooperation over this period (see Table 8.3). However, most of the fluctuations result from the floating of the EMS against other currencies, i.e. from its joint floating, which means that in fact the EMS involves fixed exchange rates only internally, i.e. among member countries.

Although this is not a system of entirely fixed exchange rates, as the joint floating changes effective exchange rates, the conditions under which small member states have to pursue their economic policies are the same as they would be under an 'absolutely' fixed exchange rate system. This follows from the fact that changes in the economic policy of a small member state influence the joint floating of the EMS against other currencies only marginally, so from this perspective exchange rates are given exogenously.

8.4.2   Purchasing power parity theory

What then determines the long-term development of exchange rates? This is an extremely comprehensive question and no attempt will be made here to provide an exhaustive answer, given that such an answer is at all possible. Instead we will focus on the effect which price developments in individual countries may have on the development of exchange rates, and this is precisely the purpose for which purchasing power parity theory may be used.

According to this theory, exchange rates move towards a level at which any currency unit provides the same purchasing power in all countries. If the volume of goods that may be bought for DEM 1000 is larger in the United States than in Germany, then Germany will import more from and export less to the United States, which causes a disequilibrium in their trade. The increase in imports increases the demand for foreign exchange and the decrease in exports reduces the supply of foreign exchange, so given floating exchange rates the currency will depreciate. If purchasing power is to be the same, the rate of exchange has to satisfy the following conditions, where P and P_f are the indices for prices in Germany and abroad, respectively:

$$E_p = \frac{P}{P_f} \tag{5}$$

E_p is the purchasing power parity (PPP) exchange rate, which ensures that goods bought in the two countries will cost the same in the same currency. If, for example, the German prices (in DEM) are twice as high as the American prices (in US\$), then the price US\$ 1.00 has to be DEM 2.00 if there is to be purchasing power parity. A different way of showing this is in terms of the following expression, which is a paraphrase of equation (5):

$$P = E_p \times P_f \tag{6}$$

When prices in US\$ are converted into DEM prices with the parity rate of DEM 2.00 per US\$, the resulting prices correspond to the German ones and the purchasing power of DEM 1000 is the same in both countries. This is the absolute version of the purchasing power parity theory in that it explains the level of the rate of exchange.

This version is based on the belief that adjustment takes place through commodity arbitrage, which levels any price differences and thus establishes one world market price for each product. Therefore this has become known as the Law of One Price. This law holds for standard products traded in highly competitive markets, e.g. precious metals and other raw materials traded on international commodity exchanges. If the US\$ price of copper is not the same on two international exchanges, arbitrage opportunities will either change copper prices or change the relative value of the two currencies in question, i.e. change the exchange rate holding between them, so that the US\$ price of copper ultimately becomes the same on both exchanges.

If all markets satisfied the Law of One Price, the absolute version of the purchasing power parity theory would of course also be satisfied. However, various conditions prevent complete international price levelling. These include 'natural' trade barriers such as transport costs and the fact that some products cannot be transported at all; they include 'man-made' trade barriers such as tariffs, import quotas, etc., which still exist. In addition, imperfect competition with product differentiation, price discrimination, etc., characterizes the markets of practically all industrial products, and of course price levelling is not always possible in such markets.

This has led to the relative version of the purchasing power parity theory, which is less restrictive. It says nothing about the level of the exchange rate but only mentions that the exchange rate is changing. If German prices increase by only 3 per cent from a given level while prices abroad go up by 7 per cent, then the value of the DEM has to increase by 4 per cent if the purchasing power holding between German products and products from other countries has to be maintained. Correspondingly, the value of DEM has to decrease against the currencies of the countries whose prices increase less than the German ones. In sum, the following equation holds:

$$e_p = p - p_f \qquad\qquad [7]$$

where lower-case letters indicate a relative change or percentage change in the variable in question, in this case a change in the exchange rate and in domestic and foreign prices. Note that the formula has been adapted to present purposes. If the change in a variable is less than 10 per cent the formula makes reasonable predictions. The exact formula is the following:

$$e_p = \frac{1 + p}{1 + p_f} - 1$$

Whether the purchasing power parity theory is in accordance with reality has been widely debated. In particular, the development of the US$ in the mid-eighties led to widespread claims that the purchasing power parity theory had met its death.

Figure 8.8 illustrates the dramatic development in the relationship between the DKK and the US$ with the Copenhagen rate for US$ diverging considerably from the parity rate. Specifically, the appreciation of 80 per cent over the period from 1979 to 1984, when the Danish rate of inflation over and above that of the United States amounted to only 12 per cent, caused a real change in purchasing power of approximately 70 per cent against Denmark.

The figure also shows, however, that, viewed over the entire period, the relative purchasing power parity theory has been satisfied, with the US$ rate at the beginning of the nineties being back to the parity rate holding at the end of the seventies. By contrast, the exchange rate between DEM and DKK closely follows the PPP rate throughout the period considered, i.e. it even does so in the short run.

The development of the US$ shows that purchasing power parity theory is a long-term theory and that one cannot expect it to be satisfied in the short run. Similar calculations with respect to other currencies corroborate this conclusion, which ultimately is a consequence of the fact that commodity arbitrage or merchandise trade reacts slowly to changes in relative prices. We will turn to this subject in Chapter 11. In the long run, however, a clear relationship exists between exchange rates and merchandise trade. This is illustrated by the fact that the appreciation of the US$ at the beginning of the eighties led to record American trade deficits from 1983 onwards and to corresponding surpluses in Europe and Japan. This trade imbalance contributed to the subsequent depreciation of the US$.

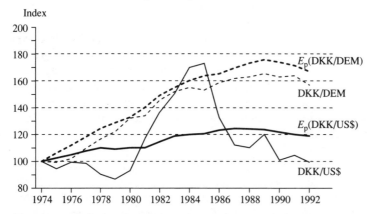

Note: The purchasing power parity rate is an index based on the relative perchasing power parity theory and calculated on the basis of the GNP deflator.

Figure 8.8 Development of DKK rate and purchasing power parity rate for US$ and DEM
Sources: OECD *Economic Outlook* and own calculations.

The purchasing power parity theory should not be used uncritically, however. Firstly, the price index selected to represent the development in prices and the point in time chosen as the starting point are of importance. If the latter involves a disequilibrium on the balance of payments, for example, then a subsequent exchange rate adjustment may be a reaction to this and not the result of purchasing power levelling.

Secondly, international payments and, consequently, exchange rates are influenced by a range of conditions other than relative price development. In the short run, as mentioned previously, these include capital movements and in the long run they include preference shifts between domestic and foreign goods, structural changes (e.g. the discovery of gas and oil supplies in the North Sea) and growth rate differences. In addition, changes in economic policy may have considerable implications for exchange rates.

Today it is generally believed that one of the most important reasons for the appreciation of the US$ at the beginning of the eighties was the difference in economic policies pursued at the time by the world's large countries. Under president Ronald Reagan the United States pursued a tight monetary policy and an expansionary fiscal policy while fiscal policy in Europe and Japan was fairly tight. This cocktail necessarily leads to an appreciation of the US$, as will be shown in Chapter 14. The historical lesson to be learnt from this experiment, which resulted in an immense disequilibrium in international trade, was that it was necessary for the large countries to coordinate their economic policies. Thus, from 1985, meetings of the so-called Group of Five (and increasingly more) have taken place between the world's leading industrial countries. We turn to this subject in Chapter 14.

8.4.3 Real exchange rates

If purchasing power parity theory were always satisfied and if price development reflected cost development then a nation's competitiveness would be constant and always the same. As shown above, however, this is far from always being the case and therefore a way of measuring deviation from purchasing power parity is needed. For this purpose the *real exchange rate* (E_r) is used, which is calculated by dividing foreign prices converted into domestic currency by domestic prices, as shown by the following expression:

$$E_r = \frac{E \times P_f}{P} \qquad [10]$$

The real exchange rate measures the relationship between foreign and domestic purchasing power and thus expresses the international competitiveness of a country, a subject to which we turn in Chapter 11. An increase in E_r, i.e. a real depreciation, means that, compared to domestic prices, prices abroad have risen in terms of the domestic currency and that the nation's international competitiveness has improved.

In a situation in which the exchange rate follows the parity value so that purchasing power parity theory has been satisfied, the real exchange rate, E_r, is constant. This is evident when equation (10) is compared to equation (6). Consequently, Figure 8.8 shows that the real DEM rate was almost constant over the period considered. It follows that exchange rate realignments within the EMS succeeded in maintaining purchasing power parity between Denmark and Germany over the same period.

While realignments within the EMS were frequent up to 1987 no realignments took place from January 1987 until the turbulence in the foreign exchange market in 1992 (see Table 8.3). This is presumably due to the fact that the participating countries pursued a policy of inflation convergence with a view to establishing a monetary union within the EU. Although inflation

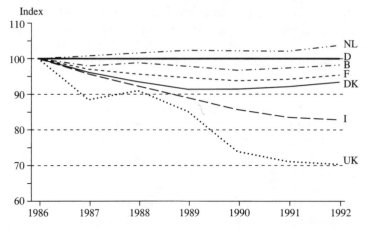

Figure 8.9 Development of some bilateral real DEM rates within the EMS after 1986
Sources: OECD *Economic Outlook* and own calculations.

rate differences were reduced over the period, marked differences still existed, which resulted in
purchasing power imbalances. Figure 8.9 illustrates this: for example, the relatively high rate of
inflation in Italy over this period reduced Italian purchasing power by more than 15 per cent.
Given this development, it comes as no surprise that although the currency unrest was triggered
by German unification, which resulted in a high German interest rate, the first countries that
had to abandon the fixed exchange rate system were Italy and the United Kingdom. The foreign
exchange market has subsequently restored purchasing power among the EMS countries.

Of course, not only does price development between two countries influence the general
competitiveness of a country, but price development in all the countries to which it exports or
from which it imports is of importance. If an index is calculated for all of these countries and if
it is used in equation (10) with the effective exchange rate then the result expresses the *real
effective exchange rate*. This may be used to measure the international competitiveness of a
country, a subject to which we deal with in Chapter 11.

SUMMARY

1. Foreign exchange markets serve as mediators of purchasing power among currencies, as a
    credit facility and as a risk-reducing instrument (forward markets).
2. In the case of floating exchange rates, market forces will produce an equilibrium at which
    current account surplus equals net private foreign lending, i.e. there will be no change in
    international liquidity.
3. Foreign exchange rates are unequivocal due to international arbitrage.
4. Historically, fixed exchange rate systems—such as the gold standard and the IMF
    systems—have been the rule, but today countries have chosen a wide range of systems with
    dominating nations opting for individually floating rates.
5. Most European nations have chosen a system of joint floating, the EMS, with internally
    fixed exchange rates.

6. In spite of frequent concern, it seems that floating exchange rate systems do not significantly reduce the volume of international trade.
7. Speculation may be very destabilizing to fixed exchange rate systems, while its effects on floating systems are still unresolved.
8. A multitude of factors influence exchange rates; in the long run the most significant factor is price developments in the individual countries. This is the basis of the purchasing power parity theory, which exists in an absolute form and a relative one.
9. The real exchange rate expresses the actual competitiveness of a country, which reflects deviance from competitiveness determined by purchasing power parity. Volatile changes in the real exchange rate is a threat to a fixed rate system.

REFERENCES AND FURTHER READING

Cassel, G. (1923), *Money and Foreign Exchange after 1914*, Macmillan, New York.
De Grauwe, P. (1988), 'Exchange rate variability and the slowdown in growth of international trade', *IMF Staff Papers*, March, 35(1), 63–84.
EC Commission (1990), 'One market one Money: An Evaluation of the Potential Benefits and Costs of Forming an Economic and Monetary Union', *European Economy*, **46**, Brussels.
Friedman, M. (1953), 'The case for flexible exchange rates', in *Essays in Positive Economics*, University of Chicago Press, Chicago.
Saviades, A. (1992), *Unanticipated Exchange Rate Variability and the Growth of International Trade*, Weltwirtschaftliches Archiv., Band 128, Heft 3, 446–463.

NINE

FINANCIAL MARKETS

As was mentioned in Chapter 8, international capital movements greatly influence the formation of exchange rates in the exchange market today. The reason for this is the extensive liberalization of international capital markets which has taken place over the past 20 years. Thus the development is towards a genuinely integrated money and capital market, a development in which the Eurocurrency market has played a decisive part.

9.1 THE EUROCURRENCY MARKET

Originally, the Eurocurrency market was an offshoot of the Cold War in the fifties. East-bloc nations placed their financial claims in European banks in order to prevent them from being frozen in American banks. In addition, an American ceiling on interest rates on deposits caused major capital flows out of the United States. During the seventies the Eurocurrency market grew tremendously and contributed significantly to the recycling of OPEC's trade surplus to (primarily) developing countries.

Eurocurrency refers to deposits in a convertible currency with banks outside the home country of the currency in question. Thus Euro-DEM are DEM deposits with banks outside Germany, e.g. in Paris, Zurich and London, and Eurosterling are sterling deposits in Paris, Frankfurt, etc. Together the parts of the money and credit markets in which Eurocurrency is bought and sold are known as the Eurocurrency market. In this market deposits are received and loans extended in currencies that differ from those corresponding to the location of the receiving banks. Eurodeposits and Euroloans are typically short term: they generally run for less than six months.

Today, and historically, the Eurocurrency market has a larger volume of trade in US$ than in any other currency. Therefore the term 'Eurodollar market' is sometimes used. This refers to US$ deposits with banks outside the United States; hence it only covers part of the Eurocurrency market, other currencies like DEM, CHF and JPY having come to play a rather significant part in the market. In fact, the prefix 'Euro' is a misnomer as the market has spread from European financial centres to Hong Kong and Singapore and on to a series of other minor countries in both Asia and Latin America (the Cayman Islands). Therefore the more adequate terms 'offshore banking' and 'external currency banking' have gained ground in the literature. However, the centre of the Eurocurrency market is still in Europe, specifically in the City of London, in which hundreds of foreign banks are represented.

9.2 EFFECTS OF CAPITAL MOVEMENTS

We first touched on international capital movements in Chapter 6, where net capital movements were shown to arise from international variation in profit rates or real interest rates. Likewise, these net capital movements were shown to have favourable welfare effects on the countries involved when capital moves from areas in which return on capital is low to areas in which it is high. At the same time, we assumed that capital movements result in total equalization of real interest rates, but, as will be seen below, this is rarely the case in the short run.

It is interesting, however, that capital movements in a given period typically flow both into and out of individual countries. In other words, net capital movements cover gross capital movements in both directions. This means that capital movements may take place without any resources being actually transferred from one country to another (see Chapter 7). Surprisingly, this may in fact involve welfare advantages as it allows investors in different countries to diversify their risk.

In Section 9.3 of this chapter, interest differentials among countries with free international capital movements are explained and at the same time the section contributes to an explanation of exchange rate fluctuations. Section 9.4 focuses on the forward exchange market, in which foreign exchange is not delivered until some time after the deal has been made. Price formation in the forward market contributes to an insight into the connection between international interest rates and capital movements. Section 9.5 combines various theories that seek to explain the connection between domestic and foreign interest rates and inflation, and provides a discussion of whether these theories can be used for exchange rate forecasting purposes. The concept of market efficiency is discussed in Section 9.6.

9.3 INTEREST DIFFERENTIALS AND EXCHANGE RATE EXPECTATIONS

Interest differentials between currencies are closely related to expectations regarding exchange rate development. In this section we will show how interest arbitrage in the exchange market harmonizes nominal interest differentials and exchange rate expectations.

9.3.1 Interest differentials between currencies

As mentioned above, the international capital market has been liberalized in recent years so that today it is quite possible that this market is the one that comes closest to satisfying the economic concept of a perfect market. Transaction costs are low, the commodity is homogeneous and the volume of trade enormous, so the market is one of extreme liquidity. This might give rise to expectations that interest differentials between currencies have been equalized as a result of the liberalization of capital movements. It is a fact, however, that short-term interest differentials still exist in spite of the liberalization (see Figure 9.1). At the beginning of the nineties the interest spread among some of the currencies remains approximately 5 percentage points, the interest rate on the most expensive currency being more than twice that on the least expensive one.

Interest differentials of this size have been possible for the simple reason that exchange rates are not invariable. Three of the countries represented in Figure 9.1 have floating currencies while Denmark has a fixed but adjustable exchange rate against the DEM. When exchange rates are not fixed, possible exchange rate losses or gains caused by exchange rate variation

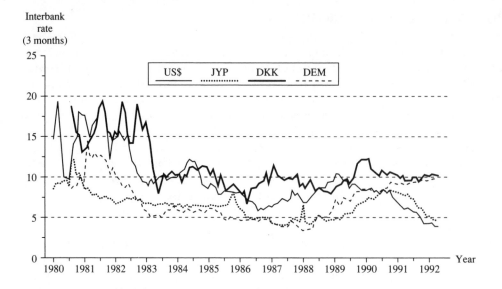

Figure 9.1 Development of short-term interest rates on various currencies since 1980
Source: Unibank A/S, Copenhagen, 1994.

during the investment period have to be taken into consideration. Consequently, it cannot be taken for granted that capital movements will equalize nominal interest rates in such a situation. We will now turn to the process of interest rate formation under exchange rate uncertainty.

9.3.2 Expected return and exchange rate expectations

Let us consider the example of a Danish firm which wants to invest DKK 1m in the best way possible for a period of one year. Further, let us assume that a DKK deposit with a bank will yield an annual interest of 10 per cent while a DEM deposit (possibly with the same bank) will yield an annual interest of 6 per cent. If the deposit is made in DKK the capital will have increased to DKK 1.1m at the end of the investment period. If, on the other hand, the deposit is made in DEM and the current DEM rate is DKK 4.00 per DEM, then the capital will have gone up to DEM 0.265m $[=\frac{1}{4}(1+0.06)]$ at the end of the same period.

However, the DEM investment can only be compared with the DKK investment if it is translated to DKK. If the DEM rate remains the same throughout the investment period, the DEM deposit will have increased to the equivalent of DKK 1.06m ($=4 \times 0.265$) by the end of the period, which of course is less than a corresponding DKK deposit would amount to. However, the firm may expect the DKK to depreciate, for example, by 7 per cent within a year and thus expect the spot rate to be DKK 4.28 per DEM at the end of the investment period. This would mean that a DEM investment would increase to DKK 1.1342 ($=0.265 \times 4.28$), i.e. to a larger amount than a corresponding DKK investment would result in. The capital increase of DKK 0.1342m, or 13.42 per cent, corresponds to an interest rate of 6 per cent and an exchange gain of 7.42 per cent divided between the principal (7 per cent) and the interest yield (0.42 per cent)

It follows that in calculating expected return on investment in a foreign currency we have to take the expected exchange rate variation into consideration, which may be quite considerable.

Consequently, the general formula for calculating the expected return on foreign currency investment is the following one:

$$i_f + e^e + i_f e^e \qquad [1a]$$

where i_f is the foreign interest rate and e^e is the expected exchange rate increase:

$$e^e = \frac{E^e - E}{E} \qquad [1b]$$

where E is the exchange rate and E^e is the expected exchange rate. Consequently, (1b) is the expected relative change in the foreign exchange rate and thus expresses the exchange gain or loss on the principal over the period in question. The last part of (1a) expresses the exchange gain or loss on the interest yield. Disregarding the exchange gain or loss on the interest yield, which is usually quite moderate, we are left with (an approximation of) the expected return on investment abroad, namely:

$$i_f + e^e \qquad [2]$$

In Table 9.1, a few examples illustrate the way in which exchange rate expectations affect the expected return on investment in a foreign currency. If the currency is expected to appreciate, the expected return will be higher than the foreign rate of interest. Likewise, the table illustrates that the approximate calculation formula (2) predicts the expected return rather precisely. If the foreign rate of interest and the expected change in exchange rate amount to less than 10 per cent, the error will be less than 1 per cent of the principal.

9.3.3   Uncovered interest parity

Now that we have shown that expected return on investment in a foreign currency consists of both an interest yield and an exchange gain or loss, we will turn to the conditions that have to be satisfied in order for equilibrium to occur in international financial markets.

If the international capital market has been fully liberalized, capital can flow to where expected return is the highest. If the agents operating in the market are not averse to risk, then the international capital movements caused by their interest arbitrage will ensure that all currencies will yield the same expected return on investment. If i is the domestic interest rate, the following expression shows arbitrage equilibrium:

$$i = i_f + e^e \qquad [3]$$

Table 9.1   Expected return on foreign currency and foreign exchange expectations

Foreign interest rate i_f	Expected change in exchange rate e^e	Expected return (approximation) $i_f + e^e$	Expected return $i_f + e^e + i_f e^e$
0.06	−0.02	0.04	0.0388
0.06	0.00	0.06	0.0600
0.06	0.02	0.08	0.0812
0.06	0.04	0.10	0.1024
0.06	0.06	0.12	0.1236

This equilibrium condition is known as the *uncovered interest parity*. It is a case of 'interest parity' because the total expected return will be the same in all countries, and it is 'uncovered' because foreign investment involves an exchange rate risk, i.e. the investor is in an 'open'— which is the same as uncovered—position. The uncovered interest parity is also known as the international Fisher effect.

As mentioned above, interest arbitrage ensures the sign of equation in equation (3) in a liberalized international capital market. This follows from the simple fact that if expected returns differ then they will result in net capital movements among countries and thus affect expected return. If, for example, the domestic interest rate is lower than the return expected abroad, then capital will be shifted to a foreign currency. This will cause a home currency depreciation, i.e. an increase in E, which in turn will reduce the expected future depreciation of the home currency, given constant expectations as regards the future exchange rate (E^e). This exchange rate adjustment may take place without any net capital movements between countries. This is the case if the current account is not affected. Thus expected domestic return and expected foreign return will be equalized.

Rearranging the elements of the interest parity in equation (3) yields

$$e^e = i - i_f \tag{4}$$

This expression of interest parity shows that the interest differential between at home and abroad equals the expected depreciation percentage. This condition is depicted in Figure 9.2, which shows that investments below the 45° curve are more profitable if made in a foreign currency. This is true, for instance, if expected annual depreciation is 2 per cent and the annual interest rate is only 1 per cent higher than the rate abroad. By contrast, investments above the 45° curve are more profitable if made in the domestic currency. Consequently, the 45° curve precisely indicates the situation in which investments at home and abroad are equally profitable. Therefore this is known as the interest parity curve.

The uncovered interest parity shows that if differences in interest rates reflect corresponding expectations with respect to exchange rate changes then it is possible to have a situation in

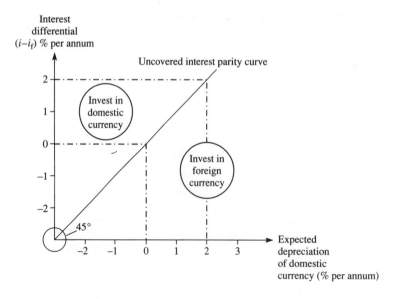

Figure 9.2   The uncovered interest parity curve

which the existence of large permanent interest differentials among countries does not necessarily result in international net capital movements. If, for example, the market expects a depreciation of the domestic currency by 2 per cent within a year, then the short-term domestic interest rate has to be 2 per cent higher than the rate of interest abroad in order to ensure arbitrage equilibrium.

Even if parities are met gross capital movements will exist. This follows from the fact that financial securities differ with respect to a number of characteristics and from the fact that investors prefer broadly composed portfolios, which reduces their risk.

9.3.4 Fixed exchange rates

The uncovered interest parity in equations (3) and (4) shows that international interest differentials can only exist under exchange rate uncertainty, i.e. in a situation with expectations of exchange losses or gains. Consequently, if exchange rates are entirely fixed the pivotal factor causing international capital movements will be the existence of nominal international interest differentials. If the rate of interest is higher in Europe than in the United States then US pension funds and firms will prefer to invest their capital in European securities, and European firms will find it profitable to borrow in the US capital market, where the rate of interest is lower.

The capital movements resulting from interest differentials also result in interest equalization: when Americans buy European securities they first have to buy European exchange for US$ and then buy the securities. As a result, money supply in the United States will decrease and, consequently, the US rate of interest will rise. The reverse process will occur in Europe, where, accordingly, the rate of interest will go down. If the citizens in the two areas consider each other's securities fully substitutable, which presupposes that they have the same knowledge of the foreign capital market as they have of the domestic one, then the flow of securities from Europe into the United States will continue until the resulting changes in money supply have created identical interest levels in the United States and Europe. At this point the flow of financial claims across the Atlantic will come to an end, as will the international capital movements.

In a *monetary union* with a common currency or a common central bank which guarantees fixed exchange rates, nominal interest rate levels among member countries will be equalized. One example of a monetary union is the United States, where interest rate variation among member states has been eliminated. Under the auspices of the EU, a number of European countries seek to establish a monetary union which is to be effective from the end of the nineties. If these countries succeed, then this will equalize interest rate variation among them. It follows that full equalization presupposes full liberalization of capital movements and harmonization of tax rules relating to taxation of interest yields.

9.3.5 Risk and portfolio theory

Investors prefer to place their capital where the expected yield is the highest, all other things being equal. However, all other things are not equal: expectations are not always met and some investments are more risky than others. Consequently, an investor will not only consider the yield on an investment but also the *risk* that it involves. Investors are usually assumed to be averse to risk, which means that given the same yield they will prefer the least risky investment. The risk involved in investing in foreign securities may have various sources. Firstly, information on special capital market conditions in other countries is limited. Secondly, a political risk is involved in that a government may decide to put a halt to payments out of a country; and, finally, there is the risk of exchange rate changes, i.e. exchange rate uncertainty. In addition, investors have to take into account, of course, the usual commercial risk relating to the foreign debtor's ability to pay.

Unexpected exchange rate development is probably the greatest risk relating to interest arbitrage among Western currencies, i.e. the borrowing in one or more currencies and the investment in others. Assessing the future risk of borrowing or investing in a currency usually involves surveying its historical exchange rate development: currencies subjected to frequent and substantial exchange rate changes are considered more risky than currencies with only infrequent and minor changes. Consequently, exchange rate risk is measured in terms of a *measure of variation*, e.g. standard deviation, which measures the historical exchange rate development. Therefore the variation measured does not reveal expected exchange rate development but merely the estimated unpredictability of exchange rates.

Figure 9.3 illustrates the expected annual percentage risk and costs of Danish public borrowing or investment in various currencies in 1992. Costs have been stated in terms of the rate of interest, changes in exchange rate expectations having been set at nil, and the risk has been estimated on the basis of weekly exchange rates. As appears from the figure, DEM, FRF and NLG had (almost) identical interest rates and variation: at the time, they all participated in the narrow band of the EMS. As the DKK participated at the same time in the EMS, the risk of borrowing in these currencies was low while the risk of borrowing in JPY and US$ was much greater: exchange rate variation relative to these currencies was larger as a result of the reciprocal floating.

If the market is considered from the point of view of a borrower, it is preferable to borrow in JPY than in US$ since the risk involved will be lower but the interest rate the same. In rejecting any combination of currencies with a higher rate of interest and a larger variation than other combinations, we are left with the *efficient frontier*, which consists of the portfolios which leave no possibility of reducing the risk without increasing borrowing costs or reducing borrowing costs without increasing the risk incurred. The answer to where the borrower should be placed on the 'frontier' depends entirely on subjective preferences, however, i.e. on perceived trade-off of risk and borrowing costs. The objective of an *investor* is to maximize return at a given risk or

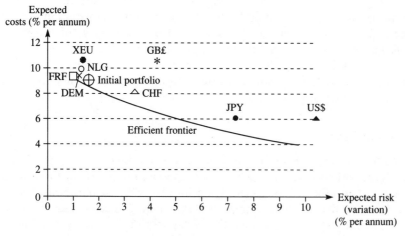

Figure 9.3 Portfolios and risk (DKK)
Source: Danmarks Nationalbank, 1992.

to minimize risk at a given return. Thus the efficient frontier will be placed over and to the left of individual currencies.

As a rule, a borrower or lender will not respectively borrow or invest in one currency. *Risk diversification*, i.e. spreading the borrowing or investments over a range of currencies, is usually an advantage since it allows the risk of 'putting all one's eggs into one basket' to be avoided. However, risk diversification is not merely a question of spreading a portfolio over low-interest, low-risk liabilities. Total portfolio risk also depends on the pattern of co-variation among currencies. If, for example, expected exchange rate changes are negatively correlated, gains from one currency may offset a loss on another. Consequently, if total borrowing is spread over a range of currencies with the same rate of interest, for example, then total exchange rate risk may be reduced to a level below that of each individual currency. For the purposes of the calculation of the efficient frontier in Figure 9.3 this was taken into consideration, which explains why the frontier is below the points of the individual currencies.

Risk diversification thus induces borrowers and lenders to spread their portfolios internationally since this allows them to reduce the risk they incur. Governments, firms, pension funds and insurance companies, for example, will compose optimum portfolios at given exchange rates and interest rate levels. If, subsequently, the domestic interest rate increases, e.g. due to a tight monetary policy, domestic and foreign borrowers and capital owners will readjust their portfolios to include a larger volume of domestic securities. Capital imports will ensue, which may affect the rate of exchange and, consequently, exchange rate expectations (compare this with the discussion of uncovered interest parity above).

The influx of capital is limited by the fact that an increased proportion of domestic securities in foreign portfolios also increase the risk incurred. Increased risk of capital loss can only be compensated for by a higher rate of interest. A country that finances continuous current account deficits by means of international borrowing will have to face increasing interest rate differentials in order to accommodate the increased risk.

Therefore, according to portfolio theory, interest rate changes have an impact on capital movements, and because each currency carries a *risk premium* (RP) the uncovered interest parity in formula (3) does not hold in the case of arbitrage equilibrium:

$$i = i_\mathrm{f} + e^\mathrm{e} + \mathrm{RP} \qquad [5]$$

An annual risk premium of 2 per cent on foreign investments in the domestic currency implies that the domestic interest rate (i) will have to be two percentage points above the sum of the foreign interest rate (i_f) and the expected depreciation of the domestic currency (e^e).

9.4 THE FORWARD EXCHANGE MARKET

The preceding section focused on exchange rate expectations and exchange rate uncertainty as well as on their effects on international capital movements and interest differentials. Firms and others with debts or claims in a foreign currency may, however, eliminate exchange rate risk. This may be done in various ways, one of which involves making use of the forward exchange market. In this market agreements are made to buy or sell foreign exchange on a fixed future date. When the agreement is made the forward exchange rate is fixed but payment does not take place until the end of the forward period. Nevertheless, regardless of the current exchange rate at this latter date, the deal will be settled at the fixed forward rate. In what follows we will discuss the three motives that account for trade in the forward market: forward cover, interest arbitrage and speculation.

9.4.1   Forward cover

The primary function of the forward market is to offer *forward cover* to exporters and importers. An advance agreement on an exchange rate allows an exporter to know the exact future revenue in the currency of his or her home country, thus avoiding taking the risk that an adverse exchange rate development may make inroads into the proceeds in this currency. Likewise, an importer may ensure that future payments will not take him or her by surprise, even if the currency of the home country has depreciated internationally.

Forward cover may also take place in the form of *currency options*. The holder of a currency option is entitled but not obliged to buy or sell foreign exchange at an agreed exchange rate on a fixed future date; thus the option is an insurance against loss resulting from an adverse exchange rate development but it does not reduce a possible gain in the case of a favourable development. Of course an option involves payment of a premium.

It is worth noting that firms trading internationally may cover their risk by other means than the two mentioned above. These, in brief, include (1) invoicing in the home currency, which, however, transfers the exchange rate risk to the other party, (2) arranging for counterclaims in the same currency to be payable on the same date, e.g. by borrowing or investing in the invoice currency for a period corresponding to that of the external commercial account, (3) inserting a foreign-exchange clause in the contract or (4) making use of governmental forward cover schemes.

Of course an exporter or importer has to take the various means into consideration if there is a need for protection from exchange rate risk. For present purposes, however, we will focus on the forward exchange market exclusively; therefore we refer the interested reader to specialist literature on the other means available.

Let us consider the example of a firm that buys a quantity of American wheat to be delivered immediately and receives a trade credit of six months to pay the bill of US$ 100 000. The forward exchange operation is illustrated in Figure 9.4.

9.4.2   Interest arbitrage

The forward exchange market may be used not only for forward cover of a firm's commercial accounts but also by firms, financial institutions and others with a certain liquidity which they want to carry interest at the best rate available. Taking as our point of departure the case of uncovered interest parity, we showed in Section 9.3. that such interest arbitrage results in equalization of expected yields on various currencies, which means that the interest parity given in equation (3) would be met. In this connection, expected exchange rates (E^e) attempted to allow for the exchange rate risk which follows from an open position in the exchange market. However, this risk may be covered in the forward exchange market by means of the forward

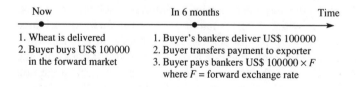

Figure 9.4   A forward exchange transaction

exchange rate (F), which is known at the time of investment. Hence, E^e in equation (1b) may be replaced with F and the expression inserted into (3), which yields

$$i = i_f + \frac{F - E}{E} = i_f + f \qquad [6]$$

where the right-hand side of equation (6) is the covered yield on foreign exchange investment, i_f is the interest yield and f is the premium obtained in the forward exchange market, i.e. the forward premium if positive or forward discount if negative.

In the same way as uncovered interest parity was established by means of interest arbitrage among various currencies, interest arbitrage in the forward exchange market may ensure that equation (6) will be met. An example may illustrate such interest arbitrage. Let us assume, for instance, that investing the liquid capital abroad will yield the highest available exchange rate covered return. Then demand for foreign exchange in the spot market will increase and E will go up. Likewise, supply in the forward market will increase and F will go down. As the home currency liquidity of domestic financial institutions, which are typically the ones carrying out such transactions, is tied up in foreign exchange, the domestic interest rate will increase. Consequently, these effects of interest arbitrage contributes to a situation in which the forward covered return on the currencies in question equals domestic return, i.e. the arbitrage equilibrium in equation (6) emerges.

This key relationship is known as *covered interest parity* since it expresses a situation in which investments in a domestic currency or in foreign currencies yield the same return, the forward exchange rate being known. It is precisely because no exchange rate risk is involved in interest arbitrage in the forward exchange market that interest arbitrage will grow considerably if the exchange rate covered return varies between countries. Consequently, covered interest parity will usually be met with great precision.

A slight revision of equation (6) yields

$$f = i - i_f \qquad [7]$$

where the forward premium or discount on the left-hand side is determined by the difference between domestic and foreign interest rates. It follows from the equation that there will be a premium on foreign currencies whose interest rates are below that of the home country and that there will be a discount on foreign currencies with interest rates above that of the home country. It is precisely because the premium or discount compensates for interest differentials among currencies that total forward covered return remains the same under arbitrage equilibrium.

The covered interest parity equilibrium given in equation (7) is shown in Figure 9.5. In positions below the 45° slope, investments in a foreign currency are attractive. This will be the case, for example, if the forward premium is 2 per cent a year while the domestic interest rate is only 1 per cent higher than the foreign rate of interest. In such a situation domestic investors will buy foreign exchange in the spot market and sell it in the forward market. This provides them with a safe gain in the exchange market, a gain that is larger than the interest loss that would result from investing in foreign assets with lower interest rates. Conversely, in positions above the 45° slope investments in the domestic currency are attractive. It follows that the 45° slope indicates the situations in which investments in the home country and abroad are equally attractive, none of them involving an exchange risk. Therefore this is known as the covered interest parity line.

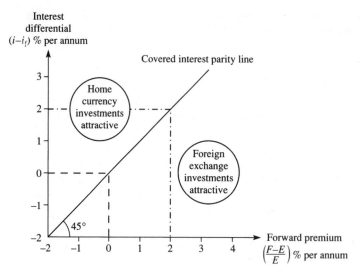

Figure 9.5 The covered interest parity line

9.4.3 Exchange rate formation and forward speculation

In principle exchange rate formation in the forward exchange market is like that in other competitive markets: exchange rates are determined by demand and supply. A graphic representation of exchange rate formation may, for example, take importers' and exporters' demand and supply of forward exchange for forward cover purposes as its point of departure, (see D_m and S_x in Figure 9.6). If these were the only ones influencing exchange rate formation, the equilibrium exchange rate, F_0, would be formed.

However, this is where foreign exchange arbitrage enters the scene. Let us assume that $\bar{F}$ is the exchange rate which, at given interest rates and spot exchange rates, yields interest arbitrage equilibrium. As F_0 exceeds $\bar{F}$, it is advantageous for interest arbitragers to sell forward exchange. As interest arbitrage transactions do not involve significant costs, the supply from arbitragers will be almost entirely elastic at $\bar{F}$, which is determined by the spot rate and interest differential as shown above.

Disregarding speculation, we obtain total supply in the forward exchange market by adding S_x and the supply curve of arbitragers, which is elastic at $\bar{F}$. Consequently, the curve will correspond to ABCD in Figure 9.6. The curve is likely to slope upwards sooner or later since, in practice, arbitragers have only limited means to invest.

The equilibrium exchange rate may now be found in the usual way, i.e. it corresponds to the point at which total demand equals total supply, $\bar{F}$. The foreign exchange turnover in the market will be OG, BC being the supply from arbitragers and the rest that from exporters. BC corresponds exactly to demand from arbitragers in the spot market.

Speculation in the forward exchange market is due to the belief of speculators that current forward exchange rates and future spot exchange rates will not be identical. If the spot rate is expected to be higher in three months than the current forward rate for delivery in three months, then speculators will buy in the forward exchange market, hoping that at a later date they will be able to sell at a profit in the spot market. The arrows in Figure 9.6 indicate this situation.

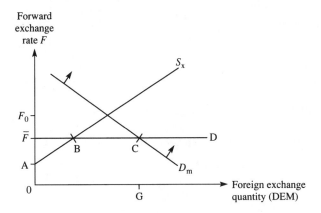

Figure 9.6   Exchange rate formation in the forward exchange market

9.5   PARITY RELATIONS

In this chapter, we have considered two kinds of parity, i.e. uncovered and covered interest parity. According to the former, the extent to which the domestic interest rate exceeds the foreign interest rate equals the expected depreciation of the home currency; according to the latter, the interest differential equals the forward premium. In Chapter 8, we considered a third kind of parity, the purchasing power parity, which holds that to the extent that the domestic inflation rate exceeds the foreign one the domestic currency will depreciate. One might then ask what the relations are that hold between these three kinds of parity. According to the American economist Irving Fisher, expectations of inflation will be transmitted in full to nominal interest rates (i), the result being that real rates (r) are independent of the rate of inflation. Implicitly this behaviour in the financial markets is contained in two of the three kinds of parity, i.e. uncovered interest parity and purchasing power parity, which are shown below:

$$e^e = i - i_f \qquad\qquad [8]$$
$$e^e = p^e - p_f^e \qquad\qquad [9]$$

where p^e is expected inflation. Equations (8) and (9) directly yield:

$$i - i_f = p^e - p_f^e \qquad\qquad [10]$$

This formulation is known as the *Fisher effect* (Fisher 1930), which implies that the interest differential between two countries corresponds to inflation rate differences, which is why real interest rates will be the same in both countries. Thus uncovered interest parity and purchasing power parity are in accordance with Irving Fisher's long-term real interest rate theory: an increase in a country's expected inflation rate brings about a corresponding increase in expected depreciation, the nominal interest rate leaving the real interest rate unaffected.

The Fisher effect implies then that real interest rates in the various countries will be equalized in the long run. Thus uncovered interest parity and purchasing power parity provide a better explanation of the motives for capital movements described in Chapter 4.

Figure 9.7 illustrates these parity relations. The Fisher effect has been drawn in quadrant I: if the domestic inflation rate is higher than the foreign one, this will bring about a corresponding interest rate differential. Quadrant II shows the covered interest parity theory: the forward

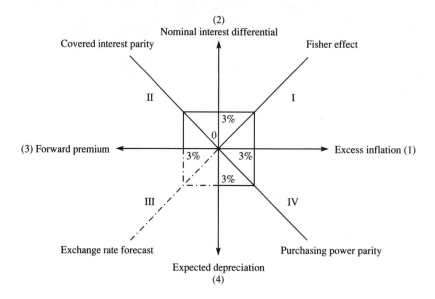

Figure 9.7   Parity relations

premium is proportional to the nominal interest rate differential. Quadrant IV illustrates the purchasing power parity theory: excess inflation causes corresponding depreciation of the domestic currency. The figure does not explicitly show the uncovered interest parity, but it explains the connection between the variables on the second and fourth axes.

If we assume, for example, that the home country has an excess inflation rate of 3 per cent above that of its trade partners, the Fisher effect will translate the 3 per cent into a corresponding nominal interest differential and from the differential it will be transmitted to the exchange market in the form of a forward premium of the same size. In addition, purchasing power parity theory predicts a corresponding fall in the international value of the home currency, which unequivocally determines the connection in quadrant III, which will also be linear. Therefore, if the three kinds of parity hold, then the forward premium will be of the same size as expected depreciation of the currency. Similarly, if exchange rate expectations in the market are correct, then the forward premium reflects the future development of the exchange rate and may therefore be used for forecasts. In practice, however, this has not been possible, as will appear from the following section.

9.6   MARKET EFFICIENCY AND PREDICTABILITY

The concept of market efficiency was developed over the seventies. It is assumed to apply to large capital markets in particular, e.g. the US share market, in which trade is lively and everyone in the market has access to full information. The exchange market is often assumed to be efficient, too, so in what follows we will examine the implications of this theory.

9.6.1   Market efficiency

The concept of *market efficiency* was introduced by Fama (1965, 1970). It refers to a market in which all accessible information is reflected in the price. In an efficient market, buying and selling by mechanical rules will yield no profit because trading prices contain all the information used in formulating the rules.

Financial markets are frequently assumed to satisfy the necessary conditions for market efficiency: a large number of rational profit-maximizing agents compete in forecasting the price development of securities correctly and all agents have access to the same information on individual securities. Except in cases in which some agents possess insider information, it is, by implication, impossible to 'beat the market'. The buying and selling quotations of everybody else already incorporates all accessible information.

If this line of thinking is applied to the foreign exchange market, forward exchange rates, being based on all the information available on future exchange rate trends, are the most reliable forecasts. This follows from the fact that interest arbitrage among market participants results in uncovered interest parity (see equation (4)), which says that exchange rate expectations equal interest differentials and, given that according to covered interest parity (see equation (7)), a forward premium equals the corresponding interest differential, we have the following result:

$$f = e^e \qquad \qquad [11]$$

This popular relation has already been established in Figure 9.7 and it also follows directly from speculative transactions in the forward exchange market. If a forward premium is less than the expected future increase in a given exchange rate, risk-neutral speculators will buy foreign exchange in the forward market until the difference has been eliminated and profit opportunities have disappeared. Conversely, if a forward premium exceeds the expected increase in a given exchange rate, then these speculators will sell the currency in question in the forward market until once again the difference has been eliminated.

As was mentioned in Chapter 8, the volume of turnover in the exchange market is enormous and transaction costs low. Thus, on the face of it, the market seems to satisfy the conditions of an efficient market. However, central banks have often intervened directly on the exchange market and in particular it used to be the case that borrowing and investments in foreign exchange by private individuals was subject to restrictions. As a result, conditions in the exchange market are not entirely comparable, for example, to conditions in the share market.

9.6.2 Predictability

As mentioned above, a forward exchange rate in an efficient market reflects the future exchange rate expectations of the market and therefore it is the best forecast of all. One might ask if this corresponds to the actual situation in the market. A number of empirical investigations of the relationship show rather unequivocally that forward exchange rates are a poor indication of future exchange rate trends. Indeed, it is so poor that the forward exchange market has come to be known as a biased one (Froot and Thaler 1990).

The following regression model illustrates the result of these investigations. In the model, the actual increase in an exchange rate, e, is explained in terms of the forward premium, f, and a normally distributed stochastic element, u.

$$e = a + bf + u \qquad \qquad [12]$$

Given an efficient market and a forward rate of exchange which predicts the future exchange rate rather precisely, the estimated parameter b equals one or is approximately one. However, the empirical estimation shows that b is not significantly different from zero, and that more often than not it is negative rather than positive (see Froot and Thaler 1990). This means that the forecast value of exchange rates is zero, actual exchange rate differences not being correlated with forward premiums.

This result also means that the exchange market is not efficient. Disagreement exists, however, as to why the theory breaks down. One interpretation of the result is that expectations are not rational and that large expectation errors are involved. Another possible interpretation is that risk premium in connection with interest arbitrage, which was mentioned in equation (5), is considerable and that it varies over time.

The lack of market efficiency results in profitable arbitrage opportunities in the market. If b equals zero in equation (12), the actual exchange rate change will not reflect the forward premium and nor, by implication, the interest differential between the currencies. Therefore a strategy to borrow in low-interest currencies and invest the revenue in high-interest currencies will be profitable since the interest differential will not disappear as a result of exchange rate losses. To the extent that b is negative the outcome will even be an additional exchange rate gain.

SUMMARY

1. International capital movements have been gradually liberalized over the past 20 years, partly through the Eurocurrency market (offshore banking).
2. Exchange rate expectations affect expected returns on investment in foreign currencies. At equilibrium, this is expressed by the uncovered interest parity: all currencies yield the same expected return! If exchange rates are fixed, interest rates will tend to equalize among countries.
3. Forward exchange markets offer forward cover against an unknown future. Due to interest arbitrage, the forward premiums or discounts equal interest rate differentials. As the forward exchange rate is known, investments in domestic and foreign currency yields the same return—the covered interest parity.
4. Forward exchange rate formation is determined by the interplay of commercial transactions, dealers and speculators.
5. Combining uncovered interest rate parity and the purchasing power parity we obtain the Fisher effect that interest rate differentials correspond to inflation rate differentials. This implies that real interest rates in various countries are equalized over time.
6. Financial markets are often assumed to be efficient, but empirical studies indicate that this is not always the case—profitable arbitrage opportunities exist!

REFERENCES AND FURTHER READING

Einzig, P. (1967), *The Dynamic Theory of Forward Exchange*, Macmillan, London.

Fama, Eugene (1965), 'The behavior of stock market prices', *Journal of Business*, **38**.

Fama, Eugene (1970), 'Efficient capital markets: a review of the theory and empirical work', *Journal of Finance*, **25**.

Fisher, Irving (1930), *The Theory of Interest*, Macmillan, London.

Froot, Kennet and Richard H. Thaler (1990), 'Anomalies: foreign exchange', *Journal of Economic Perspectives*, **3**.

Keynes, J. M. (1923), *A Tract on Monetary Reform*, Macmillan, London.

Surajas, P. and R. J. Sweeney (1992), *Profit-Making Speculation in Foreign Exchange Markets. The Political Economy of Global Interdependence*, Westview Press, Oxford.

ECONOMIC POLICY: FIXED EXCHANGE RATES

This chapter focuses on the economic goals of full employment and balance of payments equilibrium, which are sometimes referred to as internal and external equilibrium, respectively. In a number of countries, the simultaneous realization of both goals has proved rather difficult; one might say that such economies have problems 'keeping their balance'.

The point of departure of this chapter is the economic situation of a small open economy. The chapter mainly centres on the ways in which internal and external equilibria may be secured through fiscal and monetary policies when price levels and exchange rates are fixed, i.e. in the case of fixed real exchange rates. This means that we assume that exchange rate expectations are static, i.e. that exchange rates are expected not to change.

As was mentioned in Chapter 8, the fixed exchange rate policy of the EU involves *joint floating*, exchange rates of the jointly floating currencies being fixed relative to each other. However, in respect of third countries exchange rates of individual member countries vary if the exchange rates of the former float freely against EMS currencies. Such exchange rate variation against third countries is largely independent of the economic policy pursued by individual member countries.

When economic policy does not affect joint exchange rates, this is a case of economic policy within a system of fixed exchange rates. This holds for small countries but not of large ones like Germany and the United States, whose dominant influence on the exchange rates of the EMS and US$-bloc is such that they cannot be said to pursue economic policies in systems of fixed exchange rates. We will turn to this in Chapter 14.

In Section 10.1 of this chapter we will discuss the interrelationship of national product and balance of payments in an open economy. (The concepts of national product, (national) income and gross domestic product (GDP) are used interchangeably in this text.) Section 10.2 analyses international transmission of economic fluctuations, while Sections 10.3 and 10.4 describe fiscal and monetary policy, respectively. Section 10.5 introduces the IS/LM model of an open economy; finally, Section 10.6 uses the IS/LM analysis of open economies to sum up fiscal and monetary effects.

10.1 INCOME, EMPLOYMENT AND BALANCE OF PAYMENTS

This section discusses what determines national product in an open economy, given price stability both domestically and abroad as well as fixed exchange rates. The simple Keynes model may serve as a framework for an analysis of the relationship between an internal equilibrium and an external one, the rate of employment in a society correlating positively with the size of society's domestic product. Firstly, however, we will consider external equilibrium, which concerns the current account of the balance of payments. We will assume that any deficit will be financed by means of national currency reserves.

10.1.1   Net exports

Net exports are defined as exports minus imports, i.e. $X - M$. Net exports tend to decrease when income and production increase, which is due to the growth of imports in particular. Imports form part of private consumption and private investments *directly*, so when a cyclical upturn increases such consumption and investments, then the volume of imports of finished products also increases. In addition, imports of raw materials and semi-manufactured products used for production purposes have also to be included, since indirectly they form part of consumption and investments.

As total demand affects total production and income (Y), imports also depend on national product, so we assume the following linear relation:

$$M = M_0 + mY \tag{1}$$

where M_0 is the volume of imports if income equals zero and m is the marginal propensity to import (the marginal import ratio), defined as the change in imports per unit change in national product, i.e. $\Delta M / \Delta Y$.

Since one country's exports are imports to other countries, exports primarily depend on income development, and hence demand, in other countries and not on domestic demand. Therefore we assume that exports are independent of national product, i.e.

$$X = X_0 \tag{2}$$

Actually, exports are not likely to be entirely independent of national product; for example, the experience of some countries shows a *capacity effect* on exports. This means that the volume of exports drops as society approaches full employment, producers giving priority to their home market when their order books are full.

Equations (1) and (2) yield the following equation for net exports:

$$X - M = X_0 - M_0 - mY \tag{3}$$

If we disregard transfers, net exports of goods and services equal the surplus on the current account of the balance of payments. The balance of payments curve given in equation (3) is presented in Figure 10.1, which shows that the balance of payments is in equilibrium given a national product of Y_0. If the national product increases beyond this, a balance of payments deficit will emerge. This follows from the fact that a rise in income increases demand for imported goods by the import ratio multiplied by the rise in income. Therefore the larger the marginal import ratio is, the steeper the balance of payments curve will be.

The balance of payments curve expresses a fundamental *conflict* in open economies: any increase in production and level of employment is accompanied by a balance of payments deterioration. As can be seen from the figure, the conflict aggravates with increasing marginal import ratios.

Conditions other than the home country's national product influence its balance of payments. As mentioned above, these include the income development in other countries, which affects

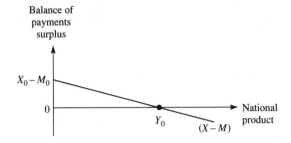

Figure 10.1   Balance of payments dependence on income

exports decisively. In addition, changes in the home country's competitiveness are of importance to its balance of payments. If, for example, Italian price and cost levels increase less than those of Italy's trading partners, then consumers in these countries will tend to substitute Italian export products for domestically produced goods, and Italian consumers will similarly tend to substitute Italian goods for import products. This increases the Italian volume of exports and decreases the import ratio, which results in a shift upward of the balance of payments curve in Figure 10.1; we will turn to this subject in Chapter 11.

10.1.2   The Keynes model of an open economy

According to J.M. Keynes (1936), the size of domestic product and national product is determined by *aggregate demand* (AD), which, in an open economy, consists of the following elements:

$$AD = C + I + G + X - M \qquad [4]$$

where C is private consumption, I is private investments and G is public purchases of goods and services. As mentioned previously, part of consumption and investments will be directed at foreign products. In equation (4) this has been taken into consideration through the subtraction of total imports.

As regards domestic demand, we will assume below that private sector demand for consumer goods depends on disposable income, $Y - T$, where T is net tax revenue, i.e. taxes minus domestic transfer incomes:

$$C = C_0 + c(Y - T) \qquad [5]$$

where C_0 is consumption at zero income and c is marginal propensity to consume, i.e. change in consumption per unit change in disposable income. We assume that taxes correlate (positively) with income, i.e.

$$T = T_0 + tY \qquad [6]$$

where t is the marginal rate of tax and T_0 is tax deduction and the income-independent part of tax revenue. Then private consumption is

$$C = C_0 - cT_0 + c(1 - t)Y \qquad [7]$$

Private sector investment demand primarily depends on interest rate and the sales expectations of firms. For the time being, we will assume that interest rate and sales expectations are given, therefore we allow investments to be independent of national product:

$$I = I_0 \qquad [8]$$

Public purchases of goods and services being the result of a politico-economic decision, the following equation holds:

$$G = G_0 \qquad [9]$$

Having determined the individual components of demand, we may now determine the size of national product that yields equilibrium in society. Equilibrium is not obtained until aggregate demand can be satisfied by means of current production, which requires total domestic product (Y) to equal planned demand (AD), i.e.

$$Y = C + I + G + X - M \qquad [10]$$

If the equations holding the individual components of demand, (7), (8), (9) and (3), are inserted into this equilibrium condition, we obtain the following expression of equilibrium national product:

$$Y = \frac{C_0 - cT_0 + I_0 + G_0 + X_0 - M_0}{1 - c(1 - t) + m} \qquad [11]$$

Figure 10.2 determines national product graphically. In Figure 10.2(a), equilibrium income is determined on the basis of the equilibrium definition in equation (10). Y_{eq} is where the curve for aggregate demand (AD) intersects the 45° curve. Production (Y_{eq}) will correspond precisely to planned demand only at this level of income, which is why stock levels remain unchanged and firms are in production equilibrium. If income is either above or below Y_{eq}, then production will either be larger or smaller than demand, and inventory change over the period will trigger production adjustment and hence income adjustment.

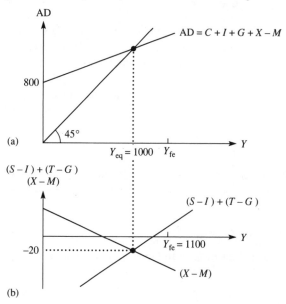

Figure 10.2   Determination of equilibrium national product

Note: The numerical values in Figure 10.2 correspond to an example where

$$c = 0.8; \quad t = 0.5; \quad m = 0.2; \quad X_0 = 200; \quad M_0 = 20 \quad \text{and} \quad (C_0 - cT_0 + I_0 + G_0) = 620$$

The investment multiplier may be calculated as follows:

$$\frac{\Delta Y}{\Delta I_0} = \frac{1}{1 - 0.8(1 - 0.5) + 0.2} = 1.25$$

Compared to that of the closed economy, the AD curve is flatter because net exports decrease with increasing national product as a result of the increase in the volume of imports. Consequently, an increase in autonomous demand, e.g. in investments, will not affect national product correspondingly since part of the increase in demand will be directed towards other countries.

This also appears from the *income multiplier*, which is smaller in the case of an open economy. Equation (11) allows us immediately to read the income multipliers to various demand changes, e.g. the investment multiplier is

$$\frac{\Delta Y}{\Delta I_0} = \frac{1}{1 - c(1 - t) + m} \qquad [12]$$

The reason why the multiplier is smaller than in the case of a closed economy is that marginal propensity to import appears in the denominator. Consequently, small open economies with high import ratios will be less sensitive to internal demand shocks from private consumption and private investments. On the other hand, part of such shocks will be reflected in the balance of payments.

10.1.3 Balance of payments surplus equals savings surplus

Above, equilibrium income was determined by relating total production and demand, but it may also be determined by means of the relationship of savings, investments and the total of the balance of payments current account. As was shown in Chapter 7, an internal savings surplus in an open economy always outbalances the surplus on the current account of the balance of payments. The definition of national product shown in the following equation reveals this clearly:

$$Y = T + C + S \qquad [13]$$

The part of national product not used by the government for net taxes is by definition spent on consumption or saving. If equation (13) is inserted into the equilibrium condition (10), the result is as follows:

$$T + C + S = C + I + G + X - M \qquad [14]$$

If C is subtracted from either side of the equation sign and the expressions are reordered, then the equilibrium condition may be expressed as

$$(S - I) + (T - G) = (X - M) \qquad [15]$$

where $(S - I)$ is private sector savings surplus, while $(T - G)$ is public sector budget surplus or savings surplus, public sector saving corresponding to the difference between net taxes and public consumption. The left-hand side states aggregate internal savings surplus in the economy, which increases with increasing national product. This follows from the fact that both private savings and taxes increase with an increase in the level of activity in society.

$(X - M)$ on the right-hand side represent current account if we disregard transfers, gifts, etc., to other countries. Consequently, the condition in (15) implies that an internal savings surplus will precisely outbalance the current account surplus so that the economy will be in equilibrium.

Figure 10.2(b) shows both savings surplus and balance of payments surplus. It is immediately obvious that only the point at which the two curves intersect each other satisfies the equilibrium condition since this is the only point at which savings surplus equals balance of payments surplus. Equilibrium income is of precisely the same size as that found by means of Figure 10.2(a). Of course, this must necessarily be the case as the equilibrium condition (15) is derived from condition (10).

However, Figure 10.2(b) has the advantage over Figure 10.2(a) in that it immediately shows the balance of payments—in this case, a deficit. Therefore we will make extensive use of this figure in the following chapters when the effects of economic policy are to be analysed.

It should be noted that equilibrium income is not necessarily the level of income that leads to full employment. If we assume that income at full employment equals $Y_{fe} = 1100$, then, given the assumptions of the numerical illustration, the situation is one with unemployment. As equilibrium income does not change so long as the individual components of demand are the same, the level of unemployment will not change either. Thus we have shown that unemployment may be a permanent phenomenon.

10.2 INTERNATIONAL TRANSMISSION OF FLUCTUATIONS

As the imports of one country are exports in the eyes of other countries, activity changes in one country will have spill-over effects on the economic activity in other countries. The above analysis shows that an increase in the volume of exports has the same effect on national product as an increase in investments, since equation (11) yields the following multiplier:

$$\frac{\Delta Y}{\Delta X_0} = \frac{\Delta Y}{\Delta I_0} = \frac{1}{1 - c(1 - t) + m} \qquad [16]$$

While the two kinds of changes have the same effect on production, their effects on the balance of payments are not identical at all. This is evident from Figure 10.3, in which a balance of payments equilibrium occurs at point A in the initial situation. An increase in investments will shift the schedule for internal savings surplus downwards, which moves the equilibrium point, for example, to point D. This results in a balance of payments deficit when the increase in income increases imports. The size of the deficit will be

$$\Delta M = m\Delta Y = \frac{m}{1 - c(1 - t) + m} \Delta I_0 \qquad [17]$$

The figure shows that the deteriorating effect of an investment boom on the balance of payments increases with increasing marginal propensity to import. By contrast, an increase in exports will improve the balance of payments, but not by the full amount resulting from the export increase. Figure 10.3 shows this: an export increase shifts the $(X - M)$ curve upwards in accordance with the increase in exports, which in this case corresponds to the segment AC. This

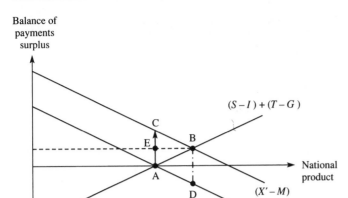

Figure 10.3   The effect of export increase

shifts the equilibrium point to B, but this improves the balance of payments by no more than the segment AE. This follows from the fact that the derived increase in national product increases imports, which reduces the balance of payments improvement. If this is taken into consideration, the adjusted balance of payments change is the following:

$$\Delta X_0 - \Delta M = \Delta X_0 - \frac{m}{1 - c(1 - t) + m}\Delta X_0$$

$$= \frac{1 - c(1 - t)}{1 - c(1 - t) + m}\Delta X_0 \qquad [18]$$

10.2.1   Boomerang effect

As mentioned previously, the fact that the multiplier is smaller in an open economy than in a closed one is the result of part of demand being directed towards other countries, in which it will create income and employment. If the level of activity in a large country rises, e.g. in the United States, then the spill-over effect on other countries may be quite considerable, which will affect the country itself positively so that the multiplier will in fact be larger when this effect is included. This boomerang effect may be substantial in the case of countries whose volume of trade with each other is considerable. The following examples illustrate this.

Let us assume that the world consists of two areas, A and B, e.g. the United States and the rest of the OECD. If income goes up in the United States, the volume of imports from the rest of the OECD will increase. Through a multiplier process the export increase will increase the national product of the rest of the OECD. This will result in increased imports, i.e. U.S. exports will go up, etc. Thus expansion (or contraction) in one country spreads to its trading partners and creates expansion (contraction) in those countries, too. Figure 10.4 shows these relationships.

As a result, international trade cycles will be highly synchronic. Therefore the leading countries, such as, for example, the United States, are crucial to international trade cycles. In popular terms, this saying is that 'when the United States sneezes, the world catches a cold'. This also means that a large country may serve as an economic locomotive pulling the world out of a slump if it pursues an expansionary economic policy. However, the price of this is balance of payments deterioration, which may result in an imbalance in international trade.

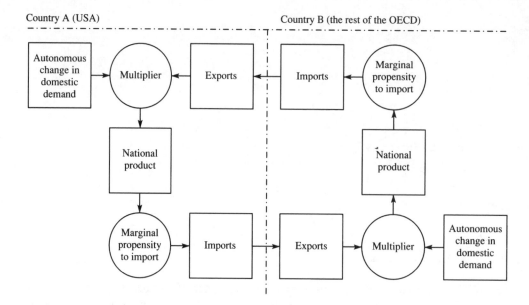

Figure 10.4 International transmission of trade cycles

This problem may be entirely avoided if a locomotive can be found that has a considerable balance of payments surplus. Japan and Germany are often pointed to in this connection. If several countries pursue a coordinated expansionary economic policy, the balance of payments problem may be avoided, however, and the expansionary effect may be reinforced. This is known as the *convoy theory*. In Chapter 14 we will treat the advantages and problems of international coordination of economic policies in greater detail.

10.3 FISCAL POLICY

As in a closed economy, fiscal policy may be used in an open economy in order to influence national product and level of employment, but its impact is stronger in a closed economy, (compare this with the discussion above on the income multiplier). What affects income, however, will also affect the balance of payments since imports are income-dependent. Consequently, an expansionary fiscal policy will increase the volume of imports and, hence, cause a balance of payments deterioration. Figure 10.5 illustrates this dilemma. Internal savings surplus and balance of payments surplus are shown as functions of national product. Point A indicates equilibrium income, savings surplus being equal to a balance of payments surplus in A. The initial situation therefore involves a balance of payments deficit and a national product that is smaller than full-employment income, Y_{fe}.

An expansionary fiscal policy, which reduces taxation and/or increases the volume of public purchases of goods and services, shifts the $(S-I)+(T-G)$ curve downwards. This allows the equilibrium point to be shifted from A to B, a point in which full employment obtains. The problem involved in pursuing such a policy is that it simultaneously increases the balance of payments deficit. An alternative, which takes balance of payments effects into consideration, would be a tight fiscal policy: this would shift the $(S-I)+(T-G)$ curve upwards. This would allow the equilibrium point to be shifted to C, where the balance of payments is in equilibrium.

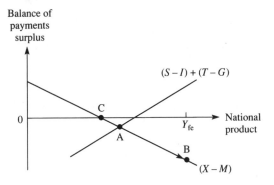

Figure 10.5   Conflicting goals of fiscal policy

The problem involved in pursuing this policy is that the level of unemployment increases simultaneously.

In sum, fiscal policy inherently involves *conflicting goals*: as fiscal policy aims at improving one goal, the other goal is necessarily put in a worse position. It follows that the combined problem of a high level of unemployment and a balance of payments deficit cannot be solved directly by means of fiscal policy. The solution to this conflict is an economic policy that is able to influence the $(X - M)$ curve, i.e. a policy that stimulates exports and/or reduces imports at a given level of activity. *Improved competitiveness* is generally what is needed for this purpose, but we will return to this in Chapter 11.

However, if fiscal measures are combined, the conflict described above may, to some extent, be eliminated. This is due to the fact that the various components of demand have different levels of import content. Typically, public consumption has a low import ratio, that of private consumption is somewhat higher, and the share of imports is high in machinery and means of transport.

The income multiplier above showed that a low import ratio increases the effect on income. Conversely, a low import ratio reduces the balance of payments multiplier, which can be seen from the following expression of the balance of payments effect of a change in public purchases of goods and services:

$$\Delta X - \Delta M = -m\Delta Y = \frac{-m}{1 - c(1 - t) + m}\Delta G_0 \qquad [19]$$

Table 10.1 shows the multiplier effect of a number of fiscal measures on both production and the balance of payments in the case of Denmark. As can be seen from the table, the various fiscal measures have a varying impact on the balance of payments and gross domestic product, which reflects the fact that the share of imports varies among the components of demand.

Changes in the number of public employees, for example, strongly affect production and employment but have little influence on the balance of payments. By contrast, a change in the public purchases of goods has a relatively stronger balance of payments effect but its effect on production is relatively weak. Consequently, fiscal policy may be used to change the composition of demand in such a way that the total volume of imports goes down. If, for example, public consumption is increased through an increase in the number of public employees and if private consumption, which has a high import content, is reduced at the same time through an increase in taxation, then this will reduce the average import ratio. This shifts

Table 10.1   Danish two-year multiplier for gross domestic product and balance of payments

Policy tool	Gross domestic product	Balance of payments
Value-added tax	−1.03	0.50
Public consumption	1.17	−0.60
Public investments in machinery	0.64	−0.87
Public investments in construction	1.31	−0.57
Number of public employees	1.45	−0.29
Pay to public employees	0.57	−0.32

Source: Modelgruppen, Danmarks Statistik, unpublished material.

the $(X-M)$ curve in Figure 10.5 upwards. Such *demand-twisting fiscal policy* improves both employment and the balance of payments and thus it solves the problem of conflicting goals.

Of course, a policy of this kind will cause structural changes in the economy: it will result in a larger public sector and a smaller private one, which, from an allocative point of view, may be an unfavourable outcome. In addition, the expansion of the public sector will be accompanied by an increased tax burden, which may reduce the incentive to save and to work, and increase wage pressure and intensify the problem of tax evasion.

In sum, demand-twisting fiscal policy has a tendency to sweep economic problems under the carpet. When the decision is finally made to give the public sector a lower priority, the employment and balance of payments problems will, in the meantime, have become even more serious.

10.4   MONEY, INTEREST RATE AND BALANCE OF PAYMENTS

Up to this point, we have disregarded the financial sector and assumed a constant interest rate. In an open economy, balance of payments transactions with other countries affect money supply and, consequently, the rate of interest. This is of importance to both fiscal policy and monetary policy but, firstly, let us consider the liquidity effect of the balance of payments.

10.4.1   Balance of payments and liquidity

All payments between the private sector and other countries affect the monetary base. The monetary base consists of the liquid claims of the private sector on the central bank and the government. It includes notes and coins in circulation and deposits made by the banks with the central bank. As the monetary base is of importance to the volume of society's money supply, the balance of payments also influences money supply and interest rate development.

Figure 10.6 illustrates the way in which exports affect liquidity. In this example, a German exporter sells a consignment of goods to the United Kingdom. He has his bankers exchange the payment received into DEM and they subsequently have the Bundesbank exchange the £ sterling into DEM. Thus exports have enlarged the monetary base in Germany, the DEM funds of the exporter having increased. Similarly, external borrowing by a domestic firm provides the home country with foreign exchange which will be exchanged into the home currency and thus increase the money base. In the case of imports and private lending to other countries, the reverse situation holds.

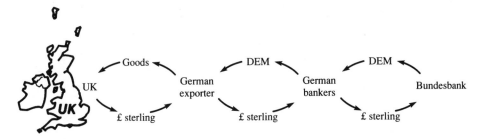

Figure 10.6   Liquidity effect of exports

Not all transactions with other countries have a liquidity effect. This holds, for example, of government transactions if money borrowed externally by the government of a country is deposited with the central bank of the country in question. In such a case, liquidity in the private sector is not affected and therefore the liquidity effect of the balance of payments corresponds to the difference between private sector payments received from and made to other countries.

10.4.2   Interest rate and capital movements

As regards liquidity, the capital account of the balance of payments is essential to economic policy. Private capital movements in particular vary a great deal from one year to the next and are highly sensitive to changes in expectations in respect of interest rate and foreign exchange conditions. In Chapter 9, we argued on the basis of portfolio considerations that capital movements would cause the expected return on investments in various currencies to be identical (see the uncovered interest parity in equation (3) of Chapter 9). This of course implies that changes in national interest levels may affect capital movements.

In this chapter, in which we assume fixed exchange rates, exchange rate expectations will be static and therefore private capital movements, B_p, are determined by the differential between domestic interest rate, i, and foreign interest rate, i_f, shown by the following expression:

$$B_p = B_p(i - i_f) \qquad [20]$$

The relationship between domestic interest rate and private net capital movements appears from the B_p curve in Figure 10.7. The figure is based on the assumption that net capital movements are zero when domestic and foreign interest rates are identical. Therefore the B_p curve intersects the interest rate axis at the foreign rate of interest. Given that we assume price stability in this chapter, nominal interest rate (i) and real interest rate (r) are identical.

If claims in the home currency and in foreign currencies are perfectly substitutable, as was assumed in connection with the derivation of the uncovered interest parity, then the B_p curve will be absolutely horizontal: this is known as perfect capital mobility, (B_p'). Capital mobility is measured in terms of the sensitivity of capital movements to interest rate or their interest elasticity, which, in this case, will be infinitely high.

In real life, however, domestic and external claims are not likely to be fully substitutable. Instead, we will be faced with *imperfect capital mobility* and the slope of the B_p curve will be positive. This may result in a difference between i and i_f so we must assume that the volume of net capital movements will increase by the interest rate differential.

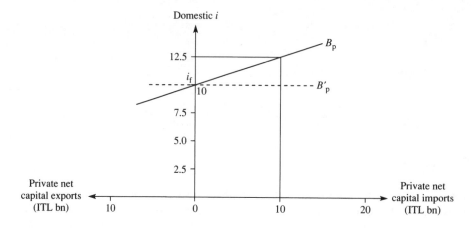

Figure 10.7   Interest rate and capital imports

For several reasons, actual capital mobility is often imperfect. First of all, with the exception of the case of a monetary union with one common currency, exchange rates are rarely entirely fixed. This gives rise to exchange rate risk and as a result external claims are never fully substitutable in a portfolio. Secondly, the political risk that tax regulation and other conditions may be altered, which may affect yields, has to be taken into consideration. Thirdly, the acquisition of foreign claims involves increased transaction costs; and, finally, the movement of financial capital among countries may be subject to restrictions. If these are very tight, as was the case, for example, in the fifties, then the slope of the B_p curve will be almost vertical. With the liberalization of exchange controls on capital movements in the postwar period, the slope of the B_p curve has become ever flatter.

Only in principle, however, does the figure show the interest rate sensitivity of capital imports, just as the position of the curve will vary with exchange rate expectations (E^e), which may be rather unstable. Given that, except in the case of a monetary union, entirely fixed exchange rates never occur in practice, fears of an Italian devaluation, for example, will cause the curve in the diagram to shift upwards so that it intersects the axis above i_f. Expectations of an annual depreciation of 3 per cent will necessitate an interest span relative to other countries of at least 3 per cent in order to ensure the same volume of capital imports as in a situation without any expectation of depreciation. A large external debt, unstable political conditions, etc., will similarly reduce the credit-worthiness of a country and necessitate a certain excess interest rate in order to maintain capital imports.

Representing capital movements as a function of the interest differential between the home country and other countries is not strictly correct. According to portfolio theory, the total stock of domestic and external claims is determined by interest differentials and thus capital movements are a *derived flow*. The following example may illustrate this. Let us assume that the Italian interest rate is 12.5 per cent while the foreign interest rate is 10 per cent and that this results in capital imports of ITL 10bn a year (see Figure 10.7). After a period with capital imports, investors in Italy and other countries will have adjusted their portfolios and capital movements will cease. By then the increase in Italy's external debt will have shifted the B_p curve upwards by 2.5 percentage points. Hence the B_p curve should be taken to represent a short-term relationship.

10.4.3 Monetary freedom of action

As in the case of fiscal policy, the activity effect of monetary policy is restricted by the fact that the multiplier is smaller in an open economy; this was shown above with respect to the investment multiplier. Likewise, as in the case of fiscal policy, monetary policy involves conflicting goals—a conflict between the goal of external equilibrium and that of internal equilibrium. If monetary policy aims at stimulating employment, then the central bank has to increase liquidity, e.g. through the purchase of bonds from the private sector, which will increase money supply and make the interest rate go down. This will trigger an increase in investments and, through the multiplier, an increase in national product and employment. However, this also increases imports and leads to a balance of payments deterioration. This is also evident from Figure 10.5, in which the increase in investments will shift the $(S-I)+(T-G)$ curve to the right, thus shifting the equilibrium point along the $(X-M)$ curve.

Apart from the effect on the current account of the balance of payments, monetary policy has a more immediate effect on capital movements than does fiscal policy. Therefore exchange market considerations will block any active control of domestic liquidity aimed at influencing the domestic activity level. Given that the principal task of monetary policy in a system of fixed exchange rates is the control of international capital movements, monetary freedom of action, e.g. as regards employment policy, is highly limited. An attempt to illustrate this has been made in Figure 10.8, which shows equilibrium in both the money market and the exchange market.

In the initial situation, the money market in Figure 10.8 is in equilibrium at the interest rate i_1; money supply is M_1^s and demand for money is M^d. In the exchange market, the equilibrium rate of exchange corresponds precisely to the parity rate, $\bar{E}$, in the initial situation, so the central bank does not intervene on the exchange market. Let us now assume that for employment policy purposes the central bank wishes to pursue an *expansionary monetary policy* and that it therefore increases money supply to M_2^s. In a closed economy, this would cause the interest rate to fall to i_2, but in an open economy, the fall in the domestic interest rate will result in capital exports (see Figure 10.7).

Capital exports will increase demand for foreign exchange to D_2, which forces the central bank to intervene with an amount corresponding to AB in order to prevent the home currency from depreciating to E_2, i.e. to an exchange rate above the parity rate. However, intervention on the exchange market also affects domestic liquidity.

When the central bank sells foreign exchange corresponding to the segment of AB, it absorbs an equivalent amount of domestic liquidity as exchange market agents pay for the foreign exchange. This causes the money supply to fall to M_1^s, which has been indicated by means of the

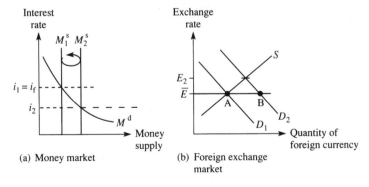

(a) Money market

(b) Foreign exchange market

Figure 10.8 Monetary autonomy

money supply arrow in the figure. Thus the two markets work like communicating vessels and the central bank cannot control both the interest rate and the exchange rate. The bank has to choose, and in a system of fixed exchange rates it has chosen to control the exchange rate rather than the interest rate, which means that the domestic interest rate has to adjust to the foreign interest rate. If the fixed exchange rate policy is abandoned, domestic liquidity may be controlled. This situation will be discussed in Chapter 12.

If the mobility of capital movements is perfect, i.e. if the B_p curve in Figure 10.7 is horizontal, then the domestic interest rate will only briefly be able to deviate from the international rate of interest. This implies that monetary policy will not be able to affect investments, so, in fact, it is not autonomous. Yet in this case monetary policy is highly effective in influencing external equilibrium, i.e. the autonomous items of the balance of payments (see Chapter 7). As will appear from Section 10.6, this makes a division of labour between fiscal policy and monetary policy possible.

The loss of autonomy of monetary policy holds primarily for small countries with liberal laws on international capital movements. In the case of large countries which influence international interest rates or countries with more restrictive regulation of capital movements, the autonomy of monetary policy has not disappeared entirely.

10.5   SIMULTANEOUS ECONOMIC EQUILIBRIUM

Sections 10.1, 10.2 and 10.3 showed the way in which equilibrium in the goods market is influenced by the opening of an economy while the opening of the domestic money market for external claims was considered in Section 10.4, where the exchange market was included. This section integrates the analyses of the three markets, using the so-called *IS/LM model of an open economy*, in which an equilibrium condition for the exchange market has been added to the traditional *IS/LM* model.

10.5.1   Equilibrium in the goods market

The *IS* curve shown in Figure 10.9 indicates the combinations of interest rate and national

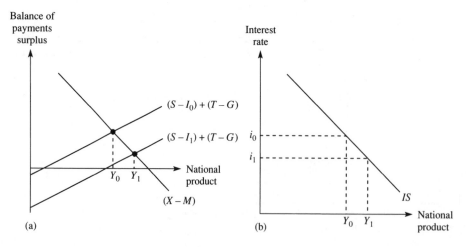

Figure 10.9   Derivation of the *IS* curve

product at which aggregate demand equals production, i.e. the ones at which the market for goods and services is in equilibrium. In an open economy, this equilibrium also exists if (planned) internal savings surplus equals balance of payments surplus (compare with the equilibrium condition (15) above).This has been shown in the left-hand figure, which illustrates the derivation of the IS curve in the case of an open economy.

Given an interest rate of i_0, private investments amount to I_0 and equilibrium income is Y_0. If the interest rate falls to i_1, lending will be less costly. This means that a number of investment projects become profitable: private investments increase,[*] e.g. to I_1, and this shifts the $(S-I)+(T-G)$ curve downwards, which in turn increases equilibrium income to Y_1. Other values of the interest rate will correspondingly lead to other points on the IS curve.

For the same reasons as in the case of a closed economy, the slope of the IS curve is negative, its slope depending on the interest rate elasticity of investments and the income multiplier. The higher the interest rate elasticity and the larger the multiplier, the larger will be the increase in income as a result of an interest rate decrease and the flatter the IS curve will be. Therefore the IS curve is steeper in an open economy since there the multiplier is smaller. This follows from the fact that part of the increase in demand that results from a fall in interest rate will be directed towards other countries, where it will create income and employment.

The figure also shows that an expansionary fiscal policy, which allows G to increase or which reduces T, will increase equilibrium income at a given rate of interest, and thus it will shift the IS curve to the right. Similarly, a fall in private saving, an increase in exports or a fall in imports will also shift the IS curve to the right. In any case, the IS curve will shift by the product of the autonomous components (G_0, T_0, S_0, I_0, X_0, M_0) and their respective multipliers.

10.5.2   Equilibrium in the money market

Derivation of the LM curve, which shows the combinations of interest rate and income at which the money market is in equilibrium, is in principle the same in an open economy and a closed one (see Figure 10.10). The left-hand side shows the money market, in which the national product of Y_0 yields equilibrium between demand for money $M^d(Y_0)$ and money supply M^s at the interest rate i_0. A cyclical upturn which increases national product to Y_1 will simultaneously increase demand for money for transaction purposes and, consequently, given the unaltered domestic money supply, force the interest rate in the money market up to i_1. In the money market, this yields a positive correlation between national product and interest rate. This has been shown by means of the LM curve in the right-hand side of Figure 10.10.

As in a closed economy, the slope of the LM curve depends on the interest rate and income elasticities of demand for money. If the slope of the M^d curve is steep, indicating low interest rate elasticity, then the upturn will result in a large increase in interest rate, which will yield a steeply sloping LM curve. Similarly, in the case of an upturn, high income elasticity in demand for money will cause a large increase in demand for money and, consequently, in interest rate, which will also yield a steeply sloping LM curve. The position of the LM curve depends, among other things, on money supply. An increase in money supply will shift the LM curve to the right, but along the LM curve the money supply is constant.

---

[*] Presumably, private consumption increases at the same time since, for example, the financing of consumer durables will have improved. Therefore private savings decrease, at a given national product, which will have the same effect on the $(S-I)+(T-G)$ curve.

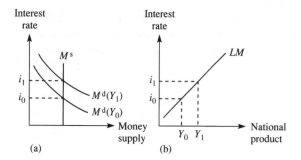

Figure 10.10   Derivation of the *LM* curve

As was shown above, the autonomy of monetary policy is rather limited in an open economy with fixed exchange rates. This is not evident from the *LM* curve itself but follows from the fact that it is difficult for a central bank to control the money supply and, by implication, to control the position of the *LM* curve, given that it has committed itself to intervene on the exchange market. Therefore we will now turn to the exchange market to investigate the interest rate and activity level conditions that may ensure equilibrium in this market.

10.5.3   Equilibrium in the foreign exchange market

As was mentioned previously, turnover in the exchange market is the result of both current items $(X - M)$ and private capital items, B_p. A current account deficit has to be counterbalanced by corresponding private capital imports if the exchange market is to be in equilibrium, i.e. if a situation is to obtain in which the central bank does not intervene on the exchange market and in which, as a result, both international liquidity and money supply are constant $(\Delta L = 0)$. Equilibrium in the exchange market and, hence, on the *autonomous items* of the balance of payments, BP_a, may then be expressed as follows:

$$\text{BP}_a = X - M(Y) + B_p(i - i_f) = 0 \qquad [21]$$

The development of the autonomous items depends on both national product and interest rate. Private capital items depend on the interest differential between the home country and other countries, which was discussed in connection with equation (20) above. Current accounts depend on national product and this relationship has been illustrated in the lower diagram of Figure 10.11. The relationship was shown in Figure 10.1, in which an increase in national product triggered an increase in the deficit on the balance of goods and services as a result of imports going up. Thus the slope of the $(X - M)$ curve was negative.

The top part of Figure 10.11 shows the BP_a curve. This indicates the combinations of domestic activity level and interest rate that ensure equilibrium in the exchange market, i.e. points in which $BP_a = 0$. An example may illustrate the slope of the BP_a curve. Given a national product of Y_0, current items will be in equilibrium. Consequently, equilibrium in the exchange market requires that capital items are also in equilibrium, which will be the case when the domestic interest rate equals the foreign interest rate, i_f (see Figure 10.7). If domestic activity increases to Y_1, this will trigger a deficit on current items, which has to be financed through corresponding capital imports in order to ensure that the autonomous items are in equilibrium. For this purpose, an increase in the domestic interest rate is required, *in casu* to i_1.

The size of the required increase in the domestic interest rate and the resulting steepness of

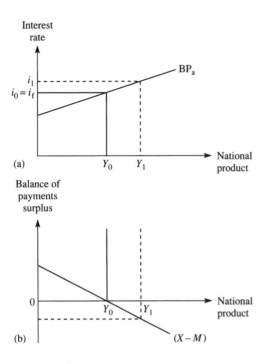

Figure 10.11   The BP_a curve

the slope of the BP_a curve depend on the interest rate sensitivity of capital movements. If capital movements are highly sensitive to interest rate, the interest rate increase required to finance the deficit on the current account will be very moderate and the slope of the BP_a curve will consequently be fairly flat. If capital mobility is perfect, the BP_a curve will be horizontal.

For all points below the BP_a curve it holds that there is a deficit on the autonomous balance ($BP_a < 0$), the domestic interest rate being too low to be able to secure the capital imports needed. As a result, the central bank has to intervene and currency reserves will be drained ($\Delta L < 0$). However, as mentioned above, intervention on the exchange market drains liquidity out of the money market. This affects money supply and, by implication, the position of the LM curve. Similarly, for all points above the BP_a curve it holds that there is a surplus on the autonomous items. In this case, intervention on the exchange market by the central bank will increase domestic liquidity and as a result the LM curve will shift to the right.

10.5.4   Simultaneous equilibrium in the three markets

The IS, LM and BP_a curves in Figure 10.12 show the combinations of interest rate and national product that create equilibrium in the markets for goods, money and foreign exchange, respectively. Consequently, simultaneous equilibrium in all three markets only obtains at one common point of intersection—in this case, at the interest rate of i_0 and the national product of Y_0. In this case, the equilibrium point involves a deficit on the current account of the balance of payments of CA_0 which is financed through corresponding capital imports.

The IS/LM model of an open economy does not work in entirely the same way as in the case of a closed economy. To illustrate this, we will consider a situation of disequilibrium. Let us assume that in Figure 10.12 the LM curve intersects the IS curve at point A. This is not a

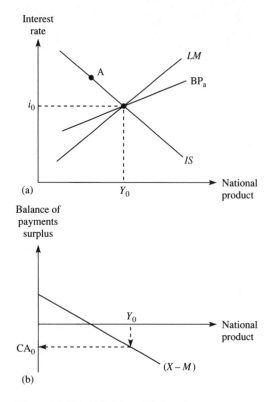

Figure 10.12   *IS/LM* equilibrium in an open economy

general equilibrium as the BP_a curve does not intersect the other curves at this point. Point A being above the BP_a curve, the interest rate is higher than that which will trigger exchange market equilibrium. Therefore capital imports exceed the volume needed for the financing of any current account deficit. When this excess supply of foreign exchange is bought by the central bank, the money supply increases. As a result, the *LM* curve will shift to the right and the interest rate will go down. When the interest rate has dropped to i_0, the exchange market will be in equilibrium and the migration of the *LM* curve will cease.

This example shows that total equilibrium depends on the intersection of the *IS* and BP_a curves. This follows from the fact that, in a system of fixed exchange rates, the central bank has committed itself to maintaining equilibrium in the exchange market; therefore this goal must have priority over the goal of equilibrium in the domestic money market (the *LM* curve).

10.5.5   Transmission of trade cycles in *IS/LM*

Figure 10.3 showed that an upswing in other countries would increase the exports of the home country and, hence, its national product. The figure is reproduced as the left-hand side of Figure 10.13; the right-hand side shows an *IS/LM* analysis of the increase in exports. Let us assume that points A in Figure 10.13 represent the initial situation of the home country. At a given interest rate, an increase in exports will increase national product by the increase in exports multiplied by the multiplier, which will shift the *IS* curve correspondingly to the right.

Given an increase in exports, the BP_a curve will also shift to the right and the shift will be even larger than that of the *IS* curve. At a given rate of interest, the autonomous items on the

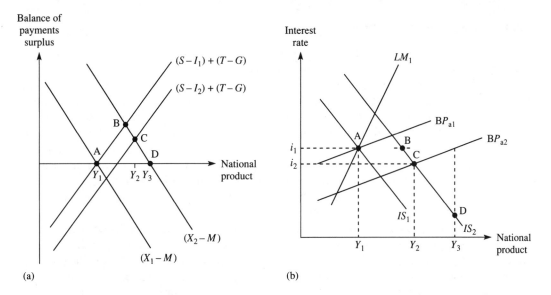

Figure 10.13   Effect of an increase in exports

balance of payments will be improved by an amount corresponding to the increase in exports; therefore a corresponding increase in imports is needed in order to recreate external equilibrium at a given rate of interest. As $\Delta M = m\Delta Y$, this will yield a shift of $1/m$ multiplied by the increase in exports, and as $1/m$ is more than the multiplier, the shift of the BP_a curve will be larger than that of the IS curve. The new equilibrium point is C, as the LM curve shifts to the right due to the liquidity effect resulting from the exchange market.

In the model of income formation shown to the left in Figure 10.13, the $(X-M)$ curve shifts upwards and, in accordance with the analysis in Figure 10.3, the equilibrium point shifts to point B. However, this is not the final equilibrium, if the financial market is included, as is the case in the IS/LM model to the right. This shows that the interest rate drops to i_2, which increases private investments and, consequently, the economy ends up in the equilibrium point C. Thus, as a result of the fall in interest rate, which stimulates the upswing, transmission of trade cycles is larger in the complete model.

The analysis in Figure 10.13 also shows that the degree of transmission depends on the slope of the BP_a curve and, hence, on the interest rate sensitivity of capital movements. If capital mobility is perfect, then, given the initial interest rate i_1, the BP_a curve will be horizontal and the conclusions reached will be the same as those obtained on the basis of the analysis of Figure 10.3. If no capital movements occur, as was roughly the case in the fifties, the BP_a curve will be vertical and the equilibrium point will be point D. That transmission is larger in this case follows from the fact that equilibrium in the exchange market is only possible if the national product is Y_3, i.e. if current items are in equilibrium. If the national product is smaller, a foreign exchange surplus results and the influx of foreign exchange will increase money supply and force the interest rate down.

10.6   FISCAL AND MONETARY POLICY

Having considered fiscal policy and monetary policy separately, we will now sum them up and compare them to each other by means of the IS/LM model.

10.6.1 Perfect capital mobility

Figure 10.14 shows the effects of an expansionary fiscal policy (FP) and an expansionary monetary policy (MP). In the initial situation, A, the domestic interest rate corresponds to the foreign interest rate, i_f. At first, an expansionary fiscal policy which shifts the IS curve to IS_2 will increase the domestic interest rate as well as national product to i_2 and Y_2, respectively. However, point B is not an equilibrium point in an open economy. The interest rate having gone up, capital imports will also increase. This increases the exchange supply so that the central bank is forced to sell its own currency against foreign exchange in order to maintain the exchange rate. This increases the money supply and shifts the LM curve to the right. Capital movements in this case being perfect, the process will continue until the domestic interest rate again corresponds to i_f and the resulting situation is C. The BP_a curve has not been included in the figure but it follows that in this case it is horizontal.

An expansionary monetary policy that shifts the LM curve to LM_2 will shift the point of intersection to D. However, in an open economy D is not an equilibrium point either. The fall in interest rate results in capital exports and, hence, in a liquidity drain, which puts the exchange rate under pressure. In order to defend the fixed exchange rate, the central bank will have to sell foreign exchange for its own currency. This reduces the money supply and shifts the LM curve to the left. If capital mobility is perfect, point D will never be reached: the economy stays in A, given the foreign interest rate i_f.

Thus, in a system of fixed exchange rates, pursuing an independent monetary policy so as to influence employment is obviously difficult. However, for the purpose of controlling capital imports, monetary policy is an effective tool. By contrast, as regards influencing employment, fiscal policy is more effective in an open economy because it reduces the 'crowding out' effect, which is entirely eliminated if capital mobility is perfect.

10.6.2 Sluggish capital movements

As was mentioned above, actual capital movements are unlikely to be perfectly mobile, and one might ask how this affects the effectiveness of fiscal and monetary policies. The principal conclusion will be that monetary policy remains as ineffective as described above while the

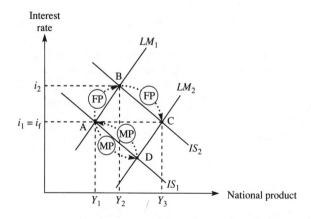

Figure 10.14 Fiscal policy and monetary policy at fixed exchange rate

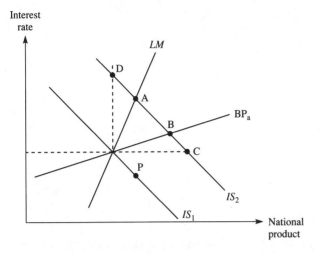

Figure 10.15   Fiscal and monetary policy, given sluggish capital mobility and fixed exchange rate

effectiveness of fiscal policy will be reduced. Figure 10.15, in which the positive slope of the BP_a curve expresses the sluggishness of capital movements, shows this by means of an IS/LM analysis.

Let us assume that an expansionary monetary policy is pursued that shifts the LM curve to the right so that it intersects the IS curve at point P. This point being below the BP_a curve, currency reserves will be drained and gradually the money supply will be reduced to the initial volume. Even if private capital movements do not occur and if, consequently, the BP_a curve is vertical, the current account deficit will force the LM curve back to its initial position.

An expansionary fiscal policy will shift the IS curve to the right and therefore the new point of intersection with the BP_a curve in Figure 10.15 is B. As explained above, the LM curve will also shift to the right and, consequently, the situation in B is one of general equilibrium. Point B being to the left of C, which is the equilibrium point under perfect capital mobility, the effectiveness of fiscal policy has been reduced.

If capital imports are precisely sufficient to finance excess imports, then the BP_a curve will coincide with the LM curve and the effectiveness of fiscal policy will be the same as in the case of a closed economy if income multiplier differences are disregarded. If no international capital movements occur, then the BP_a curve will be vertical and the equilibrium point will be point D, where fiscal policy fully crowds out private consumption.

10.6.3   Coordination of fiscal and monetary policies

Fiscal policy and monetary policy were discussed separately above and both kinds of policy were shown to contain conflicting goals in that none of them were able to solve a balance of payments problem and an employment problem at the same time. The two kinds of policy had parallel effects on the current items of the balance of payments and on national product, although monetary policy affected capital movements more directly and more effectively.

Robert Mundell, an American economist, was the first to realize that this difference between monetary policy and fiscal policy could be usefully exploited in economic policy. In a number of articles from around 1960, he showed that coordination of fiscal policy and monetary policy could result in full employment and equilibrium on the current account of the balance of payments. Figure 10.16 illustrates his line of reasoning.

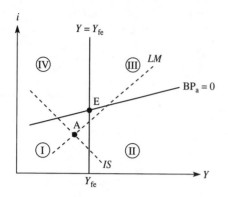

Figure 10.16   Internal and external equilibrium

The vertical curve in Figure 10.16 shows the combinations of interest rate and national income which yield *internal equilibrium*, i.e. full employment. To the right of this curve, we find excess employment and inflation, and to the left we find unemployment. The BP_a curve shows the combinations that yield *external equilibrium*, which in this case means that the autonomous items balance. Above the curve, there will be a surplus on the autonomous items and below the curve there will be a deficit. Internal and external equilibrium obtains only at point E.

If the economy is in a situation with both unemployment and an external deficit (area I), an expansionary fiscal policy may solve the unemployment problem while a tight monetary policy may finance the balance of payments deficit, as shown by the shifting of the *IS* and *LM* curves from point A to point E. Such a situation primarily calls for an expansionary fiscal policy while the extent to which monetary policy has to be adjusted depends on the position of the economy in area I. If the economy is in a situation with inflation and a balance of payments deficit (area II), its monetary policy has to be tightened, while the extent to which its fiscal policy has to be adjusted depends on the position of the economy in area II. An economy in area III is one with a balance of payments surplus and inflation, so in this case fiscal policy has to be tightened and monetary policy needs to be adjusted. Finally, an economy in area IV is one with a balance of payments surplus and unemployment, which primarily calls for relaxation of monetary policy.

Robert Mundell also showed that the means used to reach a given goal is of importance. In a situation in which the finance minister is entirely concerned with securing external equilibrium, for example, and the governor of the central bank equally focuses on securing internal equilibrium, the two goals cannot be reached at the same time. Let us assume, for example, that the economy of the country in question is in point A, i.e. in a situation with unemployment and a balance of payments deficit, and that the central bank lowers the interest rate in order to ensure full employment while the finance minister raises taxes in order to improve external equilibrium. As a result, the economy moves ever farther away from E. If, conversely, the finance minister focuses on internal equilibrium and the governor of the central bank on external equilibrium, then the economy will move towards equilibrium.

This shows that coordination of individual policies is essential if an economy is to be controlled rationally. In order to reach the goals of an economy, individual means have to be used where they are most effective. In the above model, for example, monetary policy had to be used to achieve external equilibrium and fiscal policy was needed for the purposes of internal equilibrium, the reason being that although both means affect internal equilibrium and, hence, the current account of the balance of payments, only monetary policy would additionally influence the balance of payments through an effect on cross-border capital movements.

It should be emphasized that external equilibrium is equilibrium on autonomous items and not on current items. Therefore a situation may occur in which the country in the equilibrium point E has a large deficit on the current account of the balance of payments, which will be financed through corresponding capital imports. Such a policy is not tenable for very long, however, since the external deficit of the country will increase year by year. This will make it more difficult to attract foreign capital so the interest rate will have to be increased, which will shift the BP_a curve upwards. This will necessarily hit investments and, by implication, affect economic growth.

SUMMARY

1. On the assumption that real exchange rates are fixed and in the absence of price changes, there is a fundamental conflict between production (employment) and the current account.
2. The sum of private sector savings surplus and public sector budget surplus equals the current account.
3. Export and import interact in the transmission of fluctuations between countries, in the end transmitting the impulse back to the originating country. These effects call for a coordinated international policy.
4. Apart from demand twists, fiscal policy does not, on the assumption made in this chapter, affect competitiveness and it inherently has to comply with conflicting goals.
5. The balance of payments affects money supply and interest rate, and consequently capital movements. In the case of exchange rate risk, capital mobility is imperfect and actual capital movements further depend on exchange rate expectations.
6. Monetary policy must also comply with conflicting goods. Its effect on capital movements limits active control of domestic liquidity. The central bank cannot control both interest rate and exchange rate.
7. The *ISLM* model allows an integrated analysis of the goods, money and exchange markets, which is handy for analysis of the transmission of trade cycles as well as of fiscal and monetary policies and policy coordination.
8. Coordination of economic policies is essential, and different tasks are assigned to fiscal and monetary policies.

REFERENCES AND FURTHER READING

Hansen, Alvin H. (1949), *Monetary Theory and Fiscal Policy*, McGraw-Hill, New York.
Hicks, J. R. (1937), 'Mr. Keynes and the "Classics": A suggested interpretation', *Econometrica*, **5** 147–159.
Keynes, John Maynard (1936), *The General Theory of Employment, Interest and Money*, Macmillan, London.
Mundell, Robert A. (1962), 'The appropriate use of monetary and fiscal policy under fixed exchange rates', Staff Papers, **9**, International Monetary Fund.

ELEVEN

CHANGING NATIONAL COMPETITIVENESS

The concept of competitiveness has many aspects: it may be seen (1) from the point of view of a firm, an industry or a nation, or (2) in a short-term or long-term perspective. Thus at least six different categories are relevant in this connection and this remains the case when we turn to the policies aimed at changing national competitiveness, which is the subject of this chapter.

We have already touched on the subject of competitiveness, in Chapters 2, 3 and 4. Chapter 2 concentrated on the nation, but the economic model selected excluded the problem of competitiveness as it assumes that the market mechanism works and that export and import prices are fully flexible. Neither employment nor the balance of trade presented a problem. The concept that expresses long-term competitiveness, i.e. the growth rate of an economy, was not introduced at all.

The perspective chosen in Chapters 3 and 4 was that of firms and industries. In industries with perfect competition, firms and entire national industries may either thrive or be obliterated if the price of some factors of production develops faster in the home country than in other countries. Under imperfect competition, an industry has various means at its disposal in its struggle for survival: development of interfirm relations, joint research and development, etc., which holds equally of firms. In a large number of cases, the ability of an industry to develop and organize is the best guarantee a firm has of its own survival.

This chapter focuses on the short-term competitiveness of a country and deals with the effects on the economy when competitiveness changes. Section 11.1 discusses the concept of competitiveness, including the question of how competitiveness may be measured and the actual means available if a change in competitiveness is to be achieved. The effects of competitiveness changes on employment, balance of payments, inflation and income distribution are considered in Sections 11.2 and 11.3.

The economic system contains self-regulatory mechanisms which gradually reduce problems of equilibrium. It therefore seems reasonable to ask whether politico-economic measures are necessary at all: this is the subject of Section 11.4. This also includes an exposition of various equilibrium problems and of the economic policy that will be appropriate for the solution of each individual problem.

11.1 IS COMPETITIVENESS MEASURABLE?

The oil crisis of the seventies inaugurated a long period of time which was characterized by balance of payments deficits in many countries in Western Europe. As *disequilibrium problems*, i.e. balance of payments deficits and unemployment, worsened, the concept of competitiveness became increasingly topical in the politico-economic debate at the time. Low competitiveness was singled out as one of the reasons for the balance of payments deficit, and improved competitiveness became crucial to economic policy. However, the concept of competitiveness includes a range of dimensions that is hard to concretize or define in terms of a single expression.

Put simply, competitiveness expresses the ability of home country firms to compete with foreign firms. This ability rests on several factors. First of all, a firm's level of costs is decisive. This is influenced by wages and interest rate level and also by the exchange rate, which determines the relationship between the costs of the firm in question and those of its foreign competition. Secondly, the level of productivity is important since an increase in the level of productivity decreases unit costs. Thirdly, the attractiveness of the goods in the opinion of consumers crucially depends on the quality and design of the goods produced. Finally, sales efforts also play a part, i.e. the scale of advertising, personal sales work, after-sales service, distribution, etc.

Various *indicators* may be used to measure competitiveness. If the development of competitiveness is to be measured, cost development or changes in export market shares may serve as indicators, but for the purposes of determining whether the level of competitiveness is satisfactory, the development of market shares or relative cost conditions are useless. In this case, the balance of payments is crucial.

11.1.1 A standardized balance of payments

A balance of payments deficit is often associated with a low degree of competitiveness relative to that of other countries. A current account deficit is not a good indicator of competitiveness, however, because it may increase or decrease for reasons that are unrelated to competitiveness.

The development of internal activity, for example, affects the size of the deficit. This has been shown in Figure 11.1, in which the relationship between national product and balance of payments has been illustrated. If the domestic activity level goes down, then the balance of payments will improve. However, this improvement can hardly be characterized as an improvement in competitiveness. In fact, if the domestic recession is sufficiently deep, the country in question will achieve a balance of payments surplus (see point C). Therefore the balance of payments has to be adjusted for current economic conditions. If the total of the balance of payments is calculated on the basis of national product at full employment (point B in Figure 11.1), then this yields a neutral trade cycle standard of competitiveness.

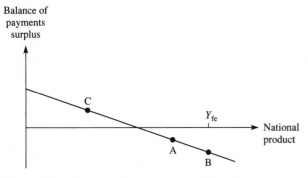

Figure 11.1   Balance of payments and competitiveness

In spite of being unrelated to changes in competitiveness, the composition of demand also affects the balance of payments. This will deteriorate, for example, if a shift in demand from public to private consumption occurs, the import content of the latter being larger than that of the former. Likewise, an international recession or an energy price increase may cause the balance of payments to deteriorate without it being attributable to deteriorating competitiveness. Thus a standardized deficit measures the extent of disequilibrium problems in the economy and, hence, the need for improved competitiveness.

Consequently, a standardized deficit may have to be adjusted now and then for permanent changes in the conditions mentioned. North Sea oil, for example, has led to permanent improvement in the British and Norwegian balances of payments, which in turn have reduced the need for actively changing the competitiveness of these countries. In addition, some countries may wish to run a balance of payments deficit in order to finance industrialization, while others with large external debts may wish to run a surplus in order to repay these debts (see the discussion in Chapter 7).

11.1.2   Market share changes

The development in the *export market share* of a given country may be considered an indicator of the attractiveness of its goods in foreign markets. However, this measurement is not without its problems.

If the market share is calculated in current prices, i.e. in the prices of the current year, a fall in export prices will immediately result in a market share reduction in spite of the fact that goods from the home country have become more competitive. The market share will not increase until the fall in prices results in increased sales.

If the market share is calculated in fixed prices, volume indices have to be used. However, these are usually vitiated by considerable sources of error. Devising a volume index that takes into consideration changes in the quality of furniture, television sets, clothes and cement plants, for example, is a rather problematic task.

If the market share is calculated at a highly aggregate level, then a fall in the share may reflect the fact that the home country largely exports to low-growth markets. In the case of Denmark, for example, this is a problem because a large part of its exports consists of agricultural products, i.e. products with a low degree of income elasticity. Thus the structural distribution of exports on goods and countries influences market share development, but it is a moot point whether a fall in market share should be conceived of as deteriorating competitiveness.

11.1.3   Price and cost development

While a standardized balance of payments and market share changes focus on competitiveness effects, this subsection will concentrate on the causes underlying competitiveness developments.

The attractiveness of home country products relative to foreign products is largely a question of price. Therefore the *relative price development* of home country goods is a more direct measure of competitiveness development. On this view, competitiveness (CP_p) may be defined as follows:

$$CP_p = \frac{E \times P_f}{P} \qquad [1]$$

P_f is a weighted expression of foreign prices calculated in a foreign currency. If this is multiplied by the effective exchange rate (E), the result shows foreign prices in the currency of the home country, which is then related to home country prices (P). A relative decrease in home country prices will improve the competitiveness of the home country, its goods becoming more attractive as a result. This indicator of competitiveness is identical to the *real exchange rate* defined in Chapter 8.

However, this competitiveness indicator is not without its problems either. Above, we mentioned some of the difficulties involved in devising a reliable volume index. Of course, similar difficulties are involved in devising a price index.

In addition, another problematic side of price indices is that changes in competitiveness do not necessarily result in price changes, therefore prices are a poor indicator under such conditions. This state of affairs holds of international markets with *perfect competition*, in which the only price is a well-defined world market price. In such a market, foreign prices, adjusted for exchange rates, always equal domestic price; thus CP_p always equals one.

This problem may be solved by using the development in *relative costs* instead. If wage costs alone are taken into consideration, then the price of a product will equal hourly wages (W) divided by average labour productivity (AP). Inserting this in the price indicator, we obtain the following result:

$$CP_c = E\frac{W_f/AP_f}{W/AP} = E\frac{W_f \times AP}{W \times AP_f} \qquad [2]$$

This *cost indicator* of competitiveness consists of three terms:[*] (1) the effective exchange rate, a devaluation or depreciation resulting in improved competitiveness; (2) relative hourly wages, a relative wage decrease in the home country likewise resulting in improved competitiveness; and (3) relative labour productivity, which improves the competitiveness of the country in which it rises (the fastest).

In practice, the cost indicator, CP_c, is the indicator that is used most often in analyses of competitiveness development, for instance it is the one used by the OECD. Information on wage development is fairly reliable, but measuring labour productivity is rather difficult and subject to considerable uncertainty. As a result, development in labour productivity is often disregarded and to the extent to which this varies among countries an index based solely on hourly wages adjusted for exchange rates will, of course, result in a distorted picture of competitiveness development.

Of course, employers' total wage costs are of interest in connection with competitiveness. These include not only direct wage costs but also indirect wage costs, which may include health insurance, statutory industrial injuries insurance, unemployment insurance, pension contribution, fringe benefits, etc. In countries like France and Germany, a large part of social schemes are financed through statutory contributions from employers. Consequently, direct wage costs have to be adjusted for such wage taxes if the costs are to be compared to those of other countries.

11.1.4 Impacts on competitiveness

Above we considered the issue of measuring development in competitiveness, we will now turn to the issue of influencing this development. In principle, two different approaches may be adopted: an internal approach or an external one.

---

[*] The expression may be rewritten as $cp_c = e + (w_f - w) + (ap - ap_f)$, where a percentage change in a variable is symbolized by a small letter. A percentage change in competitiveness is therefore the sum of a percentage change in exchange rate, foreign excess wage increase and home country excess productivity increase.

The *external approach* consists in devaluating the home country currency, which has the immediate effect of improving competitiveness. Within the EMS framework, exchange rate realignments are permitted if they have been agreed among the ministers of economic affairs from the participating countries and if the economic situation calls for this solution (see Chapter 8).

Such exchange rate changes form part of an *intended* economic policy, but others reflect the fact that, for example, exchange rates between EMS currencies and currencies floating against them change continuously. In what follows, we will be exclusively concerned with intended exchange rate changes and, in particular, with the effects of devaluing a currency. However, these effects are largely symmetrical in the case of a revaluation.

The *internal approach* consists in improving competitiveness by influencing the second and third terms of the above cost indicator, i.e. the development of hourly wages and labour productivity. In this connection, competitiveness is primarily influenced by *incomes policy*, which aims at limiting inflation through direct intervention in wage and price formation. However, part of tax and subsidy policies also affects competitiveness: special sales subsidies, export financing or export guarantee schemes, for example. Likewise, the domestic interest rate affects costs rather significantly, and labour market policy, just like research and development, is of importance in the long run.

Thus the internal approach offers a whole range of various options (supply-side policy), the effects of which differ quite considerably. In what follows, we will analyse the effects of incomes policy in particular, which is also the part of supply-side policy that aims most directly at improving competitiveness.

11.2 EFFECTS ON BALANCE OF PAYMENTS AND EMPLOYMENT

Above we showed that the relationship between domestic prices and foreign ones is influenced by the policies adopted by individual countries with a view to changing their competitiveness. Of course such policies influence import and export prices and, hence, import and export volumes in individual countries. This section discusses the effect of improved competitiveness on prices and volumes in a country's foreign trade and, consequently, on its balance of payments and level of employment.

11.2.1 The Marshall–Lerner condition

Figure 11.2 illustrates the effect of a 20 per cent improvement in the level of competitiveness on exports and imports, respectively. Export price (P_x) and import price (P_m) are stated in foreign currency, *in casu* in DEM. The two markets are assumed to be in equilibrium prior to the change in competitiveness, i.e. they are in point A.

A 20 per cent increase in the level of competitiveness will shift the export supply curve vertically downwards by 20 per cent, domestic costs decreasing in terms of the foreign currency (see Figure 11.2(a)).[*]

---

[*] This does not take into consideration that the improvement in competitiveness is unlikely to reduce exporters' costs of intermediary products by 20 per cent. In the case of a small country, import supply will be highly elastic and the fall in the price of imported goods will be moderate (see Figure 11.2(b)). If this is taken into consideration the supply curve will shift by less.

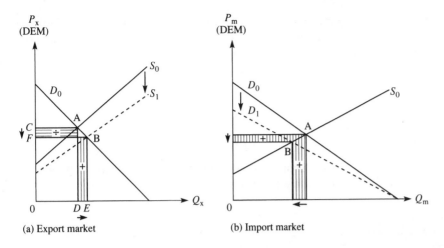

Figure 11.2   Export and import markets under a 20 per cent increase in the level of competitiveness

Since foreign demand for exports (in DEM) remains the same, the export price goes down and the volume increases.

Export revenue, which equals the area of OCAD, may change, too. If price and volume move in opposite directions, the effect on export revenue depends on export demand elasticity. If this is numerically larger than one, the revenue will increase. If it is numerically smaller than one, the revenue will decrease, and, finally, if it equals one, the revenue remains unchanged.

Figure 11.2(b) shows the import market. The supply curve is not affected by the change in competitiveness, the foreign cost level remaining unchanged in terms of the foreign currency. However, the demand curve will shift vertically downwards by 20 per cent. This is because the improvement in competitiveness reduces the domestic price level by 20 per cent relative to the foreign one. Therefore, if home country consumers, firms, etc., are to buy the same volume of imports, then the price has to fall correspondingly in terms of the foreign currency. To the extent that the increase in competitiveness increases the national product, the volume of imports will also increase and import demand will shift to the right. If this is taken into consideration, then the demand curve will shift by less than 20 per cent.

As regards the change in *import revenue* in terms of the foreign currency, the conclusion is unequivocal: the improvement in competitiveness, reducing import price (in DEM) and the volume of imports, causes import expenditure to decrease in terms of the foreign currency. Consequently, the goods and services balance $(X - M)$ will improve if export demand elasticity is elastic. However, this condition is too narrow since, as was shown above, import expenditure decreases at the same time. It is possible to show that it is sufficient for the sum of export and import demand elasticities to be larger than one, the so-called *Marshall–Lerner condition* (see Robinson 1947):

$$|e_x| + |e_m| > 1 \qquad\qquad [3]$$

Strictly speaking, this condition presupposes that supply elasticities are infinitely large and that the goods and services account is in equilibrium in the initial situation. If the initial situation involves a disequilibrum, the condition is as follows:

$$|e_x| + \frac{M}{X}|e_m| > 1$$

where M and X are the value of imports and exports, respectively, in terms of the foreign currency and prior to the change in competitiveness. If M and X are stated in the domestic currency, the condition is the following:

$$\frac{X}{M}|e_x| + |e_m| > 1$$

11.2.2 Elasticity optimism

Table 11.1 presents values of export and import elasticities of trade in manufactured goods, for selected countries. The table shows some general features, e.g.

1. Elasticities are larger in the long run than in the short run.
2. The sum of long-term export and import demand elasticities is larger than one, i.e. the Marshall–Lerner condition is satisfied. This, however, is not the case in the very short run (impact).

The fact that imports in a number of industrialized countries largely consist of intermediary products, capital goods, etc., for which no internal substitutes are available may explain why export elasticities are typically larger than import elasticities. As regards exports, the substitution possibilities available to foreign buyers are often so extensive that the elasticities are correspondingly large.

Industries in small countries are now and then said to be characterized by niche production, which allegedly is rather insensitive to international competition. On this view, domestic cost development has little bearing on the success rate of industries. However, even if niche firms have obtained considerable shares of markets of limited size and even if the most important competitive parameters are assumed to be those of product development, design, quality, etc., rather than price, there are still limits to the excess price obtainable. As is known from the theory of monopoly and monopolistic competition, a profit-maximizing firm is always to be found somewhere on the elastic part of the demand curve.

Figure 11.3 illustrates the case of a (representative) exporter facing a declining demand

Table 11.1 Price elasticities in international trade in manufactured goods

Country	Exports		Imports	
	Short run (1 year)	Long run	Short run (1 year)	Long run
United States	0.48	1.67	1.06	1.06
Japan	1.01	1.61	0.72	0.97
France	0.48	1.25	0.49	0.60
Italy	0.56	0.64	0.94	0.94
Canada	0.40	0.71	0.72	0.72
Netherlands	0.49	0.89	1.22	1.22
Austria	0.71	1.37	0.36	0.80
Norway	0.74	1.49	0.01	0.71
Switzerland	0.42	0.73	0.25	0.25

Source: Artus and Knight (1984).

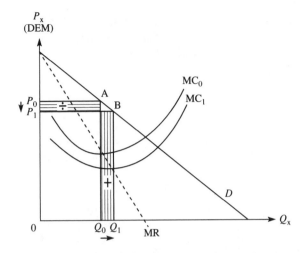

Figure 11.3 Competitiveness improvement and exports under imperfect competition

function. On the assumption of profit-maximizing behaviour (MC = MR), price and volume prior to the improvement in competitiveness are P_0 and Q_0, respectively. As, in the eyes of other countries, an improvement in competitiveness corresponds to a cost reduction, the marginal cost curve, MC_0, will shift to MC_1. The result will be a decrease in price and an increase in the volume sold. However, since the price–volume combinations prior to the change (A) and following it (B) are both to be found on the elastic part of the demand curve, export revenue will increase. Thus the niche hypothesis cannot be used, for example, as an argument against devaluation nor against a tight incomes policy.

One reason for item 2, i.e. the fact that elasticities increase over time, is that the price advantage that an improvement in competitiveness offers exporters will not affect volumes until foreign buyers have had time to analyse new offers, i.e. a time lag results. Thus, in spite of being large in the long run, elasticities may be rather small in the (very) short run. Consequently, the Marshall–Lerner condition may not be satisfied in the (very) short run. In such a case, the development in goods and services items, for example after a devaluation, will assume the shape of a 'J', as shown in Figure 11.4.

The J curve expresses a particular problem connected with changing national competitiveness: patience is essential. A certain risk exists that, for example, one devaluation may trigger

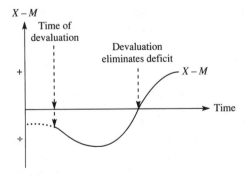

Figure 11.4 The J-curve effect

another one because the balance of payments deteriorates in the short run. This will cause competitiveness to improve more than necessary for redressing the balance of payments in the long run. Thus the danger exists that a short-term overreaction will occur which will destabilize economic policy

11.2.3 Terms of trade and competitiveness

Figure 11.2 shows that an improvement in competitiveness influences both export and import prices. This affects the international terms of trade (TOT), which are defined as the relationship between an export price index and an import price index:

$$\text{TOT} = \frac{P_\text{x}}{P_\text{m}} \quad\quad\quad [4]$$

In what follows we will describe the economic reality underlying a change in the terms of trade. An improvement in a country's terms of trade means that in exchange for a given export volume and, hence, a given input of factors of production the country may acquire more goods from abroad, which, *ceteris paribus*, is an advantage. Conversely, the essence of deteriorating terms of trade is that in exchange for a given import volume the country will have to sell a larger volume of exports. This will lead to a decrease in the country's real income. Whether an improvement in competitiveness yields improved terms of trade depends on whether the import price in Figure 11.2 falls more than the export price, and this depends on the demand and supply elasticities of exports and imports.

If the improved competitiveness is due to a devaluation, then export and import prices will increase in terms of the home country currency since after the devaluation the prices in Figure 11.2 will have to be calculated on the basis of an increased exchange rate. However, as both the numerator and the denominator of the terms of trade have to be adjusted by the devaluation percentage, it is irrelevant whether the terms of trade effect is calculated on the basis of domestic or foreign prices.

Typically, devaluation decreases TOT. However, this does not mean that devaluation is inappropriate with respect to obtaining a balance of payments improvement. When export and import prices change, volumes will also change, and since the Marshall–Lerner condition is satisfied (see Table 11.1), the balance of payments improves.

11.2.4 Employment effect

However, the balance of payments effect that is predicted by the elasticity analysis is not the final effect. The change in competitiveness affects national product and employment and thus causes a derived effect on imports. Figure 11.5 illustrates this.

Let us assume that in the initial situation the country has a balance of payments deficit of PESOS 10bn, which corresponds to point A in Figure 11.5. On the assumption that the elasticity condition is satisfied, an improvement in competitiveness of 20 per cent, for example, will result in a balance of payments improvement, say, of PESOS 15bn (AB). This of course means that the $(X-M)$ curve shifts vertically by PESOS 15bn to $(X-M)_1$.

Through a multiplier process, the demand increase of PESOS 15bn will increase national product to OC. As a result, imports will increase by the marginal propensity to import multiplied by the increase in income. This reduces the immediate balance of payments improvement shown in Figure 11.5 from PESOS 15bn to PESOS 10bn. At the same time any

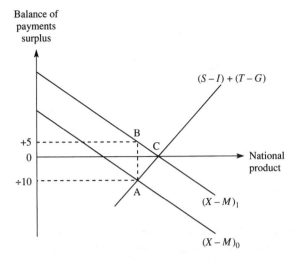

Figure 11.5   Competitiveness and national product

deficit on public budgets $(T-G)$ will be reduced since a national product increase results in larger tax receipts and less unemployment benefit expenditure. In addition, the increase in net exports has an interest rate-lowering effect, which stimulates investments and national product (see the *ISLM* analysis in Figure 10.13).

Thus a policy of this kind, which is intended to change national competitiveness, both increases the level of employment and reduces budgetary and balance of payments deficits. This distinguishes it from fiscal and monetary policies in that it does not involve conflicting goals.

If there is full employment in the initial situation, however, then the policy has to be supplemented with a tight fiscal or monetary policy which releases the resources needed by the industries that face international competition. This appears from the following national account identity:

$$Y = C + I + G + (X - M) \qquad [5]$$

If Y is at its maximum level, which corresponds to full employment, then $(X-M)$ can only rise if $(C+I+G)$ simultaneously fall equally as much.

11.3   EFFECTS ON INFLATION AND DISTRIBUTION

As was mentioned in Section 11.1, competitiveness may be improved either through an internal approach or through an external one. While the two approaches have the same balance of payments and employment effects, their price level effects differ. Consequently, their distribution effects also differ.

11.3.1   Direct and derived effects on price

Figure 11.6 illustrates both direct and indirect price effects of respectively incomes policy (a) and devaluation (b). The AS curve represents short-term aggregate supply and AD is the corresponding aggregate demand curve. The reason for the upward slope of the AS curve is partly identical to the one that we find for the upward slope of the supply curves of individual firms. In the short run, an increase in production has to be the result of more labour being used

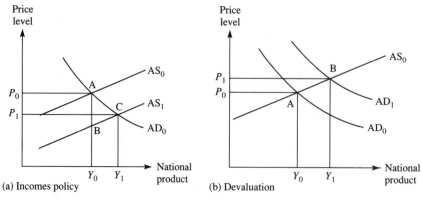

Figure 11.6   Direct and derived price effects

at a given capital stock, which puts the law of diminishing returns into operation. The decreasing marginal productivity increases marginal costs to firms, and the increase in costs will be reflected in prices. Like the supply curves of individual firms, the AS curve is constructed for given wage and productivity levels.

The explanation of the AS curve is the same in the case of both open and closed economies. The AD curve, however, needs further explanation in the case of an open economy. In particular, in addition to interest rate and real balance effects, the *competitiveness effect* is of importance.[*] If the price of home country goods goes up while that of foreign ones remains the same, then consumers in the home country will shift part of their purchases to foreign goods, i.e. the volume of imports will also go up. At the same time consumers in other countries will reduce their purchases of goods from the home country and buy goods from other countries instead. Consequently, the volume of home country exports will fall. Both these factors reduce net exports and thus contribute to the downward slope of the AD curve.

In Figure 11.6, there is equilibrium at point A in the initial situation, where the price level is P_0 and the national product Y_0. If an incomes policy is pursued that reduces all costs by 10 per cent, then the aggregate supply curve **shifts downwards** by 10 per cent, i.e. by the segment AB in Figure 11.6(a), to AS_1. GDP does not change immediately but the economy gradually moves to point C, with national income increasing to Y_1. This triggers a derived price increase, which results from the movement along the aggregate supply curve from point B to point C.

Figure 11.6(b) illustrates the corresponding effects in the goods market in connection with an exchange rate change. If the devaluation does not affect home country costs, then the GNP deflator remains unchanged and there will be no direct price effect on the AS curve.

By contrast, the devaluation will cause aggregate demand to shift to the right to AD_1. This is because, at the home country price level of P_0, the devaluation increases the volume of exports and reduces demand for imports (see Figure 11.2). If the Marshall–Lerner condition is satisfied, net exports $(X-M)$ increase and this will lead to an increase in aggregate demand. The resulting equilibrium in the goods market will be at point B, and if it is a devaluation by 10 per cent, then the increase in national product will be the same as in the case of the incomes policy in Figure 11.6(a). Therefore a derived price increase similarly results from the movement along the aggregate supply curve from point A to point B.

---

[*] The interest rate effect emerges when an increased price level increases turnover and, hence, demand for money. The real balance effect emerges when an increased price level reduces the value of citizens' claims on the government, the central bank and other countries. The interest rate effect particularly affects investments, while the real balance effect reduces private consumption.

Even though the devaluation has no direct price effect on the GNP deflator, a rise in consumer prices will take place. As was mentioned above, the reason for this is that home country import prices increase by the devaluation percentage. If the import share of consumption is 30 per cent, then the increase in consumer prices will be 3 per cent, which is equivalent to an immediate fall in real wages.

Likewise, an incomes policy which reduces home country costs by 10 per cent will reduce consumer prices by only 7 per cent. Thus an immediate fall in real wages by 3 per cent also results in this case.

11.3.2   Derived cost increase

In the case of a devaluation, the immediate increase in consumer prices and the resulting temporary inflation present no genuine problem. In fact, the point of a devaluation is precisely to have the change in prices stimulate consumers to switch from foreign goods to domestically produced ones. By contrast, the effect on domestic costs is crucial to wage competitiveness. If the domestic cost level is not affected, then the entire devaluation becomes a real devaluation and competitiveness improves correspondingly regardless of the size of direct and derived price increases (see equation (2) above).

However, fear of wage impacts has prevented numerous governments from applying the devaluation tool against a balance of payments deficit. Two factors in particular point to such impacts.

Firstly, an increase in consumer prices will cause the real earnings of employees to fall. The reaction in the labour market may be a demand for compensation, i.e. for higher earnings, and if the demand is met, this will start an inflationary process. Of course the process will be triggered automatically if wage agreements include cost-of-living clauses.

The derived increase in earnings will result in further increases in domestic prices, which may start the wage–price spiral. This has caused extensive fear that wage impacts will be so heavy that within a short period the entire advantage of devaluating will be swallowed up by corresponding domestic cost increases. Therefore the use of *statutory instruments* including a tight incomes policy is often considered a precondition for a successful devaluation.

Secondly, the devaluation will increase the level of employment. If the labour market is in equilibrium in the initial situation, then the devaluation will lead to a disequilibrium which will cause nominal increases in employees' earnings. Therefore, in a situation with full employment the devaluation needs to be supplemented with a tight fiscal policy in order to keep wage costs at rest.

The discussion above shows that restoring a balance of payments is much more difficult in a situation with full employment than otherwise since fiscal tightening further reduces disposable real earnings. In a situation with heavy cyclical unemployment, however, a balance of payments improvement resulting from such competitiveness-changing policies will make an expansionary fiscal policy possible, which may reduce the decrease in after-tax real earnings.

11.3.3   Aspects of redistribution

When devaluation and incomes policy reduce domestic costs relative to the price of goods traded internationally, an increase in profits will occur in industries facing international competition, i.e. in industries in which firms either export or compete with imports. In the long run, the expansion of these industries will eliminate such excess profits unless, of course, the firms are monopolists. Thus, in the short run, competitiveness-changing policies reduce the proportion of payroll costs in these industries and, hence, in the entire economy.

The expansion increases the demand for labour specifically for these industries. This may force up earnings in fields in which structural lack of labour results. Thus employees in these industries will also benefit from the increase in profits.

If the balance of payments deficit is the result of domestic costs increasing faster than foreign costs, then profits and earnings increases in the industries facing international competition have been smaller than in other domestic industries. In this case, a competitiveness improvement may be considered a return to normal conditions.

Improved competitiveness will result in losses on loans in foreign currency. In the case of a devaluation, debt service on foreign currency loans increases in terms of the domestic currency by the devaluation percentage. In the case of incomes policy, debt service on foreign currency loans remains unchanged in terms of the domestic currency but since incomes decrease the real burden on these loans increases. Of course claims in foreign currency yield gains when competitiveness improves.

As was mentioned in Chapter 9, companies in high-interest countries obtain an advantage by borrowing in foreign currency. Such an interest advantage reflects the risk of devaluation and of related exchange rate losses. Thus exchange rate losses resulting from devaluation do not in full constitute losses to the firms concerned since these have partly included such losses in their borrowing costs.

Although a devaluation of 10 per cent increases foreign currency loans in terms of the domestic currency by 10 per cent, society's debt burden does not necessarily increase by 10 per cent since export prices also increase. If foreign debt increases by 10 per cent and export prices by 7 per cent, then an increase in the volume of exports of only 3 per cent will be sufficient for repayment of the debt increase, which means that the real burden increases by only 3 per cent. This also shows that firms competing internationally frequently reap profit increases which by far exceed the increases in foreign debt service.

To the extent that a realized improvement in national competitiveness is unexpected, it will result in redistribution of domestic fixed-interest loans. Devaluation will cause losses to creditors, since prices increase, while incomes policy will cause losses to debtors, since prices will decrease. In general, firms and their owners are net debtors, and, consequently, a devaluation gives them a further advantage. By contrast, employees are net creditors through their pension funds, so incomes policy provides them with creditor gains.

11.4   COMPETITIVENESS-CHANGING POLICY: WHY AND HOW?

In the preceding sections, we considered the most significant effects of changing competitiveness. In what follows, we will address the issues of whether intervention of this kind is needed and of how competitiveness-changing policy may be coordinated with other economic policy.

11.4.1   Market sluggishness

Firstly, we will consider the market forces that automatically start operating when the economy is in disequilibrium. Let us assume that in the initial situation a country, the home country, is in both internal and external equilibrium. Further, we will assume that the home country interest rate and rate of inflation are the same as in other countries. The home country now experiences a fall in its volume of exports, which causes a decrease in foreign exchange supply. Alternatively, we might have considered a fall in the volume of private capital imports, e.g. one that resulted from an increase in the foreign interest rate (note arrow 10 in Figure 11.7). The current account of the balance of payments and exchange market equilibrium are restored through three mechanisms.

Firstly, an *incomes adjustment mechanism* will start to operate. When the volume of exports goes down, domestic product also goes down, and so does, by implication, the volume of imports. Consequently, the current account deteriorates by less than the volume of exports (see arrows 1 and 2 in Figure 11.7).

Secondly, a *liquidity effect* operates. When the volume of exports and national product decrease, the interest rate is put under downward pressure, which results in capital exports. Consequently, the home country central bank has to supply the foreign exchange necessary to maintain the exchange rate. This will drain the monetary base by an amount of the same size as the balance of payments deficit; compare this with the discussion of the liquidity effect of the balance of payments in Chapter 10. This in turn leads to a fall in the money supply, which will cause the domestic interest rate to rise (arrows 11 and 12).

An interest rate increase has two effects which both contribute to reducing excess demand for foreign currency: (1) an increase in the rate of interest reduces real investments and, consequently, forces down national product (arrows 13 and 14), which in turn reduces the volume of imports and thus improves the current account of the balance of payments; and (2) an increase in the domestic rate of interest causes a fall in the volume of capital exports (arrow 15). In particular, it is worth noting that the decrease in the money supply does not stop until the deficit in the exchange market has been eliminated. It is not until then that an equilibrium has been restored between demand for and supply of foreign exchange at the given rate of exchange, so until this point the home country will face deterioration of its international liquidity.

Thirdly, a *price adjustment mechanism* steps in. When the level of activity falls, the rate of increase of domestic prices and that of earnings also fall. This improves competitiveness, which is of benefit to exports and import-competing production. Thus price adjustment reinforces incomes adjustment and the liquidity effect (see arrows to 3 to 8 in Figure 11.7).

In sum, a balance of payments deficit affects the incomes inflation rate and money supply and in so doing it sets various adjustment processes in the economy in motion which help eliminate the deficit.

A similar conclusion holds as regards internal equilibrium. The fall in the level of employment which results from the fall in the volume of exports and investments (arrows 1 and 14) is ultimately neutralized because the international competitiveness of business becomes ever stronger as long as the rate of increase of domestic price and earnings is lower than that of other countries. If sufficient time elapses, the final result of these automatic market forces may be internal as well as external equilibrium. However, the sluggishness of the automatic mechanisms will often speak in favour of a politically controlled adjustment process.

11.4.2 Choice of economic policy

Chapter 10 discussed the conflicting goals involved in pursuing a fiscal policy, which does not allow both a balance of payments equilibrium and full employment to be secured. However, competitiveness-changing policy is not capable of securing both goals in any given situation either. The problem was briefly touched upon above, where we mentioned that such a policy would have to be supplemented with tight fiscal policy in a situation with full employment.

As a rule, realizing two goals requires two different means; Figure 11.8 illustrates this problem. The vertical curve (fe), which intersects the income axis at the point where full employment income obtains, and the horizontal income axis (Y) divide the figure into four areas whose economic balance problems differ.

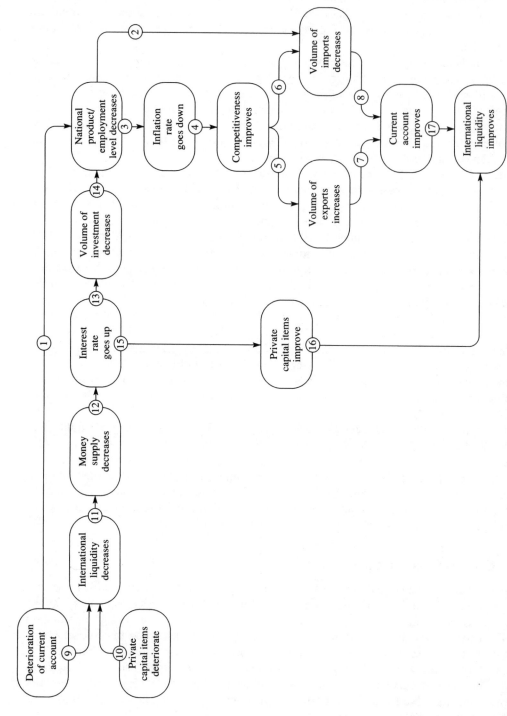

Figure 11.7 Automatic balance of payments adjustment under fixed exchange rates

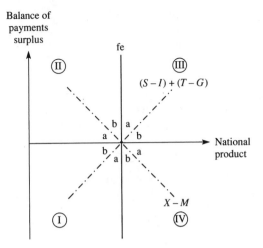

Figure 11.8 Fiscal and exchange rate policy

In area I, there is unemployment and a balance of payments deficit. The figure shows that the economic policy relevant for handling these problems involves a devaluation which causes the $(X-M)$ curve to shift upwards, and that in area Ib this policy has to be supplemented with an expansionary fiscal policy, whereas a tight policy is needed in area Ia. In the early eighties, Denmark was in area Ib, which meant that competitiveness-improving policies could be accompanied by an expansionary fiscal or monetary policy.

In area III, the situation is precisely the reverse, with both inflation and a balance of payments surplus. In this case, economic policy has to give priority to a revaluation supplemented with a fiscal adjustment. The adjustment needed depends on whether the economy is in area IIIa or IIIb. During various periods, Germany has been in this situation and consequently revalued its currency.

In area II, there is unemployment and a balance of payments surplus. This was the situation in The Netherlands and Germany in the mid-eighties and in Denmark in the early nineties. In such a situation, the right medicine is an expansionary fiscal policy supplemented with exchange rate policy. Whether the currency should be revalued or devalued depends on the size of the balance of payments surplus.

In area IV, we find inflation and a balance of payments deficit. This was the situation of several European countries in the seventies. The economic policy required is that of a tight fiscal policy supplemented with an exchange rate realignment, the nature of which depends on whether economic activity is in area IVa or IVb.

Figure 11.8 shows, firstly, that two different means are usually required for the realization of two goals. Only when given a position on one of the two broken curves will one means be sufficient to achieve both internal and external equilibrium. Table 11.2 summarizes the economic problems involved in each of the four cases and the economic policies required to solve them.

Secondly, Figure 11.8. shows that different problems require different solutions. The objection is widely raised, for example, that devaluation and incomes policy are of no use if other countries pursue the same policies. However, only countries with a balance of payments deficit need to restore their competitiveness. Countries with a balance of payments surplus typically have to revalue their currency or to pursue an expansionary economic policy. That some countries run surpluses is a consequence of the fact that any country's balance of

Table 11.2 Economic problems and relevant policies

	Economic problem		Economic policy	
Area	External	Internal	Primary	Supplementary
I	Deficit	Unemployment	Devaluation	Fiscal adjustment
II	Surplus	Unemployment	Expansionary fiscal policy	Exchange rate adjustment
III	Surplus	Inflation	Revaluation	Fiscal adjustment
IV	Deficit	Inflation	Tight fiscal policy	Exchange rate adjustment

payments deficit has to be offset by corresponding surpluses in other countries. Therefore improved competitiveness in deficit countries will contribute to reducing any disequilibrium in international trade.

SUMMARY

1. Competitiveness may be defined at various levels of aggregation and in various time perspectives. Chapter eleven focuses on short-run national competitiveness.
2. In order to measure competiveness, a standardized balance of payments must be defined. Changes in competitiveness may be measured in terms of change in export market shares, and this is determined by the relative wage development, the effective exchange rate and relative labour productivity. This leaves the nation with an external and an internal approach to improved competitiveness.
3. Whether improved competitiveness translates into an improved goods and services balance depends on whether or not the Marshall–Lerner condition is met. In general it is met, which gives rise to 'elasticity optimism'. Elasticities increase over time, following a change in competitiveness—the J-curve effect.
4. Both exchange rate changes and incomes policy affect inflation. Devaluation increases prices, and often has further wage impacts, which has prompted statutory instruments such as an incomes policy.
5. Distribution is changed in favour of profits in the international sector of the economy, and by an increased debt burden on loans in foreign currency. The debt burden on the economy as a whole, however, is increased far less. In general, creditors will lose and debtors gain from an improvement in national competitiveness.
6. If the economy is in disequilibrium then income, liquidity and price adjustments will redress it. However, the process takes time, which justifies active economic policy.
7. A combination of fiscal policy and competitiveness-changing policies may remedy any combination of external and internal disequilibrium.

REFERENCES AND FURTHER READING

Artus, J. R. and M. D. Knight (1984), 'Issues in the assessment of exchange rates of industrial countries', Occasional Paper 29, IMF, Washington, D.C., July.
Lerner, A. (1944), *The Economics of Control*, Macmillan, London.
Marshall, A. (1923), *Money, Credit, and Commerce*, Macmillan, London.
Robinson, Joan (1947), 'The foreign exchanges', in *Essays in the Theory of Employment*, Macmillan, London.

TWELVE

ECONOMIC POLICY UNDER FLOATING EXCHANGE RATES

In the preceding chapters we showed that a balance of payments problem may be solved by means of incomes policy or devaluation. However, instead of devaluating occasionally, a country may opt for the short-cut of letting the exchange rate of its currency float, in which case using the exchange rate as a politico-economic tool becomes impossible. As will be shown below, a floating currency does not automatically secure equilibrium on the current account of the balance of payments but only on the autonomous items.

During the currency crisis in the early seventies, the major industrialized countries chose to let their currencies float, and since that time the major currencies have been floating against each other (see Chapter 8). Figure 12.1 shows the development of the value of the US$ from 1960 onwards against DEM, JPY, £ sterling and DKK. After 1973, exchange rate variability has been considerably more marked than it was before that time. From 1960 until 1973, fluctuations were minor ones, which was in accordance with the Bretton Woods fixed exchange rate system in force at the time. Since 1973 exchange rate fluctuations have been substantial. The period of 1980 to 1985 is particularly noteworthy because the value of the US$ rose considerably against the European currencies shown in the figure, but it rose little against the JPY. It should be noted that even though the DEM curve does not rise very much from 1980 to 1985, as compared to those of £ sterling and DKK, its percentage rise is above 60 per cent, the exchange rate level being low in 1980. However, the value of the US$ increases somewhat more against the DKK, which was devalued against the DEM during this period. After 1985 the situation gradually changed so that in 1992 exchange rates against the US$ largely corresponded to those of 1980. Of course the large exchange rate fluctuations after 1973 and the resulting market-based fluctuations in the competitiveness of individual countries put the minor adjustments made under fixed exchange rate systems into perspective.

In this chapter and the following one, we will consider the advantages and disadvantages of floating exchange rates. The analysis in Section 12.1 aims at answering the question of whether exchange rate flexibility reduces the international transmission of trade cycles. Section 12.2 explains why monetary policy is more effective and, as a result, more extensively used by countries with floating exchange rates than fiscal policy, while the ineffectiveness of fiscal policy is explained in Section 12.3. Section 12.4 compares the effects of monetary and fiscal policies under floating exchange rates. The section shows that fiscal policy is the better means in certain employment and balance of payments situations while in other situations monetary policy is to be preferred, and that sometimes an economy may benefit from combining the two. Finally, Section 12.5 provides an analysis of the reasons for the large fluctuations seen under floating

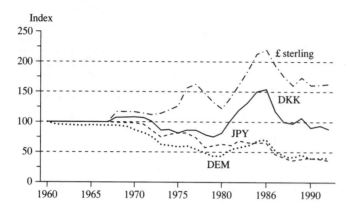

Figure 12.1   Exchange rate development against the US$ in four industrialized countries, 1960–92
Source: OECD.

exchange rates and, in addition, the section discusses whether this is a decisive argument against floating exchange rates. Except for its final section this chapter applies the same method as the previous ones—the comparative-static analysis. This means that we compare initial and final equilibrium, but not the dynamic paths in between.

Like the two preceding chapters, this present one focuses on the problems of a small country. In Chapter 14 we will broaden our perspective to include large countries as well. In addition, the present chapter is based on the assumption that wages are not affected by the domestic activity level. Consequently, nominal exchange rate changes are also real ones. Therefore our analyses are based on a short-term view. In Chapter 13 we will include medium- and long-term views, which allow for price and wage flexibility.

12.1   INTERNATIONAL TRANSMISSION OF FLUCTUATIONS

On the basis of economic theory, the assumption was widely made in the sixties that transition to full exchange rate flexibility would cause international transmission of trade cycles to cease, i.e. would cause a state of *immunity*. This contrasts sharply with the analysis in Chapter 10, which showed that under fixed exchange rates economic activity will spread internationally. The economic theories and the reality of the sixties were strongly characterized by international capital immobility; in fact, capital immobility is still characteristic of a large number of less industrialized countries. In what follows, we will first present the reasoning underlying the argument for immunity and then consider some factors that, nevertheless, cause transmission.

12.1.1   Immunity without capital movements

Under floating exchange rates a country may be immune to external disturbances if international capital movements are insignificant. Figure 12.2 illustrates this. In the initial situation, the domestic economy in Figure 12.2(a) is at point A, where the current account of the balance of payments is in equilibrium. An increase in exports caused by an international upswing will shift the balance of payments curve to $(X-M)_1$. Under fixed exchange rates the new equilibrium point will be B, where the current account of the balance of payments shows a surplus.

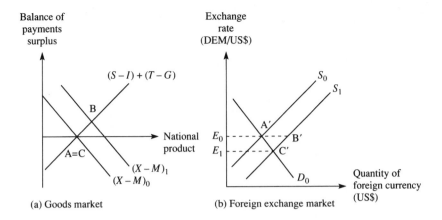

Figure 12.2   Effect of an increase in exports under floating exchange rates: no capital movements

Under floating exchange rates the increase in exports will affect the exchange rate (see the exchange market illustrated in Figure 12.2(b), where the foreign currency is US$ and the domestic currency is DEM). At first, the equilibrium point is A', given the exchange rate of E_0. The increase in exports increases the supply of foreign exchange to S_1. Given the exchange rate of E_0, the resulting excess supply of foreign currency will correspond to A'B', which under fixed exchange rates will be bought by the central bank but under floating exchange rates will force the exchange rate down to E_1 and thus shift the equilibrium point to C'. This appreciation of the DEM will deteriorate the sales conditions of German industries facing international competition and therefore the balance of payments curve will not shift to $(X-M)_1$ but will remain at $(X-M)_0$. This follows from the fact that current items have to be in equilibrium when capital mobility is non-existent. Therefore, if an increase in exports causes a potential balance of payments surplus, then the currency appreciates and prevents the emergence of the surplus.

Consequently, we may conclude that an export shock has no effect on production and employment. Under the assumptions made, the economy is isolated from international trade cycles.

12.1.2   Immunity under capital movements

Under the assumption that the international interest rate, i_f, and exchange rate expectations, e^e, remain unchanged, i.e. the expected return on assets denominated in foreign currency remains the same, the above conclusion holds even if capital flows freely among countries. This situation has been analysed in the *IS/LM* diagram shown in Figure 12.3.

Compared to the analysis of the situation under fixed exchange rates, the new aspect of this *ISLM* analysis is that exchange rate changes cause the *IS* curve to shift, net exports $(X-M)$ depending on real exchange rates. Real depreciation (appreciation) will shift the *IS* curve to the right (left). This argument presupposes, however, that the Marshall–Lerner condition is satisfied (see Chapter 11).

If point A in Figure 12.3 is taken to be the initial equilibrium point, then at a given exchange rate an increase in exports will cause the *IS* curve to shift from IS_0 to IS_1. If i_f and e^e are unaffected, then the uncovered interest parity, $i=i_f+e^e$ (see Chapter 9), predicts that the domestic interest rate also remains unaffected. In the case of a small country, a constant i_f is a realistic assumption. We assume that $e^e=0$ in *final* equilibrium. This corresponds to an

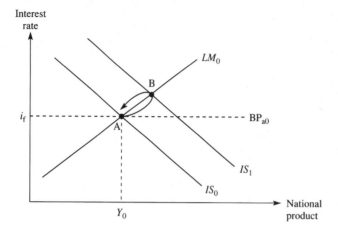

Figure 12.3 Effect of an increase in exports under floating exchange rates: perfect capital mobility and $e^e = 0$

assumption of *static formation of expectations*, so that the actual exchange rate represents the best guess of the market on the future exchange rate, $E^e = E$.

Under floating exchange rates the autonomous items of the balance of payments are always in equilibrium, which explains why domestic money supply is not affected by the exchange market. Consequently, the *LM* curve is not affected by the increase in exports.* Only the exchange rate is able to restore equilibrium in the goods market, as well as in the money and exchange markets. An appreciation will cause the *IS* curve to revert to IS_0, which restores equilibrium at A, but at a higher value of the domestic currency.

It is important to note that under fixed exchange rates the position of the *LM* curve is determined endogenously, as no single country is able to control both its money supply and its exchange rate. Consequently, equilibrium obtains in the points of intersection of the *IS* and BP_a curves. However, under floating exchange rates, control of the money supply is regained, and since the exchange rate is endogenous the position of the *IS* curve is determined endogenously. As a result, equilibrium obtains in the point of intersection of *LM* and BP_a curves. It should be emphasized that the increase in exports and the derived increase in the interest rate will cause an appreciation. In the period of adjustment, in which the interest rate is higher than i_f, a currency depreciation will be expected because $e^e > 0$.

12.1.3 Transmission—all the same

Experience since 1973—a period during which exchange rates have been floating more or less freely—shows, nevertheless, that trade cycles still spread internationally. Several factors may account for this. Firstly, exchange rates have not been moving freely consistently throughout the period: floating has been managed because central banks have intervened on the market, buying or selling currency. This has particularly been the case since September 1985, when the five leading industrial countries entered the so-called Plaza agreement, committing themselves to control their mutual exchange rates through coordinated intervention (intervention on the

---

* This is not strictly true as appreciation of the domestic currency reduces the domestic consumer price level and, hence, the demand for money, which causes the *LM* curve to shift to the right.

exchange market). The primary purpose of this commitment was to exert influence on the balance of payments disequilibria of the countries involved (see Chapter 14).

Secondly, the way in which trade cycles are accompanied by interest rate changes are of importance. If an upturn in the United States, for example, is accompanied by an American interest rate increase, then the increase in American imports will be accompanied by an influx of capital. This will either reduce the appreciation of other currencies against the US\$ or eliminate this appreciation entirely. Therefore the $(X-M)$ curve in Figure 12.2(a) or the IS_1 curve in Figure 12.3 will not shift back to their initial positions and, consequently, transmission will result. If the American interest rate increase is considerable relative to the domestic increase in exports, capital will flow to the United States and not from the States. In this case, the domestic currency will depreciate, but in both cases trade cycles are transmitted to other countries.

Thirdly, the increase in exports may affect e^e, i.e. exchange rate expectations, preventing the economy from returning to the equilibrium point A in Figure 12.3. If the increase in exports is considered not to be permanent, but *temporary*, this may lead to expectations that the exchange rate will revert to its initial level when exports once again decrease. During the export boom such depreciation expectations may cause the interest rate to increase, compare with $i = i_f + e^e$. This means that in an IS/LM diagram, like the one in Figure 12.4, the BP_a curve will periodically shift upwards, e.g. to BP_{a1}, when the currency appreciates. At a given LM curve, C becomes the equilibrium point, IS_1 reverting to IS_2 instead of IS_0. The reason for the transmission to the domestic economy is that the expectations of depreciation limit the actual appreciation and, as a result, the increase in exports is not fully neutralized. This means that as long as the export booms there will, in the equilibrium point C, be expectations of a depreciation.

Since one or several of these provisos are usually in force in real-life situations, a small country will, under floating exchange rates, receive economic shocks from other countries. At this point it seems reasonable to pose the question of whether monetary and fiscal policies can usefully serve to dampen external and internal shocks.

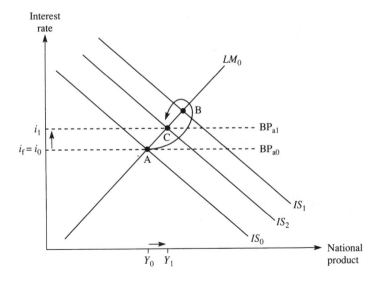

Figure 12.4   Transmission under expectations of depreciation

12.2 MONETARY POLICY

The liberalization of capital movements which has taken place since the Second World War has gradually weakened the monetary autonomy of countries with fixed exchange rates (see the discussion of this subject in Chapter 10). Interest rates have been linked to the international interest rate level and monetary policy has gradually become a question of controlling capital movements relative to other countries and, hence, of controlling currency reserves. The position of monetary policy under floating exchange rates is a different one. In such a case, monetary expansion will be speeded by the exchange market, which will reinforce the increase in income. Thus while the efficiency of fiscal policy decreases under freely floating exchange rates (see Section 12.3), that of monetary policy increases. In large part this explains why monetary policy has again occupied a prominent position in economic policy after the collapse of the fixed exchange rate system and why the breakthrough of monetarism, which attaches great importance to monetary policy, occurred in the seventies.

Figure 12.5 illustrates the monetary autonomy of a small open country: the international mobility of capital and the flexibility of exchange rates determine the degree of autonomy. Capital mobility is indicated on the horizontal axis while exchange rate flexibility is indicated on the vertical axis.

The combination of fixed exchange rates and extremely low capital mobility is one that prevailed immediately after the Second World War. This allowed individual countries extensive freedom of action in the pursuit of independent monetary policies. The narrow restrictions on capital movements, for example, made it possible for individual countries to pursue expansionary policies for the sake of internal equilibrium.

As appears from the figure, transition to more freely floating exchange rates and liberal-

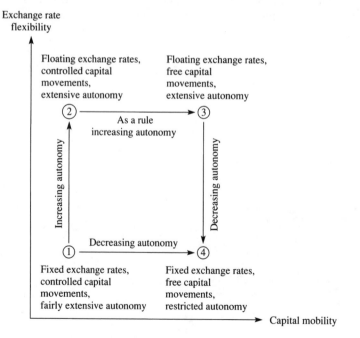

Figure 12.5 Monetary autonomy
Source: Det Økonomiske Råd: Dansk økonomi, September 1985.

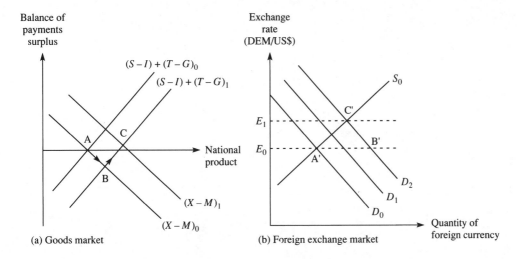

Figure 12.6   Expansionary monetary policy under floating exchange rates

ization of international capital movements increase monetary freedom of action. This is shown in Figure 12.6, in which point A is the initial situation in the goods market and point A' is the initial situation in the exchange market. The current account of the balance of payments is in equilibrium and, hence, the capital items are in equilibrium at the exchange rate of E_0.

If the monetary policy pursued is expansionary, e.g. the German central bank buys bonds from the private sector, then the interest rate will drop, which will have two effects:

1. The demand for investments will increase, which will cause the $(S-I)+(T-G)$ curve to shift to the right. Given an unaltered exchange rate (E_0), the resulting equilibrium will be at point B, i.e. income will be larger and there will be a deficit on the current account of the balance of payments. At the same time, the increase in imports will increase demand for foreign exchange to D_1.
2. The fall in interest rate will make investments in foreign securities, repayment of foreign debt, etc., more profitable. This capital export will increase demand for foreign exchange to D_2.

Thus an expansionary monetary policy triggers an increase in demand for foreign exchange and increases the value of foreign exchange to E_1. This depreciation of the domestic currency improves domestic competitiveness and, consequently, the $(X-M)_0$ curve shifts to $(X-M)_1$. The resulting equilibrium is at point C, where production has increased and the country runs a balance of payments surplus. The increase in national product raises demand for money and thus forces the interest rate up again. This will stabilize capital exports and the new equilibrium in the exchange market will be at the exchange rate of E_1.

The magnitude of the increase in income that results from a given increase in the money supply depends, among other things, on *capital mobility*. Capital exports will increase with capital mobility, and, as a result of the depreciation of the domestic currency, the expansion of the domestic industries facing international competition will likewise increase with capital mobility. Figure 12.7 illustrates the case of perfect capital mobility by means of the *IS/LM* technique.

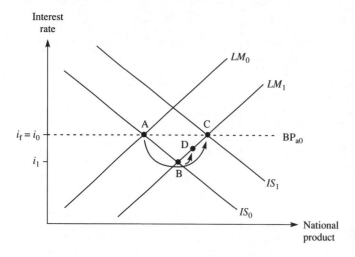

Figure 12.7   Effectiveness of monetary policy under floating exchange rates and perfect capital mobility

The immediate effect of an expansionary monetary policy is to shift the nation from point A, the initial position, to point B. The drop in the domestic interest rate from i_0 to i_1 will result in readjustment of portfolios to the advantage of foreign securities. The depreciation of the domestic currency caused by the concomitant capital export will improve the current account of the balance of payments by an amount that precisely corresponds to the exported capital. As a result of the improvement in competitiveness, the IS curve shifts to the right and the equilibrium point will be C, given an unchanged interest rate. Thus an expansionary monetary policy is reinforced by the increased activity in industries facing international competition.

In the above analysis, the crucial factor is the assumption that $e^e = 0$ in the new equilibrium point C, i.e. that expectations are static. If the increase in money supply is considered to be of a permanent nature, it may be reasonable to expect the depreciation of the domestic currency to be of a permanent nature as well; this expectation may, for example, be based on the belief that an increase in money supply will cause long-term domestic price increases and, according to purchasing power parity theory, lead to a depreciation. This relationship and the precise determination of the long-term equilibrium exchange rate will be dealt with in greater detail in Chapter 13, where we will include price and inflation trends.

However, if the increase in money supply is considered to be temporary, then the current increase in exchange rate will also be considered to be temporary and will be expected to revert to the initial exchange rate. Therefore the depreciation under the expansionary monetary policy will be expected to be followed by an appreciation, when money supply again begins to decrease. The new equilibrium will, in this situation, not be point C, as the expected appreciation ($e^e < 0$) keeps the domestic interest rate below the international rate of interest. This corresponds to a drop in BP_{a0} in Figure 12.7 and to the equilibrium point D for example, instead of C. The fact that monetary policy is less effective in this case is based on the reduced incentive to capital movements due to an expected appreciation. This, again, causes a smaller actual depreciation.

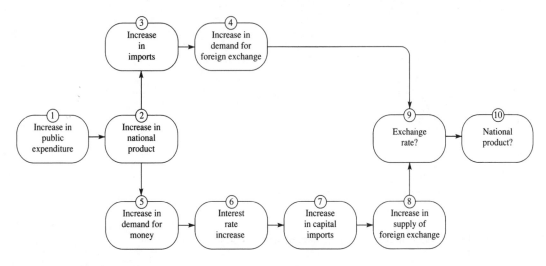

Figure 12.8   Effects of fiscal policy under floating exchange rates

12.3   FISCAL POLICY

While monetary policy is more effective under floating exchange rates than under fixed ones, the effectiveness of fiscal policy is rather more uncertain. This uncertainty is illustrated diagrammatically in Figure 12.8, which shows sequential effects of fiscal policy. An increase in public purchases of goods and services, which has increased aggregate demand, is assumed to have triggered the sequence illustrated. The figure is based on the assumption that the policy pursued is purely fiscal, i.e. any increase in the budgetary deficit is financed through the sale of government bonds so that the money supply remains unaffected.

The sequence of items 2 to 8 is the same under both fixed and floating exchange rates: the increase in demand for money for transaction purposes forces the interest rate up and the supply of foreign exchange is increased through capital imports. At the same time the increase in the level of activity causes an increase in imports and in the demand for foreign exchange. If the increase in demand exceeds the increase in supply, then, given fixed exchange rates, the money supply will decrease and this will dampen the effects of fiscal policy. Conversely, if the increase in the supply of foreign exchange exceeds the increase in demand for foreign exchange, then the money supply will increase and reinforce the effects of fiscal policy.

Item 9 is specific to floating exchange rates. The effects on exchange supply and demand will be reflected in an exchange rate change. If the increase in exchange demand exceeds the increase in supply, then the exchange rate will go up, i.e. the result will be a depreciation. This will stimulate exports and limit imports, and thus increase national product. Conversely, if the increase in exchange supply exceeds the increase in demand, then the result will be an appreciation, which will trigger a decrease in exports and an increase in imports, and thus restrain the original increase in income.

The crucial issue is the interest rate sensitivity of capital movements. If the sensitivity is low, then an expansionary fiscal policy will be followed by a depreciation, which increases fiscal effectiveness. However, if the sensitivity is high, then the increase in capital imports will be large. As a result, the currency will appreciate and this will weaken the effectiveness of fiscal policy.

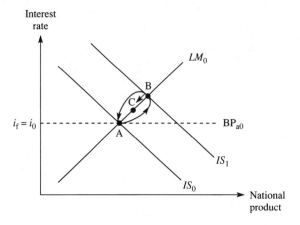

Figure 12.9   Fiscal policy under floating exchange rates and perfect capital mobility.

If capital flows entirely freely among countries, then, given that $e^e = 0$, the international interest rate level determines domestic interest rate, and in this case an expansionary fiscal policy will trigger massive capital movements, which will result in an appreciation (see Figure 12.9). Concurrently with the increase in public expenditure (IS_0 to IS_1) and the resulting trend towards interest rate increase, capital imports will cause an appreciation that precisely ensures that the decrease in exports and the increase in imports prevent the national product from increasing. Therefore, in the new equilibrium point, the following holds: (1) the national product is unchanged, (2) interest rate equals the international interest rate level, (3) the expansion of the public sector has crowded out production in the industries that are subject to international competition ($\Delta G = -\Delta(X-M)$). The budgetary deficit corresponds precisely to the increase in the deficit on the current account. This shows that, in theory, there are good reasons to claim that the root of the large foreign trade deficit of the United States in the eighties was the American budgetary deficit.

As in the case of monetary policy, the result depends on the effect of fiscal measures on exchange rate expectations; this, in turn, depends to some extent on whether the measure is considered to be of a temporary or a permanent nature. If the increase in public spending is expected to be permanent, then static expectations may be a realistic assumption in the new equilibrium. In this case, the lower exchange rate that has emerged will also be expected to hold in the future, and the result will be the total ineffectiveness of fiscal policy as shown in Figure 12.9.

If the market expects the fiscal expansion to be *temporary*, the appreciation should be expected to be temporary, too. In the longer run, when fiscal policy is again contracted, the exchange rate will be expected to revert to the original one. The fiscal expansion is consequently followed by expectations of a depreciation ($e^e > 0$) that keeps the domestic interest rate above the international. In Figure 12.9, this corresponds to an upward shift of the BP_a curve, and the economy changes only to, for example, point C on the unaffected LM curve. The temporary fiscal policy is more effective because the incentive to capital movements is reduced, and so is the succeeding appreciation.

The above examples illustrate that exchange market expectations may be important for the effect of economic policy. If a policy change is thought to be temporary, exchange rate reactions, and hence employment effect, will differ from the case where it is thought to be permanent. Economic policy is not only a question of politicians' *actual* decisions, but very much a question of their *signals* concerning future policy.

Table 12.1 Effectiveness of fiscal and monetary policy under floating exchange rates

	Fiscal policy	*Monetary policy*
Temporary ($e^e \neq 0$)	Some effectiveness	Some effectiveness
Permanent ($e^e = 0$)	Ineffective	Highly effective

12.4 CHOICE OF ECONOMIC POLICY

A comparison of Sections 12.2 and 12.3 yields the principal conclusion (shown in Table 12.1). If a politico-economic measure is needed to restore employment, then fiscal policy should not be used unless a signal is issued that the measure is temporary and the market believes in this signal. By contrast, monetary policy is effective regardless of whether the measure is considered to be a temporary one, but an expected permanent monetary change yields more perceptible effects.

Comparing these conclusions to those drawn under the assumption of entirely fixed exchange rates ($e^e = 0$), we see that the ranking of the two policies has changed on the basis of their effectiveness with respect to production and employment: under floating exchange rates monetary policy has regained its strength while the effectiveness of fiscal policy has been reduced.

12.4.1 Ends and means

The preceding discussion of effectiveness has not included the effects of the measures used on the current account of the balance of payments. To throw some light on this aspect, we will consider a situation in which an external shock has created unemployment and a balance of payments deficit. Given fixed exchange rates, only an expansionary fiscal policy will affect employment and the balance of payments, but the classic problem of conflicting goals will be inherent in this policy: if priority is given to unemployment, then the balance of payments will deteriorate.

Under floating exchange rates, both (temporary) fiscal policy and monetary policy can restore employment but the effects of the two kinds of policy on the balance of payments are not the same. Under an expansionary fiscal policy the currency appreciates and the balance of payments deteriorates, while an expansionary monetary policy results in depreciation of the currency and, consequently, improves the balance of payments. The appropriateness of using one of the two kinds of policy in order to achieve both a balance of payments equilibrium (($X - M) = 0$)) and full employment ($Y = Y_{fe}$) appears from Table 12.2.

Table 12.2 Matching of goals and means

	$Y < Y_{fe}$	$Y > Y_{fe}$
$(X - M) < 0$	Expansionary monetary policy	Tight fiscal policy
$(X - M) > 0$	Expansionary fiscal policy	Tight monetary policy

Note: Fiscal policy is assumed to change Y, i.e. $e^e \neq 0$.

The table may lead to the conclusion that, depending on the economic situation in question, politicians have to use either fiscal policy or monetary policy. It is rarely as simple as that, however, one of the reasons being that typically more goals are involved than the two shown in Table 12.2, and, as a result, all means will be needed.

Even in the case of only two goals, however, two different means may be needed. Let us assume, for example, that the goal of full employment has been attained ($Y = Y_{\text{fe}}$) but that there is a deficit on the balance of payments. In this situation, one possibility is to make use of both fiscal and monetary policy and to have the conflicting employment effects neutralize each other.

If fiscal policy and monetary policy are not balanced against each other, some of the goals may not be achieved. One of the classic examples illustrating this is that of American fiscal and monetary policy in the early eighties. While the central bank tightened monetary policy in order to fight inflation, political promises of reduced taxation and wishes for increased armament led Congress and the President to introduce extensive fiscal measures to expand the economy. As a result, the US$ appreciated considerably, as can be seen from Figure 12.1, which caused subsequent balance of payments deficits and external debt. One consequence of this development, which was highly negative from the point of view of the American industries which faced international competition, was a widespread demand for the introduction of *protectionist measures* against, for example, countries in South-East Asia.

12.5   UNSTABLE EXCHANGE RATES

As was mentioned in the introduction, large exchange rate fluctuations have characterized the period since 1973. This brings us to two crucial questions: firstly, what are the *causes* of these large fluctuations and, secondly, what are the *effects* of such fluctuations.

12.5.1   Causes of exchange rate fluctuations

A range of theoretical explanations have been offered for large exchange rate fluctuations. Some of these explanations will be touched on below while others will be dealt with in Chapter 13. However, most of them take the uncovered interest parity:

$$i = i_{\text{f}} + \frac{E^{\text{e}} - E}{E}$$

as their point of departure.

Under fixed exchange rates, the relevant authorities decide on an exchange rate. This may, for example, be E_0 in Figure 12.10, which indicates the spot rate at time t_0 as well as the exchange rate expected to be valid one year later. If the fixed exchange rate system is entirely reliable, then the expected future exchange rate will be the same as the present one ($E_0^{\text{e}} = E_0$). Given that the expected exchange rate change in this case equals zero, domestic and foreign interest rates are identical ($i = i_{\text{f}}$).

When *currencies float freely*, exchange rates are unrestricted. Given domestic and foreign interest rates, the uncovered interest parity will be satisfied at infinitely many levels of E. If the annual German interest rate is 5 per cent and the annual American interest rate is 10 per cent, then a spot rate of $E_1 = 2.0$ DEM/US$ corresponds to the expected exchange rate $E_1^{\text{e}} = 1.9$, and, similarly, $E_2 = 1.5$ corresponds to $E_2^{\text{e}} = 1.425$, etc. (compare the two dotted lines in Figure

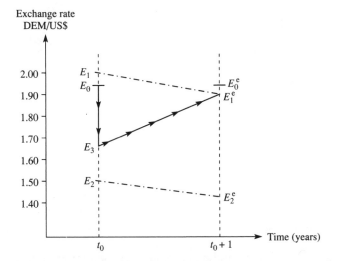

Figure 12.10   Various possible exchange rate developments under floating exchange rates

12.10.) The spot rate and expected future spot rate being tied together in this way, it seems reasonable to look for the causality involved, i.e. which of the two rates determines the other one.

Even though each rate influences the other, the predominant view is that E is determined by expectations. This may be illustrated in terms of the effect of a tighter German monetary policy in an equilibrium situation with identical German and American interest rates, $E = E_0$ and $E^e = E_0^e$. Given an unchanged American interest rate, the German interest rate increase will cause expectations of a future DEM depreciation corresponding to the difference in interest rates. The tight monetary policy, however, will immediately cause an appreciation of the DEM, attracting foreign capital to Germany. Gradually the exchange rate will move as indicated by the bold-faced line $E_0 E_3 E_1^e$ in Figure 12.10: a short-term DEM appreciation and a subsequent depreciation, assuming the expected exchange rate to be E_1^e.

Short-term exchange rate fluctuations being more violent than long-term ones, the spot rate 'overshoots the mark'. This phenomenon, which is actually known as *overshooting*, is ascribed to the fact that money and exchange markets adjust much faster than the goods market. Chapter 13 explains this in detail.

Apart from changes in interest rate differentials among countries, changes in exchange rate expectations, E^e, also affect spot rates. If the agents operating in the market make use of any relevant and accessible information that may affect the future exchange rate then the resulting expectations are known as *rational expectations*. Such information may include expected changes in inflation rates, or in fiscal and monetary policies, or various supply shocks and political events, etc. However, if such information is to form the basis of exchange rate forecasts, then the agents in the market have to have a model that indicates effects on foreign exchange.

If the agents in the market do not have such a model 'at their disposal' and thus do not attribute importance to fundamental economic factors such as inflation rate differences, balance of payments trends, changes in economic policy, etc., or if they are guided by entirely different models, then the exchange rate will not be controlled by fundamental economic relationships but rather by past exchange rate development and arbitrariness. Given that the agents in the

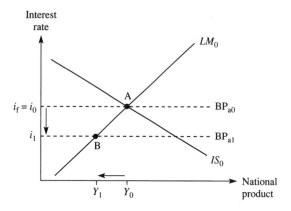

Figure 12.11 Expected monetary tightening and exchange rate

market are continuously bombarded with 'news', it should come as no surprise that exchange rates may fluctuate substantially.

The theory of rational expectations holds that exchange rate formation is driven by expectations. Figure 12.11 presents an example of how market expectations of a reduction in money supply may affect the current exchange rate and, consequently, economic activity for some time to come.

The German Bundesbank sets targets for the future growth of German money supply, believing a narrow correlation to hold between the trend of money supply on the one hand, and inflation, on the other. If, for a period of time, actual money supply significantly exceeds the money supply planned, the market may expect money supply to be tightened in the future, e.g. in half a year. As explained above, the agents in the market will then expect the DEM to appreciate in the course of the coming half year. As a result, investors in Germany and other countries will begin to purchase DEM securities and to sell securities of other denominations. The demand for DEM will gradually increase the value of DEM, for example, in relation to US$ and at the same time the German interest rate will be forced down on account of the increase in demand for German financial assets. The rate of swaps from US$ to DEM will be precisely such that the German interest rate will be consistently below the American rate of interest and that the gap between them will correspond exactly to the expected rate of DEM appreciation. If we assume that Germany is 'small', then i_f will remain unaffected and therefore the BP_{a0} curve will shift downwards to BP_{a1} and the equilibrium point of the economy will shift from A to B, appreciation shifting the IS curve leftwards. It should be noted that the LM curve does not shift since the money supply has not yet been altered.

It follows that mere expectations of future changes in economic policy may affect exchange rate formation and economic activity. Changes like the ones described in Figure 12.11 only take place if the agents in the market make use of an 'economic model' in which a tight monetary policy leads to appreciation.

In the above analyses, we have presented exchange rate changes caused by domestic conditions. This implies that if the home country and other countries are subjected to symmetrical economic impacts (changes in fiscal and monetary policies, etc.) then such fluctuations will not occur. If interest rates increase equally in the home country and abroad as a result of monetary tightening, then future exchange rate relations among the countries will remain unaffected and current exchange rate relations will not change. Thus exchange rate instability may largely be ascribed to the fact that countries do not coordinate their economic development and, in particular, their monetary policies with each other, the result being that large international capital movements cause large exchange rate fluctuations. We will return to this problem in Chapter 14.

12.5.2   Efficiency losses as a result of exchange rate variation

The outcome of any assessment of whether the transition to floating exchange rates has had negative effects on economic efficiency depends crucially on the extent to which actual fluctuations have been expected. If fluctuations are fully expected and the parity conditions dealt with in Chapter 9 have been fully satisfied, then no real economic losses result. If, for example, the market holds confident expectations of a domestic depreciation of 5 per cent a year, then the domestic interest rate will correspondingly be 5 per cent above the foreign interest rate in accordance with the uncovered interest parity. Consequently, borrowing costs will be the same regardless of currency. In addition, purchasing power parity theory predicts that the domestic inflation rate will be 5 per cent higher than the foreign one. Thus the increased costs incurred by exporters will be covered by their receipts from increased export prices and, as a result, their real profits remain unaffected.

If exchange rate fluctuations cannot be fully predicted, however, then they will affect economic activity. Although we established in Chapter 9 that not all parity conditions will ever be fully satisfied, a comparison of actual exchange rate changes (e) and forward premium (f) gives some indication of whether the exchange rate fluctuations were expected. The reason for this is that if both the uncovered interest parity ($i = i_f + e^e$) and the covered interest parity ($i = i_f + f$) hold then $f = e^e$ has to hold. Thus the best exchange market forecast of future exchange rate changes is that provided by the forward premium (see Chapter 9)

If we compare the values of e and f (as a proxy for e^e) in the period from 1960 to 1993, then a clear picture emerges: prior to 1973 no marked fluctuations occurred, but after 1973 e fluctuated much more than f. This may be interpreted as a sign that a considerable proportion of actual fluctuations are unexpected (see De Grauwe 1989).

Such unexpected exchange rate fluctuations may lead to efficiency losses and, consequently, to a decrease in the rate of economic growth if they act as barriers to international trade and to factor mobility. Risk-averse firms and individuals will of course reorganize their economic activities and replace more risky foreign activities with less risky domestic ones, the international division of labour deteriorating as a result. The risk incurred may of course be reduced, e.g. through the use of the forward and options markets. Although this will reduce the problem, it does not remove it entirely since there are costs involved in using these means. Although the arguments for such reductions in international trade and factor mobility may seem plausible, no positive empirical signs of any relationship between increased exchange rate variation and reduced international trade and factor mobility have yet been observed.

The possibility of economic efficiency losses under increased exchange rate variation, however, is no decisive argument against floating exchange rates. Even though a system of fixed exchange rates may stimulate international trade in reducing the risk involved, fixed exchange rates may increase the fluctuation of other variables, e.g. employment. Flexible exchange rates will not cause any efficiency losses if they are driven by 'basic' economic conditions. If, however, exchange rates are driven by 'speculators' on the basis of continuously changing conceptions of future exchange rates and without any relation to basic economic factors, then the costs of exchange rate flexibility will be very real ones. In any case, there will be a trade-off between economic efficiency and macro-economic stability. We will examine the relationship in greater detail in Chapter 13.

SUMMARY

1. Since the early seventies major currencies have been floating and exchange rates have been subjected to violent changes. A flexible exchange rate regime leaves economies more immune to external shocks than a fixed regime.
2. In the real world, a number of factors hamper immunity, including interest rate changes over the trade cycle, which causes exchange rate adjustments.
3. This raises the question of the effects of economic policy, and in a floating regime monetary policy assumes a prominent position because it influences exchange rates without neutralizing liquidity effects from the exchange market.
4. Fiscal policy, on the other hand, more or less loses its effectiveness, depending on the sensitivity of international capital movements. High sensitivity will change the exchange rate and cause the goods and services account to upset the fiscal policy.
5. The fact that money and exchange markets adjust much faster than goods markets give rise to overshooting, i.e. comparatively violent short-term exchange rate fluctuations causing the spot rate to miss the mark.
6. Spot rates are also affected by changes in exchange rate expectations, and, consequently, so is overall economic activity.
7. Contrary to expected fluctuations in exchange rates, unexpected ones cause inefficiency, i.e. economic losses. In itself, this is not an argument against flexible exchange rates, only against speculation-driven flexible exchange rates.

REFERENCES AND FURTHER READING

De Grauwe, Paul (1988), 'Exchange rate variability and the slowdown in growth of international trade', *IMF Staff Papers*, **35**(1).
De Grauwe, Paul (1989), *International Money, Postwar Trends and Theories*, Clarendon Press, Oxford.
Dornbusch, Rudiger (1976), 'Expectations and exchange rate dynamics', *Journal of Political Economy*, **84**, 1161–76.
Fleming, M. (1962), ' Domestic financial policies under fixed and under floating exchange rates', *IMF Staff Papers*, November, **9**, 369–379.
Frenkel, Jacob A. and Assaf Razin (1987), 'The Mundell–Fleming model a quarter century later', *IMF Staff Papers*, **34.4**.
Friedman, Milton (1953), 'The case for flexible exchange rates', *Essays in Positive Economics*, University of Chicago Press, 157–203.
IMF (1984), 'Exchange rate volatility and world trade', IMF Occasional Paper 28, Washington, D.C.
Mundell, Robert (1967), *International Economics*, Macmillan, New York.

THIRTEEN

INFLATION AND ECONOMIC POLICY

The exposition of Chapters 10, 11 and 12 was based on the assumption of fixed prices and wages. Effects on price level—or effects of price level changes—have been mentioned only sporadically. However, at least in the long run, the assumption of fixed prices is unrealistic (see Figure 13.1), which shows inflation rates in the United States, Japan, Germany and Denmark from 1960 to 1994. As appears from the figure, the beginning of the period with floating exchange rates was particularly characterized by increasing international inflation, but after 1973 the situation changed. One typical objection against floating exchange rates is that they are more inflationary than fixed exchange rates. However, the figure shows that this claim is not generally true: the rate of inflation was higher at the end of the sixties than in the early nineties.

This chapter primarily aims at investigating whether the conclusions drawn in the chapters on fixed and floating exchange rates change in the long run when price and wage levels are endogenous variables. Section 13.1 briefly presents inflation theory in the case of a closed economy, while Sections 13.2 and 13.3 present the modifications necessary in the case of an open economy with fixed or floating exchange rates, respectively. Section 13.4 addresses the aspects peculiar to a system with 'fixed but adjustable exchange rates'. Section 13.5 reviews the possibility of economic management under inflation. Finally, Section 13.6 concludes the chapter with a discussion of key elements determining a country's choice between fixed and floating exchange rates.

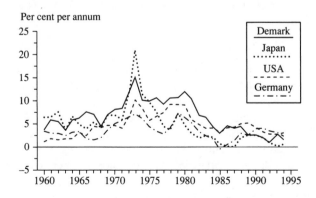

Figure 13.1 Inflation rates in four industrial countries, 1960–94
Source: OECD: Economic Outlook.

13.1   INFLATION IN A NATIONAL PERSPECTIVE

The conditions that influence inflation in a closed economy also exist in the case of a small open economy. However, the overall effect of inflation sometimes differs in the case of an open economy because supplementary mechanisms are at work, which will appear from the following section.

In 1958 A.W. Phillips, a New Zealand economist, published an article in which he showed on a statistical basis that a stable and inverse relationship held between nominal wages increases and the level of unemployment in the United Kingdom in a period of one hundred years (see, for example, P_5 in Figure 13.2). Gradually, similar results were reached for other countries. The implication was that a high level of unemployment involved moderate earnings increases or even decreases, while a low level of unemployment involved substantial increases in earnings.

In the sixties the Phillips curve was extensively interpreted as reflecting a causal relationship which might form the basis of the fiscal and monetary management of an economy: if some inflation was accepted, tax reliefs or a low rate of interest could be used to increase the level of employment.

13.1.1   The vertical Phillips curve

As belief in the stability of the Phillips curve led to increasingly expansionary monetary and fiscal policies, i.e. to upward movement along the curve, its stability broke down. Suddenly, inflation rates that had characterized low levels of unemployment occurred at high ones. The phenomenon of coexisting high unemployment levels and high inflation rates was termed *stagflation*.

This discredited the original Phillips curve. Gradually, the view became predominant that one had forgotten to take into consideration the expectations of the labour market parties with respect to future inflation rates. If inflation has persisted for a long time, labour will expect it to continue. Therefore, at a given level of employment, demands will be raised for increased earnings; in a situation in which inflation is expected, firms will be less likely to refuse pay increases since they will have included such increases in their budgets. On this line of reasoning, the Phillips curve is not stable. A given unemployment percentage does not correspond to one rate of inflation but to infinitely many, each corresponding to an expected rate of inflation. This relationship may be expressed formally as follows:

$$p = p^e - f(U - U_N) \qquad [1]$$

This means that any current rate of inflation (p) is determined by the expected rate of inflation (p^e) adjusted for labour market pressures ($f(U - U_N)$), where U and U_N respectively express actual and 'natural' levels of unemployment. If an actual level of unemployment is above the 'natural' level, this will dampen inflation, yielding an inflation rate below the expected rate. Conversely, if the level of unemployment is below the 'natural' level, the rate of inflation will exceed the expected rate. Figure 13.2 shows three 'expectation-augmented' Phillips curves corresponding to expected inflation rates of 5, 10 and 15 per cent, respectively.

The expectation-augmented Phillips curves may be conceived of as short-term Phillips curves, each holding only under given inflation expectations, which presumably are largely determined by previously recorded inflation rates: if the actual inflation rate has been 5 per cent for quite

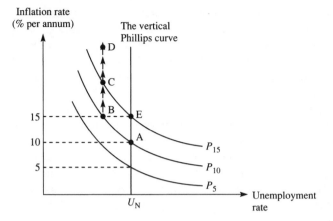

Figure 13.2   Expectation-augmented Phillips curves

some time, then the expected inflation rate will gradually also become 5 per cent. The 'natural' level of unemployment is precisely the level that corresponds to both actual and expected inflation rates (see Friedman 1968).

The level of employment that corresponds to the 'natural' unemployment level is often interpreted as society's maximum level of permanent employment. This is due to the fact that any attempt to reduce the level of unemployment to a level below the 'natural' one, e.g. by means of fiscal or monetary policy, requires a continuous increase in nominal demand because the rate of inflation will go up and thus make it difficult to maintain even the existing level of employment. If the initial situation is point A in Figure 13.2, where both the actual and expected inflation rates are 10 per cent, then an expansionary economic policy will push society to point B, where the inflation rate is 15 per cent. However, as the rate of inflation expected by employees is below the actual inflation rate, the rate of pay increases will gradually be pushed up in an attempt to maintain expected real earnings. Thus inflation accelerates.

Only if the authorities allow nominal demand to increase concurrently with the rate of inflation will it be possible to maintain real demand and consequently the level of employment. However, if this happens, inflation expectations will be disappointed again, and gradually society will move from B to C to D, etc., the rate of inflation increasing all the time. At some point, such an inflationary trend becomes unacceptable and demand will have to be curbed. As a result, the level of unemployment rises again.

Not until a situation has been reached in which the actual and expected rates of inflation are identical will the changes in inflation expectations come to an end. In this case, a long-term equilibrium exists. In any society, there is one level of unemployment (the 'natural' one) that corresponds to long-term equilibrium, i.e. an equilibrium exists for combinations of this level and any rate of inflation. Thus the Phillips curve becomes vertical in the long run.

13.1.2   Internationalizing inflation

Purely national explanations of inflation are no longer satisfactory. Like other economic phenomena, inflation has been internationalized. Various explanations have been offered for why inflation accelerated at the same time in a large number of countries from the end of the sixties (see Figure 13.1). One of these explanations attributes this to a full-employment policy in the sense of Keynes, holding that this policy really caught on in various countries at this time. Another explanation attributes the phenomenon to the increases in energy and food prices that hit all countries at the same time, e.g. in 1972–74, and contributed to inflation in the seventies. A third explanation emphasizes that international inflation originates in a few countries and that it spreads from there to other countries. The United States and American monetary policy until 1973 have been singled out in particular (see Chapter 14).

A fourth explanation of international inflation emphasizes that the exchange market is in equilibrium under floating exchange rates so that an expansionary monetary policy does not, in this case, drain foreign currency reserves. Under fixed exchange rates, however, countries often abstained from pursuing expansionary economic policies precisely because they involved foreign currency problems. Thus the fourth explanation argues that a system of floating exchange rates reinforces any inclination to unrestrained economic policy. This explanation does not fit well with real world figures, which show decreasing inflation rates after 1973 (see Figure 13.1).

13.2 INFLATION UNDER FIXED EXCHANGE RATES

To the extent that international inflation is not due to simultaneous occurrences in all countries but, on the contrary, originates in a few dominant countries, it is appropriate to ask how it spreads among countries. Various channels exist through which international conditions may affect aggregate demand and aggregate supply of goods and services in a small country.

13.2.1 Inflation transmission under fixed exchange rates

One mechanism contributing to the dispersion of inflation is that of the international transmission of trade cycles, which was mentioned in Section 10.2 of Chapter 10. Increased demand for imports in the world's large countries automatically leads to increased employment in small countries in industries facing international competition. This may sow the seeds of demand-driven inflation in any small country thus affected.

Firstly, a Phillips curve reaction occurs in that the increase in the level of employment causes increased prices. Secondly, a *liquidity effect* is generated as a result of the improvement in the current account and of any capital influx. The central bank in the small country in question buys the surplus foreign exchange and in so doing provides the private sector with additional national liquidity. On the assumption of imperfect capital movements, the increase in liquidity causes a fall in the domestic interest rate, which provides the basis for further increases in activity level and prices.

In addition, a recovery in the leading countries may affect the price levels of goods traded internationally. This affects both demand and supply in small countries. The increased prices of imported intermediary products reduce supply and result in supply inflation. At the same time, the increased prices of finished products yield competitive advantages which stimulate demand in industries facing international competition and which force prices up in these industries.

Finally, inflation may spread internationally as a result of the existing internationalization of price and wage formation. The Common Agricultural Policy of the EU provides one example of such internationalization and the OPEC cartel another. However, internationalization may be more indirect than in these examples: wage formation in countries competing with each other may be interdependent. If, for example, labour agreements have been reached in Germany which allow for supernormal pay increases, then this may affect pay claims in Denmark and Austria, because corresponding pay increases will constitute no threat to Danish and Austrian jobs.

Thus the international transmission of inflation is heavily dependent on how open and how interdependent national economies are. In the case of countries trading extensively with each other and with considerable reciprocal business investments, e.g. the United States and Canada, or the member countries of the EU, inflationary development in one country spreads very soon to any such partner country.

13.2.2   The horizontal Phillips curve

In Section 13.1 above, we showed the way in which the activity level in a closed economy influences the rate of inflation. This holds equally of an open economy; however, the causal relationship may alternatively be inverted, i.e. changes in the rate of inflation may affect the level of activity.

This is shown in Figure 13.3, in which P' is a short-term Phillips curve. Let us assume that in the initial situation society is at point A, where the rate of inflation is 5 per cent. The trading partners, against whose currencies the currency of the home country is fixed, have precisely the same inflation rates. If the home country is hit by a supply shock in the form of wage increases that have been agreed by the labour market parties and, after adjustment for productivity increases, are above those of other countries, then the short-term Phillips curve shifts upwards and in the short run society lands at point B for example.

As was shown in Chapter 11, a productivity-adjusted wage increase rate which year by year is above the rates of other countries will gradually result in deterioration of the home country's international competitiveness and, consequently, decrease its net export volume. This is illustrated in the figure, in which wage increase causes the balance of payments curve to shift from $(X-M)_0$ to $(X-M)_1$ during the first time period. The equilibrium point shifts from A to B' and the national product falls. This increases unemployment and reduces the rate of inflation to B' in Figure 13.3(b). The *ISLM* analysis in Chapter 8 showed that, given a fixed nominal money supply, a decrease in real money supply leads to decreasing investments as a result of an increasing interest rate. This provides a further explanation of the decrease in production and employment.

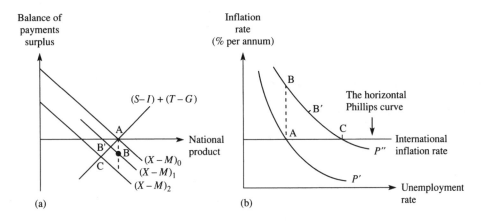

Figure 13.3   Effects on national product and inflation rate when wages increase

Since price and wage increase rates at point B' are still above those of other countries, domestic competitiveness will deteriorate and national product decrease. The deterioration of competitiveness does not come to an end until unemployment has reached a level at which price and wage increase rates are in harmony with those of other countries. This will happen at point C.

The conclusion to be drawn from this analysis is that in the long run the rate of inflation can not deviate from the international rate. This is entirely consistent with *purchasing power parity theory*. This result may be taken to mean that, apart from the vertical Phillips curve, a horizontal Phillips curve exists that holds under fixed exchange rates.

13.2.3   The Phillips point

Figure 13.4 illustrates both the vertical Phillips curve and the horizontal one. In the long run, the vertical curve links unemployment to the 'natural' level, while the horizontal curve links the rate of inflation to the international rate. Taken as one, the two links do not leave much freedom of action to the national economy, which in the long run is linked to the intersection of the two curves. This is at point A in the figure, which we have termed the *Phillips point*.

The arrows show that 'disequilibrium' characterizes all other points than A. Let us assume that the economy is, for instance, at point B. As the unemployment percentage at this point is below the natural level of unemployment, inflation will accelerate. Given that the rate of inflation is at the same time above the international rate, the concomitant deterioration of competitiveness will force up the level of unemployment. Therefore, at some point in time, the level of unemployment will be above the natural level (point C). Then the rate of inflation will decrease but that of unemployment will continue to increase until the international and domestic price increase rates coincide. However, when this happens inflation will still decelerate, the level of unemployment being above the natural level, and the rate of inflation will fall below the international rate (point D). This reduces the level of unemployment and at some point in time this will once again be below the natural level (point E); consequently, inflation accelerates again, etc. This dynamic process is usually assumed to converge towards the equilibrium point of A. However, nothing precise can be said about the process without knowledge of the adjustment mechanisms involved.

If an open economy has chosen to pursue a fixed exchange rate policy, then the Phillips point theory easily leads to economic fatalism as neither fiscal nor monetary policy allows politicians

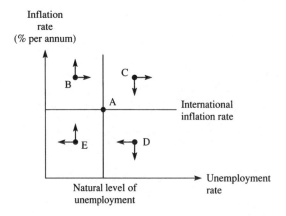

Figure 13.4   The Phillips point

a choice in the long run between inflation and employment. However, given that expansionary effects, e.g. of fiscal policy, are eroded only slowly by the diminished competitiveness, it is important to notice the long-term aspect of this conclusion.

13.3   INFLATION UNDER FLOATING EXCHANGE RATES

As is evident from the preceding analysis, the large inflation rate differentials among the industrialized countries included in Figure 13.1 can only be maintained in the long run if exchange rates are adjusted regularly within the framework of a fixed exchange rate system or if, alternatively, the market mechanism is allowed to neutralize these differentials through floating exchange rates, which will allow these countries to maintain their competitiveness. In the case of the industrialized countries included in Figure 13.1, inflation differentials are not particularly marked; however, if the inflationary development in Brazil, for example, had been included the resulting picture would have been very sharp indeed.

13.3.1   Nominal shock

Under fixed exchange rates, the long-run inflation rate of a country is determined by inflation rates in the countries with which it trades. By contrast, a small country whose currency floats will be protected from international inflation, which means that it will be able to decide on its own position on the vertical Phillips curve. A nominal shock will be now used to illustrate this.

Let us assume that neither the home country nor other countries have experienced any inflation for a long time ($p = p_f = 0$). Nominal and real exchange rates have not changed and interest rate levels are identical. Against this background, the home country unexpectedly expands its money supply. Figure 13.5 shows the effect on interest rate, exchange rate and national product in the extreme case of *full price flexibility* in both the short and the long run. The increased money supply will immediately result in corresponding increases in the domestic price level. This is based on a quantity theoretical point of view in that $MV = PY_{fe}$, where Y indicates the velocity of money. As Y always equals Y_{fe} due to the assumption of full price flexibility, M and P will move proportionally. Consequently, real money supply (M/P) remains unaffected and the LM curve in Figure 13.5(a) does not shift.

Purchasing power parity theory predicts that at the same time the increased price level will immediately cause the currency to depreciate correspondingly in nominal terms, the result being that the price of foreign goods remains the same in terms of the domestic currency. Thus the real exchange rate, E_r in Figure 13.5(b), remains unaffected and, consequently, the IS curve also remains unaffected. It follows that the equilibrium point of A holds both before and after the change in monetary policy. The only difference between the two situations consists in the nominal depreciation and the increased domestic price level. All real conditions are unaffected.[*] Thus, in the long run, individual countries may select their own price level (and rate of inflation), which, accordingly, will be immune to inflationary waves from other countries.

---

[*] The example provided only involved a single change in the money supply and, consequently, only a single price level change and nominal exchange rate change. Therefore the rate of inflation will remain zero. If the growth rate of money supply had been increased from zero to 5 per cent per annum, for example, then the final result would still present no real changes but it would include an inflation rate of 5 per cent and depreciation of the currency by 5 per cent. At the same time the nominal interest rate would increase by 5 percentage points.

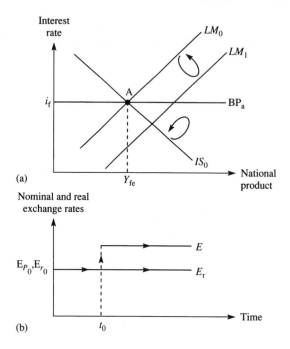

(a)

(b)

Figure 13.5   Monetary policy in the long run under floating exchange rates

Thus solid theoretical arguments speak in favour of the purchasing power parity theory being satisfied in the long run if economies are subjected to nominal shocks, e.g. changes in the money supply. In fact, empirical investigations support this conclusion to some extent (see Chapter 9 and below). However, both theoretical and empirical evidence now show equally well that the theory does not hold in the short run. The best explanation for this is to be found in the phenomenon of 'exchange rate over-shooting', which means that in the short run exchange rates over-react to nominal shocks.

13.3.2   Over-shooting—short-term adjustment

The phenomenon of over-shooting was first described by Dornbusch (1976). His model may be seen as a hybrid between the long-term model above and a short-term model. The phenomenon is due to the fact that price adjustment in the real market and earnings adjustment in the labour market are slow because of various earnings and price rigidities, e.g. due to long-term contracts, while interest rate adjustment and exchange rate adjustment in the money and exchange markets, respectively, are extremely fast. Thus, in the short run, financial markets may 'live their own lives' with equilibria that are out of step with the long-term equilibrium in the goods market. This is often seen as the explanation why the US$ was strongly overvalued in the mid-eighties. We will now discuss the phenomenon in greater detail and in so doing we will build on the *ISLM* analysis (see Figure 13.6).

Since production and prices will not react in the very short run, an increase in the money supply leads to a corresponding increase in the real money supply (LM_0 shifts to LM_1). If equilibrium is to be restored in the money market, then a fall in the interest rate is necessary (i_0 has to shift to i_1) because neither production nor price increases will contribute to an increase in demand for money. In this situation, the decreased interest rate makes it an advantage to invest

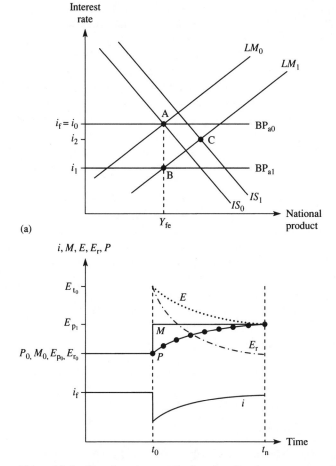

Figure 13.6   Overshooting nominal and real exchange rates under a nominal shock

abroad, which will cause the home currency to depreciate. The extent of immediate capital outflow and depreciation has to be precisely such that domestic assets become profitable again. At given rates of interest, this is only possible if the depreciation of the home currency is so large that it creates expectations of a subsequent appreciation corresponding to the interest differential. This follows from the uncovered interest parity, $i - i_f = e^e$. If $i_f = 10$ per cent and $i = 6$ per cent, then the value of the expected appreciation has to be 4 per cent ($e^e = -4$ per cent). Consequently, the BP_a curve shifts downwards by 4 per cent in such a case.

The conditions at B will trigger two processes in the goods market. Excess demand for goods characterizes the situation at B since this point is to the left of IS_0. Therefore firms will draw on stocks and this will gradually lead to a process of production expansion. In addition, because the depreciation of the currency is real, which amounts to improved competitiveness, the IS curve will shift to the right, e.g. to IS_1. Concurrently with the increase in production, demand for money increases and consequently the interest rate goes up to i_2 ($= 8$ per cent). At given expectations of appreciation (4 per cent), investments in the home country are more profitable than investments abroad. As a result, capital influx causes the currency to appreciate even further. As the exchange rate approaches the new long-term exchange rate, appreciation expectations diminish and the interest differential is reduced.

Since the volume of production at point C is larger than that at Y_{fe}, prices and wages will gradually react and thus affect the *IS* and *LM* curves. The *IS* curve will shift to the left because the original improvement in competitiveness is being eroded by wage increases, and *LM* will also shift to the left, because price increases reduce the real money supply. Price adjustments will continue until the level of employment once again corresponds to the natural level, i.e. $Y = Y_{fe}$. In the long run the real interest rate will remain unchanged which leaves the BP_a curve unaffected. (Since we have only assumed a single change in the money supply, the long-term effect on the rate of inflation and on inflation expectations (p^e) remains unaffected, and, consequently, nominal and real interest rates are identical: $i = r + p^e$. If the growth rate of money supply had increased, the rate of inflation and inflation expectations would gradually increase and nominal interest rate would become higher than the real interest rate.)

Figure 13.6(b) illustrates the development over time in nominal and real exchange rates, nominal and real interest rates, and in price level. The figure shows that at the time of the shock, t_0, the nominal value and the real value of the currency depreciate by identical percentages, the price level being constant. The nominal exchange rate subsequently moves towards the level of E_{p_1}, which indicates the new purchasing power parity rate. With the increase in prices the real exchange rate moves back towards the initial value of E_{r_0} ($= E_{p_0}$). This shows that both exchange rates over-shoot their long-term equilibrium (by $E_{t_0} - E_{p_1}$ and $E_{t_0} - E_{r_0}$, respectively). In addition, it is clear that the short-term adjustment of the exchange rate can be the reverse of the adjustment expected under the purchasing power parity theory, the currency appreciating while the domestic price level increases relative to the price level in other countries.

The model above also explains a phenomenon that has often been observed, that of nominal and real exchange rates being positively correlated.

13.3.3 Long-term shifts in real exchange rates

As opposed to nominal shocks, i.e. changes in the money supply, real shocks lead to permanent changes in exchange rates. Examples of real shocks include demand manipulation through fiscal policy, differences in productivity growth rates among various countries and changes in the prices of raw materials (oil), which affect countries differently.

Chapter 12 discussed the case of fiscal policy. On the assumption of constant money supply, a permanent change was shown to have no long-term effect on national income. Expansionary fiscal policy causes an appreciation, which leads to balance of payments deterioration and, consequently, leaves room for expansion of domestic demand. In the absence of derived price and wage effects, domestic prices remain unchanged: nominal and real appreciations are identical and lasting.

Diverging productivity growth among countries may lead to real changes in exchange rates. Japan is a case in point, its fast productivity growth being a major contributor to the JPY real appreciation by 25 per cent against the DEM and by 100 per cent against the US$ (1960–86) (see De Grauwe 1990).

The impact from productivity growth on the real exchange rate depends on productivity growth being slower in protected industries including services than in internationally competitive industries. For the purposes of securing earnings and, in the long run, factors of production, price increases will be stronger in the domestic industries. Purchasing power parity is in principle only valid for internationally traded goods. If we assume the law of one

Table 13.1 Consequences of real exchange rate changes

	Denmark	*Germany*
Nominal interest rate (i and i_f)	10	6
Expected nominal exchange rate change (e^e)	4	4
Expected inflation rate (p^e and p_f^e)	3	0
Expected real return to Danish investor (r^e)	$10-3=7$	$6+4-3=7$
Expected real return to German investor (r_f^e)	$10-4=6$	$6-0=6$

price to be in operation, the parity will be satisfied for industries competing internationally and they will face a constant real exchange rate. However, if the general price index is used in the calculation of real exchange rates, then it will appreciate. This is because the Japanese price level is pulled upwards by the domestic industries. As a result, the appreciation of the real exchange rate is a measurement paradox: being the result of vigorous productivity increases in the internationally competitive industries, it will not hurt Japanese competitiveness.

The divergence of general price developments, which is not mirrored in the exchange rates, implies real interest rate differentials among countries. Of course, this eliminates the real interest rate equalization which, in the general case, would follow from international capital movements (see Chapter 4). Table 13.1 shows a case in which the purchasing power parity between Germany and Denmark is not satisfied. Under liberalized capital movements, interest arbitrage will equalize expected return on the two currencies and the uncovered interest parity will be satisfied. However, this implies that real return received by investors in the two countries will differ. International capital movements will *not* equalize real return in various countries.

13.4 FIXED BUT ADJUSTABLE EXCHANGE RATES

Most known fixed exchange rate systems have been based on fixed but adjustable exchange rates, adjustments taking place when specific conditions were met. In the IMF system, the condition to be met was that of a 'fundamental disequilibrium'; in the EMS there has to be mutual agreement among member countries. In addition, fixed exchange rate systems allow demand and supply to function between intervention limits. In brief, they contain elements from both fixed and floating exchange rate systems. Given unchanged parity exchange rates, they become fixed exchange rate systems whenever intervention limits are hit. In between, the systems serve as floating exchange rate systems, although exchange rate expectations reflect the existence of intervention limits. If parity adjustments are easily brought about and if the distance between intervention limits is large, then such systems are rather similar to ones of floating exchange rates.

In a fixed exchange rate system of this kind, i.e. one in which exchange rates are not entirely fixed as they are in a monetary union, monetary policy does not lose its effectiveness entirely. There will be a certain latitude between intervention limits, and even more so if parity rates are easily adjusted. In addition, the system allows appreciation/depreciation expectations and, consequently, domestic interest rates may differ from the international rate of interest. Even without expected parity rate changes, fluctuations between intervention limits may cause $e^e \neq 0$. In such a hybrid system, fiscal policy loses some of the effectiveness that it commands under a system of totally fixed exchange rates (see Chapter 12).

Since parity rate adjustments may currently lead to regained competitiveness, inflation rates are not linked to those of competing nations.

13.4.1 A currency crisis

A country may experience a currency crisis if it faces inflation rates that are higher than those of its trading partners but attempts to stick to the exchange rate parity (see Figure 13.7). Let us assume that in spite of excess inflation and balance of payments trouble, the initial situation is at point A: the exchange rate parity is credible and the interest rate equals the international one, i_f. Continued disequilibrium gradually nourishes expectations of a devaluation, which reflect lack of confidence in the ability and willingness of the authorities to defend the parity rate. At the going interest rate, investors prefer foreign assets, i.e. the country concerned faces capital exports. Excess demand for foreign currency drains its international liquidity and reduces the money supply. The interest rate will go up unless the central bank sterilizes the effect by purchasing bonds. However, sterilization implies that the interest rate differential is smaller than the expected exchange rate loss on the home currency. Capital exports will continue and so will the depletion of the country's international liquidity. Eventually, the vain struggle has to be given up and the interest rate will increase sufficiently to compensate for the expected devaluation, i.e. it will shift to i_1 in Figure 13.7. Sustained defence of an overvalued currency may turn out to be very expensive in terms of high interest rates and unemployment.

In order to move from B to A, politicians have to alter economic policy in a credible way, i.e. they have to announce a tight fiscal policy, an incomes policy, etc., and a declared fixed exchange rate policy. If this removes devaluation expectations, the interest rate may go down and the level of employment increase. Of course, the question is whether announcing this is a sufficient way of establishing credibility or whether it takes a sustained and consistent economic policy. In the latter case, economic improvements will occur gradually. Entering a monetary union that has formalized admission criteria is one way of establishing credibility and moving from B to A as a result.

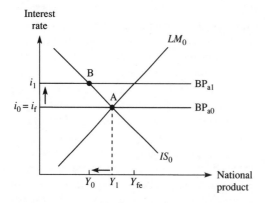

Figure 13.7 The logic of a currency crisis

13.5 ECONOMIC MANAGEMENT UNDER INFLATION

Having presented the economics of an open economy with variable price level under alternative exchange rate systems, we will now summarize the possibility of economic management in the long run and the short run.

13.5.1 The inflation trap

In Chapters 10 and 12, we showed that, under fixed exchange rates and perfect capital mobility, monetary policy loses its effectiveness while fiscal policy becomes highly effective. These conclusions were turned upside down under floating exchange rates.

In this chapter, we have shown that inflation will present obstacles to any policy in the long run. Under floating exchange rates an expansionary monetary policy will boost inflation and, consequently, reduce real money supply and hence employment: the economy will be bound to return to its natural level of unemployment. Nothing changes except the rate of inflation and the nominal exchange rate.

Under fixed exchange rates an expansionary fiscal policy will boost inflation in the short run and gradually erode international competitiveness. Unemployment will increase until it has returned to the 'natural' level and the inflation rate equals the international one.

A fixed exchange rate system detracts 'one' degree of freedom from economic policy as floating exchange rates allow management of the inflation rate. The advantage is questionable, however, as the level of employment and the distribution of incomes and wealth are left unaffected by inflation in the long run, at least if the inflation rates had been expected.

Similar problems infect policies of international competitiveness. Improved competitiveness will improve the level of employment and increase the rate of inflation so that, in the long run, the economy will revert to its natural level of unemployment. Nevertheless, this kind of policy may be useful, e.g. if natural unemployment implies a current account deficit. The deficit may be eliminated if the policy is supplemented with a tight fiscal policy that eliminates the derived inflationary effect.

Until this point, we have assumed the initial position to be one of long-run equilibrium, i.e. the Phillips point in the case of fixed exchange rates, or some point on the vertical Phillips curve in the case of floating exchange rates. The realism of this assumption may be questioned, however: why should a country pursue an economic policy at all if its economy is in internal equilibrium? This would correspond to placing a bull in a china shop: any movement would spell disaster.

13.5.2 Management in the short run

Obviously, it is important that politicians are informed about the natural unemployment rate so that they can avoid long-term inflationary problems under floating exchange rate systems and balance of payments deficits under fixed exchange rate systems. If a country is not in a long-term equilibrium position, it is—or may be—appropriate to resort to economic policy. An unemployment level above the natural one calls for an expansionary policy and vice versa. If applied in this way, economic policy supplemented with the automatic adjustment mechanisms may restore long-term equilibrium, as has been shown in Chapters 10, 11 and 13.

13.6 FIXED OR FLOATING EXCHANGE RATES?

On the basis of the aim of efficiency, Section 12.5 in Chapter 12 listed a number of arguments favouring a fixed exchange rate system, which was assumed to promote international trade and investments. Similarly, automatic exchange market equilibrium is an efficiency argument in favour of floating exchange rates: international reserves are not required and, consequently, there will be no loss of interest. From an efficiency point of view, fixed exchange rates are probably preferable, but this should be balanced against the increase in macro-economic instability.

The fundamental macro-economic goals are quantitatively and qualitatively identical. Under floating exchange rates, the exchange market is always in equilibrium and the need for international liquidity is very limited. Nevertheless, current account equilibrium is a goal in this case as well, as it was in the case of fixed exchange rates.

We have mentioned the issue of policy effectiveness at various places above. Fully fixed exchange rates deprive a small country of exchange rate policy and renders its monetary policy impotent while fiscal policy remains an effective tool. Under fixed but adjustable exchange rates, and even more so under freely floating exchange rates, monetary policy becomes effective while fiscal policy weakens. Exchange rates become more or less endogenous and subject to market supply and demand. In sum, it is highly uncertain which system leaves more room for management.

13.6.1 Joining a monetary union

In a monetary union with irrevocably fixed exchange rates, the possibility of realizing economic goals crucially depends on three conditions. The first one consists of the *harmonization of politico-economic goals*, in particular of inflation rates. If inflation rates differ widely among member countries, high-inflation economies will face unemployment problems and will have to adjust their economic policies to the goals of the union.

The second condition consists of the *absence of violent asymmetrical shocks*, which have very different effects on national target variables. An example of this would be a change in consumer preferences in respect of goods produced in the member countries. Another would be external price increases in raw materials, which will influence member countries differently due to differences in business structures. Negotiated wages provide a final example if they increase (much) faster in one country than in some of the other countries. Of course wage and price differentials among member countries will equalize in the long run as increasing unemployment dampens inflation. However, the establishment of mutual wage and price levels in the union takes time and unemployment may be unequally distributed during long periods of time (compare with the position of the new versus the old 'Länder' in Germany). If all agents in a union, come to behave rationally through a learning process, then any negative consequences of labour market shocks may be either avoided or dampened including not just political authorities but also labour and trade unions. External shocks such as oil price increases will hit member countries uniformly and only cause slight changes in competitiveness if the countries have diversified and similar business structures (see Kenen 1969).

The third crucial condition is that of economic flexibility, which helps absorb asymmetrical shocks. A high degree of *labour mobility* among member countries will help iron out different shock-induced tendencies in employment levels. Labour moving from unemployment-stricken areas to high-activity countries will tend to equalize activity and employment levels. This was first shown by Mundell (1961), who introduced the concept of 'optimum currency areas'.

Similarly, a high degree of *price flexibility* in the member countries will reduce the need for exchange rate adjustments. Price and wage adjustments will quickly restore relative competitiveness, making deviation from full employment a short-run phenomenon (compare with the vertical Phillips curve).

Abolition of the exchange rate policy will place emphasis on competitiveness adjustment through incomes policy, i.e. through the management of prices and wages. Unions may reasonably be expected to take wage and price development in other member countries into consideration when they raise their wage demands. To some extent, this will compensate for the loss of exchange rate policy.

In sum, countries that agree on politico-economic goals and have similar economic structures including the degree of diversification and flexibility should consider forming an economic and monetary union. Such a step would reduce uncertainty in international trade and investments and save the costs of exchanging currency. If the conditions are not satisfied, it would seem the better solution to opt for a system of floating exchange rates in order to preserve macro-economic stability.

SUMMARY

1. Factors that influence inflation in a closed economy are also at work in a small open one. Thus expectation-augmented Phillips curves and the vertical long-run Phillips curve are still relevant.
2. Purely national explanations of inflation no longer suffice: simultaneous global shocks or inflation spread from originating countries are supplementary hypotheses.
3. Under fixed exchange rate regimes inflation spreads internationally because of the Phillips curve, liquidity and international price effects.
4. As the inflation rate cannot, in the long run, deviate from the international level, the Phillips curve turns horizontal. As the vertical one is still valid, the Phillips point results, around which the economy gravitates in the short run.
5. Under flexible exchange rate regimes the small open nation can freely choose its position on the vertical Phillips curve as nominal shocks will not influence the real money supply, nor the real exchange rate in the long run.
6. While purchasing power parity holds in the long run, the phenomenon of over-shooting explains why this is not the case in the short run. Short-run adjustments may even be the reverse of the long-run ones.
7. Fixed exchange rates are probably preferable from an efficiency point of view, but they give rise to increased macro-instability—there is no obvious choice.
8. The conditions for successfully joining a monetary union includes a similarity of economic structures, factor mobility and price flexibility.

REFERENCES AND FURTHER READING

De Grauwe, P. (1990), *International Money. Postwar Trends and Theories*, Clarendon Press, Oxford.

Dornbusch, R. (1976), 'Expectations and exchange rate dynamics', *Journal of Political Economy*, **8**, 1161–76.

Friedman, M. (1953), 'The case for flexible exchange rates', in *Essays in Positive Economics*, Chicago, University Press, Chicago.

Friedman, M. (1968), 'The role of monetary policy', *American Economic Review*, **58**, 1–17.

Kenen, P. (1969), 'The theory of optimum currency areas: an eclectic view', in R.A. Mundell and A.K. Swoboda (eds.), *Monetary Problems of the International Economy*, Chicago University Press, Chicago, pp. 41–60.

Mundell, R. A. (1961), 'A theory of optimum currency areas', *American Economic Review*, **51**, 509–517.

Nielsen, J. U.-M., H. Heinrich and J. Hansen (1992), *An Economic Analysis of the EC*, McGraw-Hill Book Company, Maidenhead.

Phillips, A. W. (1958), 'The relation between unemployment and the rate of change of money wage rates in the United Kingdom, 1861–1957', *Economica*, Nov, 283–99.

FOURTEEN

INTERNATIONAL COORDINATION

The relationships between nations develop in many ways, pulling them into networks of mutual dependence. This includes economic aspects in the form of, for example, the rapidly growing volume of international trade and capital movements. Whether economic goals such as full employment, growth and stable prices can be realized increasingly depends on a nation's economic environment including the economic policies pursued by other nations.

The preceding chapters dealt with economic policy in a small open economy, i.e. in a country that has no influence on production, inflation, etc., in other nations. The essential conclusion was that the effectiveness of macro-economic policies depends on the given exchange rate system. Table 14.1 shows the short-to-medium term effectiveness of these policies, given perfect international capital mobility, and static exchange rate expectations.

Countries like Germany, Japan and the United States are highly important in the global economy. In order to investigate the way in which the economic policies pursued by large countries influence their economic environment, the small country assumption is abandoned in Section 14.1, where the issue is discussed in a short-to-medium term perspective and in the light of alternative exchange rate systems. In the case of large countries, it seems reasonable to assume that coordination of their economic policies will yield positive welfare effects. Section 14.2 deals with this issue.

In 1973 the world's major currencies began floating, but this did not mean that fixed exchange rates came to an end. Instead, groups of countries, such as the members of the EMS, have fixed exchange rates within their group but float jointly against other currencies. Section 14.3 discusses joint floating, which in the extreme case involves a monetary union, and the ways in which it influences macro-economic relationships. Economic coordination is of particular interest in this connection. It has two aspects: (1) internal coordination among member states and (2) joint external coordination *vis-à-vis* the rest of the world. Section 14.4 highlights the history of economic coordination.

This chapter deals with short- and medium-term development, i.e. cyclical matters. It does not deal with long-run adjustment aiming at full employment.

Table 14.1 Effectiveness of economic policies in a small country

	Fixed exchange rates	*Floating exchange rates*
Fiscal policy	Effective	Entirely ineffective
Monetary policy	Entirely ineffective	Effective

14.1 INTERDEPENDENCE

The macro-economic models presented in Chapters 10 to 13 all related to *dependent* economies in the sense that trade in goods, services, securities and foreign exchange influences these economies.The economic effects discussed, however, were all directed inwards: none of them were effects produced by the country in question and influencing other countries. In brief, the models were devoid of *inter*dependence. They were realistic for countries such as Ireland or Sweden, which have GNPs of less than 1 per cent of global GNP, but hardly for countries with significant shares of global GNP (the American GNP amounts to around 30 per cent of global GNP).

In order to find out whether a country's economic freedom of action is influenced by interdependence, we will define a global two-country model. For present purposes, the United States constitutes the home country and Europe the foreign country. The analysis is based on an assumption of perfect capital mobility between the two countries.

14.1.1 The nominal anchor

In Chapter 10, the concept of 'fixed exchange rates' was taken to mean that a small country had decided unilaterally to fix its exchange rate against other currencies and that it had taken responsibility for the rate, relying on intervention on the exchange market. In this sense, the fixed exchange rate system was *asymmetrical*. Fiscal policy was shown to be potent while monetary policy was impotent. In the two-country model, it is necessary to be explicit about where responsibility for maintaining the exchange rate should be placed. It may rest with (1) the United States, (2) Europe, or (3) both countries in a joint symmetrical system agreed on by the two parties.

The choice made is crucial to the economic management of global monetary policy and, consequently, to the way in which international liquidity is created. In economic theory, this choice has been termed the problem of the *nominal anchor*. In order to illustrate the problem, we will consider the monetary markets in the two countries (see Figure 14.1). On the assumption that the fixed exchange rate of US$ against ECU is perfectly credible, no expectations of devaluation will exist. Therefore, due to the uncovered interest rate parity, interest rates in the two countries will be identical. A joint interest rate may take on any one of a large number of

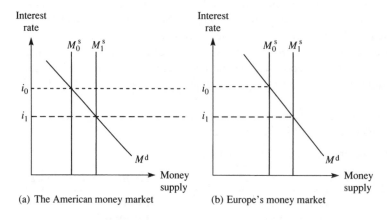

(a) The American money market   (b) Europe's money market

Figure 14.1   The anchor-country problem

values, however, and, consequently, any one of a large number of different volumes of money supply in the two countries will be compatible with a fixed exchange rate. Two examples would be an interest rate of i_0 and the corresponding money supply of M_0, or i_1 and M_1. Given such an extensive range of possibilities, it is worth asking how monetary policy should be designed.

In the *asymmetrical* case, one (dominant) country takes responsibility—by implicit or explicit agreement—for the monetary policy to be pursued. Under the Bretton Woods system (1944–73), the United States played this part while the other participating nations were obliged to ensure that parity exchange rates against the US$ were observed. In the European Monetary System, Germany has played a similar part. In the *symmetrical* case, the monetary policies of all countries involved have to be coordinated and maintaining exchange parities is a mutual problem.

Let us assume that the initial situation involves a joint i_1 and that the Europeans want to fight inflation by means of an increased interest rate. The European central bank sells European securities, which causes a drop in money supply to M_0 and an increase in the rate of interest to i_0. The interest rate differential induces investors to sell American securities and buy European ones. In the foreign exchange market ECU will consequently be in excess demand and US$ in excess supply.

In a symmetrical system, this will drain American ECU reserves, as the American central bank buys US$, which will decrease American money supply and force the American interest rate up. The European central bank will similarly buy US$ and sell ECU, which will increase money supply and force interest rates down in Europe. The final result is a joint interest rate but one that is at a higher level than the initial rate of interest. In addition, the money supply has decreased in the United States and even in Europe, where the derived increase cannot fully neutralize the initial reduction. Consequently, the global money supply has decreased.

In sum, a contractionary monetary policy in one country is transmitted to the other, and the mutual obligation to intervene is equivalent to acceptance of common monetary goals. Without this acceptance, the exchange rate parity will be questioned, the result being exchange speculation.

In an asymmetrical system, the situation is a different one. If the United States is the anchor country, the operation described above will have no impact on the global rate of interest nor on American money supply. Because the American central bank is not responsible for the exchange rate it can design a monetary policy that takes nothing but American policy objectives into account. Thus, when the European interest rate increase spreads to the United States, the American central bank will neutralize it through the buying of American securities, which will stabilize the money supply and the interest rate in the United States.

In Europe, exchange market intervention will be more extensive than in the symmetrical case and the derived increase in money supply will fully neutralize the initial decrease. As a result, the global interest rate remains unchanged.

If the United States had been responsible for the exchange rate, the European monetary contraction would have been fully transmitted to the global interest rate level and, by implication, to the American interest rate level.

14.1.2 Fixed exchange rates

Given the above analysis of responsibility for intervention, we can now investigate the ways in which fiscal and monetary policies are transmitted from one country to another in the world

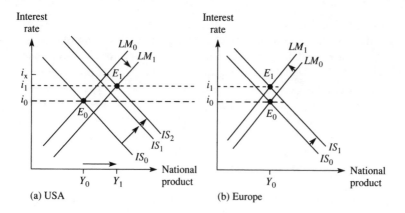

Figure 14.2 Fiscal policy in interdependent economies under a symmetrical fixed exchange rate system

economy. Firstly, we will analyse fiscal policy in a symmetrical system. An expansionary American fiscal policy presents a global increase in demand, which translates into a global increase in production and interest rate according to the IS/LM model. Figure 14.2 shows this.

Figure 14.2(a) depicts the American economy, which is in equilibrium in the initial situation at point E_0. As a result of the expansionary fiscal policy, the IS curve shifts to IS_1. At a given international interest rate, the increase in American national product will induce imports, i.e. European exports. This causes the European IS curve to shift to IS_1 in Figure 14.2(b), which in turn produces a feedback effect on the American IS curve, which now moves to IS_2 due to increasing European imports. Let us assume that the transmission of international demand results in IS_2 in Figure 14.2(a) and in IS_1 in Figure 14.2(b).

Since the United States (only) constitutes part of the global economy, the American interest rate will not rise to i_x. Instead, the international interest rate will increase to somewhere between i_0 and i_x, for instance i_1, if money supply is assumed to remain unchanged. As a result of mutual exchange market intervention, American money supply will increase and European money supply decrease to LM_1 in (a) and (b), respectively. Table 14.2 summarizes the effects on these two large countries.

The effect on American national product is certain to result in the short term as well as in the medium term. In Europe, increasing exports will make Y go up while the increasing interest rate will crowd out investments; the total effect may either be positive or negative, depending on the slopes of the IS and LM curves as well as on the relative size of the two countries.

Both countries will face rising interest rates, and the United States will also see price increases, due to the rise in GNP. In Europe, the sign of the change in income determines the price change, according to the Phillips curve.

Table 14.2 Effects of American expansionary fiscal policy under a symmetrical fixed exchange rate system

	USA	Europe
National product (Y)	↑	?
Current account ($X-M$)	↓	↑
Interest rate (i)	↑	↑
Consumer prices (P_c)	↑	?

Table 14.3 Effects of a US expansionary monetary policy under a symmetrical fixed exchange rate system

	USA	Europe
National product (Y)	↑	↑
Current account ($X-M$)	?	?
Interest rate (i)	↓	↓
Consumer prices (P_c)	↑	↑

In an asymmetrical system, in which Europe is obliged to maintain the exchange rate, the United States is under no such obligation. Therefore American money supply remains at LM_0. In Europe, the extent of the monetary contraction will be larger in order to raise the European interest level to that of the United States, i.e. i_x. Consequently, the American GNP increases less than it would in the symmetrical case and the European GNP declines more than it would in that case. In the asymmetrical system, Europe benefits from a solid reserve of international liquidity, US$, and thus the United States performs the role of a *reserve currency country*.

Let us now imagine that the United States, which pursues an expansionary fiscal policy, is responsible for maintaining the foreign exchange rate. In this case, the American central bank has to purchase ECU in the exchange market, which forces American money supply up. The European monetary policy remains unchanged, i.e. the LM curve is left unaltered. Due to increased exports, the European IS curve will now shift to the right: both European interest rate and production will increase.

Under the assumption of a symmetrical system, an expansionary monetary policy in either of the two countries will increase global money supply, leading to a lower global interest rate and a higher volume of world production in the short-to-medium term. The expansionist country will produce excess supply of its own currency and, as a result, will face a subsequent contraction in money supply, which in part will offset the initial expansion. Due to the decreasing global interest rate, the nation that is passive in respect of monetary policy will see an inward capital flow leading to an increase in money supply: an expansionary monetary policy is inflicted on this country. Table 14.3 summarizes the situation.

Both countries face increases in production, exports and imports. Net effects on their current accounts depend on the interest rate sensitivity of demand, on marginal taxes and on the propensity to import and consume in the two countries. If the change in the balance of payments of one country is known, then that of the other country is also known: the amounts will be the same but they will have opposite signs.

In the asymmetrical case, in which Europe is responsible for maintaining the exchange rate in the face of American monetary expansion, the signs in Table 14.3 will still be correct. Quantitatively, however, American income rises even more because no exchange market intervention neutralizes the increase in American money supply.

Finally, if the United States is responsible for securing the exchange rate, its expansionary monetary policy will have absolutely no effect because its exchange market intervention will neutralize it entirely, the only result in this case being the draining of American ECU reserves. This corresponds to the small-country case described in Chapter 10.

Under the Bretton Woods system, which was mentioned in Chapter 8, the international exchange rate system was dollar-based in the sense that countries would peg their respective currencies to the US$. It is clear from the analysis above that American monetary policy was the driving force behind international interest rate levels at the time and that it influenced production, inflation rate and balance of payments in the countries participating in the system. Since these countries were obliged to intervene on the exchange market, they were of course interested in holding suitable amounts of US$ as a reserve currency (see Section 14.4).

14.1.3 Floating exchange rates

In Chapter 10 we showed that fiscal policy in a small economy is impotent under floating exchange rates and static exchange rate expectations since currency appreciations neutralize expansionary effects. Figure 14.3 shows the case of two large countries.

Let us assume that an expansionary American fiscal policy causes IS_0 to shift to IS_1. Given an unchanged national and global money supply, this addition to global demand will force up the international interest rate from i_0 to i_1. As i_x is above i_1, the United States will receive capital flows from Europe and the US$ will appreciate. As a result, IS_1 shifts leftwards to IS_2. Similarly, ECU depreciates relative to US$, which stimulates European exports, causing IS to shift to IS_1 in the case of Europe. The effects appear from Table 14.4.

The combined effects of the ECU depreciation and the rising American GNP lead to an improvement in the European balance of trade and a similar deterioration of the American trade balance. Consumer prices in Europe rise as American imports result in increased activity and ECU depreciation increases import prices. In the United States, the appreciation of the US$ and the increase in activity influence P_c in different directions. The net effect depends on the import share contained in the American consumers' baskets.

Table 14.4 Effects of one country's fiscal policy in the case of two interdependent economies under floating exchange rates

	USA	Europe
National product (Y)	↑	↑
Current account ($X-M$)	↓	↑
Interest rate (i)	↑	↑
Consumer prices (P_c)	?	↑

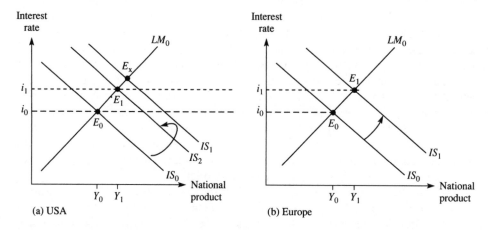

Figure 14.3 Fiscal policy in interdependent economies under floating exchange rates

Table 14.5 Expansionary monetary policy in two interdependent economies under floating exchange rates

	USA	Europe
National product (Y)	↑	↓
Current account ($X-M$)	?	?
Interest rate (i)	↓	↓
Consumer prices (P_c)	↑	↓

A country that pursues an expansionary monetary policy will cause global money supply to increase and, consequently, cause the international interest rate to fall. In addition, its currency will depreciate. The other country, which remains passive, will face an appreciation of its currency and, hence, a decline in its GNP. Since changes in economic activity and in exchange rates are counter-active, the effect on the balance of payments is uncertain. The effect on consumer prices, however, is unequivocal: in the United States, both the depreciation and the activity expansion will stimulate price increases, while the reverse will be the case in Europe. These results appear from Table 14.5.

14.1.4 Summing up

Some of the fairly safe conclusions relating to economic policy in large countries are the following:

1. Compared to the case of small countries, fiscal policy is less effective under fixed exchange rates and more effective under floating exchange rates.
2. Contrariwise, monetary policy is most effective under floating exchange rates, while under fixed exchange rates it is totally impotent to non-anchor countries. Anchor countries may influence GDP through monetary policy.
3. The monetary policy of an anchor country will influence production and inflation in other nations in the same way as it influences production and inflation in the anchor country. By contrast, while the fiscal policy of other countries is transmitted, international transmission of an anchor country's fiscal policy is doubtful at best.
4. Under floating exchange rates a country's fiscal policy will be transmitted to another country but the balance of payments will be affected inversely. Monetary policy triggers a 'beggar thy neighbour' effect on prices and economic activity, i.e. an expansionary monetary policy in one country causes production level price levels to go down in another country.

14.2   IS COORDINATION PROFITABLE?

The main conclusion to be drawn from Section 14.1 is that nations are highly interdependent regardless of whether exchange rates float or have been fixed. Macro-economic models have thrown some light on global interdependence (see Table 14.6, which is based on a study of 12 econometric models and highlights the interaction between the United States and the other OECD countries).

The effects largely reflect our conclusions, which were based on simpler models with floating

Table 14.6 OECD interdependence

Effects				In the United States				In the other OECD countries			
Changes in economic policy		Y (%)	P_c (%)	o (per-centage point)	BPi (US$ billion)	Y (%)	P_c (%)	e (per-centage point)	BPi (US$ billion)	US$†(%)
G_{USA}	+ 1% −	1.2	0.3	1.1	− 13.1	0.4	0.3	0.4	6.9	1.4
$G_{OECD-USA}$	+ 1% −	0.2	0.5	0.4	5.3	1.5	0.3	0.6	− 7.1	− 0.4
M_{USA}	+ 4% −	1.2	0.9	− 1.6	− 2.8	−	− 0.3	− 0.5	0.7	− 6.4
$M_{OECD-USA}$	+ 4%	0.1	− 0.5	− 0.3	0.1	0.6	0.5	− 1.1	− 0.2	3.2

Note: Any effects indicate changes compared to a situation with unchanged economic policy after a period of two years—average of 12 models.
† A positive US$ exchange rate change indicates an appreciation of the US$.
Source: Frankel and Rockett (1988). In the present case, the table is based on *The Economist*, 26 September 1987.

exchange rates (see Section 14.1). An expansionary American fiscal policy translates positively into economic activity in the other OECD countries, and vice versa. An expansionary monetary policy has limited effect. The reason why the results differ slightly from those in Section 14.1 is probably that the econometric models are more sophisticated than the *IS/LM* model, e.g. as regards the formation of exchange rate expectations.

Mutual interdependence is largely due to the fact that unilateral policy changes cause interest rates to differ among countries as a result of the uncovered interest parity. Any resulting imbalances caused by exchange rate changes may lead to unwanted disruption to international trade.

Let us consider an example of this. An international depression would call for coordinated expansionary fiscal policy. However, a unilateral expansion will hurt the trade balance and government finance in the active country, while the passive nations will face increasing economic activity, improved government finance and a positive change in the balance of trade. In such a situation the individual country may tend not to take action, either because it fears that no one else will follow or because it expects a free ride when the others decide to move. Consequently, the remedy is an agreement obliging all the countries to coordinate expansionary fiscal policies.

The advantages of cooperation also extend to monetary policy. The combination of a tight monetary policy and an expansionary fiscal policy in the United States in the early eighties is a splendid example of poor coordination. This policy mix caused a strong appreciation of the US$, which in turn contributed to a severe American foreign trade deficit. In order to curb depreciation, a large number of countries tightened their monetary policies, triggering a tendency towards escalating interest rate increases. Thus it is possible to point to recent instances of uncoordinated economic policy which has left the countries involved in positions worse than the ones in which they originated. In economic theory, this problem has been dealt with in *game theory* (the classic contribution is Hamada (1974); see also de Grauwe (1990)) under the heading of 'the prisoners' dilemma'. The theory shows that two decision-makers who act without coordinating their activities will both be worse off than they would if they had permitted coordinated decisions. Below, the argument will be applied to economic policy decisions in two countries.

14.2.1   The countries' dilemma

Let us assume that both countries, as in the early eighties, face rather high inflation rates due to a supply shock. Anti-inflation measures are either a very tight monetary policy leading to controlled price increases in the short run or a moderately tight monetary policy that cures the disease in the long run. The choice of policy depends on the costs resulting from each, which include increases in the level of unemployment. Figure 14.4 illustrates the trade-off in terms of a short-run Phillips curve (Ph).

Both countries will be at point A immediately after the supply shock, i.e. the inflation rate will be 10 per cent and the level of unemployment 4 per cent. A moderately tight monetary policy (B) curbs the inflation rate to 8 per cent and increases the level of unemployment to 6 per cent. In this case, one percentage point of the rate of inflation is traded off against one percentage point in the level of unemployment. If the monetary policy is very tight (C), the trade-off is less favourable: a decrease of three percentage points in the rate of inflation against an increase of four percentage points in the level of unemployment.

Let us assume that the two trade-off figures, 1 and 0.75, hold for the United States and Europe if the two countries adopt the same policy. A coordinated policy will have no impact on the exchange rate of ECU/US$ and, consequently, no derived inflation results from import prices. Table 14.7 illustrates the two cases of coordinated policy in a pay-off matrix.

If the United States adopts a very tight policy while Europe opts for a moderate one, an interest rate differential will result and the exchange rate will change (see Table 14.6). The US$ appreciation reduces American import prices and increases European ones. On the assumption that the derived price effects curb American inflation by three percentage points, the trade-off in the United States will be 6 percentage points of inflation against 4 percentage points of unemployment, corresponding to a pay-off ratio of 1.5. If we assume that increasing import

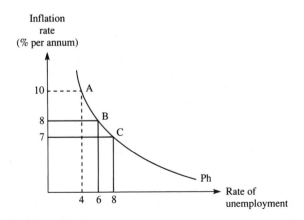

Figure 14.4   Costs of anti-inflation policy

Table 14.7. Pay-off matrix for monetary policies

Europe	USA	
	Moderately tight	*Very tight*
Moderately tight	(1;1)	(0;1.5)
Very tight	(1.5;0)	(0.75;0.75)

prices push inflation upwards by two percentage points in Europe, the combined effect on inflation will be zero: Europe will have increased its level of unemployment without receiving anything in return. In the matrix, a tight European policy and a moderate American one have symmetrical effects.

The pay-off matrix clearly illustrates the advantage of coordinating moderately tight policies. This yields the most favourable pay-off in both countries. The countries' dilemma is the following: if they do not coordinate their policies, they will both opt for a very tight policy and end up in the bottom-right corner, where trade-off is worse than in the upper-left one. In the case of non-coordination, very tight monetary policy is a *predominant strategy*, i.e. the preferable strategy regardless of the strategy of the other country. To illustrate this point, let us adopt a European view.

If the United States adopts a moderately tight policy, then Europe would have a trade-off of 1.5 if it opts for a very tight policy and of 1 if it opts for a moderate policy. If the United States pursues a very tight policy, then Europe must do the same in order to avoid the inflationary effects of the resulting depreciation.

The argument in this section has been based on somewhat unrealistic assumptions. For instance, in real world politics, Phillips curves are unlikely to be stable. Further, the presentation does not take into consideration that cases of uncoordinated policies will have employment effect due to international transmission

14.2.2 Arguments against coordination

If coordination is to be successful, a number of conditions have to be satisfied. First of all, the political goals of the two governments have to be compatible. If the United States suffers from a negative balance of payments and Europe from high unemployment rates, then both parties may wish to devalue their currencies. Of course, no coordination can achieve these conflicting goals. In fact, rounds of retaliating interest rate reduction are quite possible in such a situation, which would prevent exchange rate changes and, in addition, speed up inflationary pressure in both countries. Contrariwise, if Europe wants the ECU to appreciate as a means of curbing inflation, the two countries would have some common interests in coordinating their policies. This should not be taken to imply that cooperation cannot be successful if countries have different goals but the likelihood is reduced (see De Grauwe 1990).

Secondly, it is imperative that the two countries have a shared understanding, or model, of international transmission of real and monetary shocks and that shocks are predictable. In general, if economic policy is to be successful, such preconditions have to be satisfied, but in the case of international relations they are even more crucial.

Thirdly, the agreement reached between the two parties has to be binding. The basis for international coordination is agreement among central banks and governments in several countries. In addition parliaments—and pressure groups—will also be involved, in the typical case, particularly if the topic is fiscal policy. This always poses a potential threat to the implementation of agreements. In general, coordination may suffer from weak credibility due to indefinite decision lags and the resulting imprecision of timing. By contrast, central banks in most countries enjoy a fairly high degree of political independence, which makes coordination of monetary policy much easier than that of fiscal policy.

The risk that an agreement is violated may be reduced if efficient supervision is possible, i.e. if the joint policy is quantifiable as it would be if, for example, country X is to cut public expenditure by 100 bn currency units. Likewise, supervision is easier to enforce if only a limited number of countries participate.

14.3   MACRO-ECONOMIC POLICY UNDER JOINT FLOATING

We have illustrated the way in which economic impulses are transmitted among major countries and shown that countries may acquire gains from coordination. A basic distinction throughout has been that between fixed and floating exchange rate systems, represented in the real world by the Bretton Woods period up to 1973 and the subsequent period, respectively. However, the latter period has also been characterized by *joint floating*: the currencies of the world's major countries float against each other while minor countries have pegged theirs to one of the major currencies.

One example is that of the EMS, which constitutes one aspect of EU cooperation and which is to develop into a monetary union with one common currency unit (ECU). This means that inside the union, exchange rates will be fixed irrevocably but externally the ECU will float against the currencies of other countries.

The advantages and disadvantages of membership of a monetary union or of any other fixed exchange rate system were outlined in Chapters 12 and 13, where the reasons for efficiency gains versus possible losses due to increased macro-economic instability are given.

14.3.1   Efficiency gains

Allocative efficiency is enhanced for two reasons. Firstly, the formation of an economic union eliminates transaction costs related to currency transactions among member countries. Exchange charges disappear and firms save resources previously spent on foreign exchange management. Such gains increase with the volume of payments among member countries.

Secondly, a monetary union removes any exchange rate uncertainty among member countries. If we assume that exchange rate uncertainty impedes the international mobility of goods and factors of production, then a union provides a basis for allocative efficiency gains.

Compared to a system based merely on irrevocably fixed exchange rates, a monetary union with one common currency presents some advantages. Firstly, it offers total elimination of transaction costs. Secondly, it offers increased price and wage transparency since prices and wages are stated in one currency. This may promote the competitiveness of goods and labour markets. Thirdly, financial markets may deepen and become more efficient due to scale effects. Fourthly, a common currency provides the union with a high degree of credibility because it makes it difficult for members to opt out. This in turn renders interest rates on securities with comparable characteristics uniform. Finally, a common currency may become an international reserve currency. To the extent that non-member countries hold the common currency as international liquidity, the union gains international seigniorage (see Commission of the European Communities 1990).

14.3.2   Macro-economic coordination

Members of an economic union renounce the possibility of pursuing exchange rate policies. In this section, we will examine the macro-economic mechanisms of joint floating in order to assess whether the lack of exchange rate policy inflicts losses on member countries.

Let us assume for the time being that the member countries of a monetary union keep their independent central banks. If one of the major countries pursued an expansionary monetary policy, then this would serve as an expansionary monetary policy in all the member states because of the common currency (or the irrevocably fixed exchange rates). The policy would stimulate income in the union partly due to a depreciation of the common currency and the derived increase in net exports.

This would appear to be profitable but in the given situation some member countries may have no wish to expand. In fact, they may be hit by inflation as a result of the expansion. As in the case of 'the countries' dilemma', which was illustrated in Figure 14.4, coordination of the monetary policy of member countries will be a necessity. In a monetary union, coordination is crucial as independent monetary policies are incompatible with a credible fixed exchange rate system.

It seems unlikely that an anchor country should be entrusted with the joint monetary policy of the union. Consequently, a common central bank system will have to be established. This system will have two main tasks: the handling of monetary policy with respect to inflation and sharing the responsibility for external exchange rate policy. Although a common currency eliminates national monetary autonomy, member countries gain influence on joint monetary and exchange rate policy.

Monetary policy affects production and inflation in all member countries in the same way. However, as regards fiscal policy, no such definite conclusion can be reached; sometimes it will have a 'beggar thy neighbour' effect. The underlying argument is easy to grasp if we assume that the union is insignificant in the world economy and that it consists of merely two countries, e.g. Norway and Sweden. Let us assume that Norway adopts an expansionary fiscal policy in order to increase her level of employment. As a whole, the union will experience an expansionary fiscal policy and its freely floating currency will appreciate. In Chapter 12 we showed that the loss of competitiveness renders fiscal policy inefficient, leaving the union's GNP unchanged. Thus the Norwegian expansion is to the detriment of Swedish activity, which will suffer from declining exports. Table 14.8 summarizes the effects on demand components in the two countries.

Figure 14.3 showed that the net effect on Y is positive and not zero if the union is a large one. The explanation for this is that a large union affects global interest rate and, consequently, reduces appreciation. It follows that the 'beggar thy neighbour' effect does not necessarily occur. This is also valid in the case of a small union if exchange rate expectations do not correspond to the simple version in which they are based on static expectations (see Nielsen *et al.* 1992).

The expanding country will gradually face price increases and the passive one falling prices. Thus relative competitiveness changes to the advantage of the latter and, over time, this country will restore its volume of production and level of employment. Given that fiscal policy in one country may affect production and inflation in other member countries, coordination is required in a monetary union. Countries pursuing expansionary fiscal policies will face a deteriorating balance of payments and a negative development in government finance. Formally, however, no member country is subject to any restrictions as regards its balance of payments or its international liquidity. Therefore it may be tempted to pursue an (overly) expansionary fiscal policy.

Table 14.8   Effects of expansionary fiscal policy in a small monetary union

	G (1)	$(X-M)$ relative to the partner country (2)	$(X-M)$ relative to the rest of the world (3)	$C+I$ (4)	$Y=(1)+(2)+(3)+(4)$ (5)
Norway	↑	↓	↓	↑	↑
Sweden	0	↑	↓	↓	↓
The union	↑	—[†]	↓	0	0

Note: We assume static exchange rate expectations and perfect capital mobility internally and externally.
[†] Not defined.

Consequently, some constraints are needed on national fiscal policy if undesirable developments in the exchange rate or on the current account of the whole union are to be avoided. Such constraints may take the form of limits to budgetary deficits and of a ban on monetary financing of public sector deficits, which would protect the joint monetary policy.

If the member countries all face problems of the same kind, e.g. unemployment, then coordinated fiscal expansion may take place, which may be supplemented with monetary expansion. In such a case, individual countries are more likely to comply with common budgetary restrictions. A joint expansionary fiscal policy may be implemented either through national budgets or through the budget of the union. In the latter case, the union's budget has to be substantial if the effects of the policy are to make themselves felt. The budget of the EU, for example, amounts to no more than 1 per cent of EU GNP, so this budget will not be applicable for such purposes.

A union of global significance faces coordination problems at two levels: (1) externally, i.e. in relation to other major agents, and (2) internally, i.e. among member countries. Solving internal problems is a precondition for speaking with a single voice and for effective participation in the global coordination dogfight.

In sum, the macro-economic stability of a country may be eroded by participation in a monetary union since this involves loss of economic autonomy. National monetary policy and exchange rate policy disappear and fiscal policy becomes subject to constraints. The importance of the loss of autonomy depends on the degree of economic flexibility still left and on the kinds of shock to which the country is exposed (see Chapter 13). The costs of the loss of autonomy decrease with the decreasing likelihood of asymmetrical shocks and with increasing degrees of wage and price flexibility in the country.

14.4   HISTORICAL LESSONS

The thirties were characterized by increasing protectionism, competitive devaluations, exchange control, etc., and, hence, by shrinking international trade and lost opportunities for growth resulting from international specialization. This was truly a period of 'the countries' dilemma'. The early post-war period saw both the founding of a number of international institutions and the signing of agreements designed to promote growth and employment. The prevailing ideology favoured liberalization of financial markets and trade on the basis of international coordination, which was seen as a means of countering the kind of misery experienced in the thirties. Some prominent examples are the Bretton Woods agreement, which established the IMF and the World Bank, the OEEC (later the OECD), GATT and the European Communities.

14.4.1 The Bretton Woods system

The Bretton Woods exchange rate system was based on two-step convertibility (see Chapter 8). Firstly, the United States guaranteed that participating central banks could exchange US$ for gold at a fixed rate, namely US$ 35.00 per ounce. Secondly, the central banks could buy and sell their home currencies against US$ at an official, fixed exchange rate. Thus free convertibility and fixed exchange rates were used to reap the efficiency gains outlined in Section 14.3.

The participating nations subjected themselves to the rules of this game. Thus the system was an example of international coordination. The outstanding feature of this system was the asymmetrical organization that made one nation, i.e. the United States, the anchor country.

If such a system is to survive, two conditions have to be satisfied. The anchor country has to supply sufficient international liquidity without jeopardizing gold convertibility. In addition, the other participating nations have to design monetary policies that are in accordance with the asymmetrical nature of the system. Consequently, the monetary policy of the anchor country guarantees low inflation rates while the policies pursued by the other countries exclusively aim at observing exchange rate parities.

As regards gold convertibility, it presented a threat to the system that the global gold supply was exogenous, i.e. it depended on new discoveries, etc. Growing international trade would spur demand for international reserves (US$) outside the United States. Without similar growth in the American gold stock, developments would lead to declining confidence in gold convertibility. During the period from 1958 to 1972, the ratio between the American gold stock and circulating US$ decreased from 2 to 0.2. *Gresham's law* predicts that, where two kinds of currency exist together, 'bad money drives out good money', the latter being extracted from circulation. It follows that the price of gold would increase in private markets relative to the price of US$. In order to avoid a spread between the official exchange rate of US$ 35 per ounce and the private one, central banks jointly sold part of their stocks on private markets. However, private demand continued to increase and in 1968 the policy was discontinued. The United States suspended the exchange of US$ against gold and thus the Bretton Woods system was reduced to a dollar standard in 1968.

As regards the adaptation of monetary policies to that of the anchor country, it was a problem throughout the sixties that countries did not consider external equilibrium a primary economic goal. If deficit countries in an asymmetrical fixed exchange rate system are hit by external shocks, which affect employment and the balance of payments negatively, then external equilibrium has to be controlled if the credibility of exchange parities is to be maintained. Devaluation is against the spirit of the system, and wages policy works too slowly, so the only policy option left is one of internal contraction, which of course increases unemployment. As a country gives higher priority to (full) employment, currency speculation will gain ground and gradually destroy the country's international liquidity. Of course surplus countries face a luxury problem since they can enjoy watching their international reserves accumulating.

The United States began to focus on internal objectives as well. Thus it led an expansionary and inflationary policy in the sixties. As a result, the US$ was overvalued and was subjected to speculation. As was shown in Section 14.1, an expansionary monetary policy in the anchor country is transmitted to the other countries in an asymmetric system. In the present case, the derived inflationary pressure harmed countries such as Germany, Switzerland and Japan, which faced conflicting goals: the internal goal of low inflation rates and the external goal of fixed exchange rates against the US$. Of course, the efficient policy would have been one of revaluation, which runs counter to the basic idea of the whole system. Consequently, the late sixties saw continued speculation against the US$, which was finally devalued under the Smithsonian agreement of 1971. However, there was little confidence in the revised parities and the Bretton Woods system ultimately broke down in 1973 as the major currencies began floating.

In sum, the long-term failure of the system has been ascribed to two factors in particular: (1) American monetary policy was too expansionary and, consequently, supplied the global economy with excessive amounts of US$ and (2) the participating countries generally changed their priorities, giving a low priority to external goals. In brief, no willingness existed to adapt economic policies to the requirements of an asymmetrical fixed exchange rate system.

14.4.2   Floating exchange rates and Group coordination

The 1973 transition to floating exchange rates was followed by continued liberalization of capital movements, which resulted in violent and unforeseen exchange rate fluctuations among the major currencies. The result of this was economic efficiency losses (see Chapter 12).

Throughout the eighties, the leading industrialized nations took an increasing interest in coordinating their economic policies. One reason for this was the growing imbalance in international trade, which left the United States with a sizeable deficit. The imbalance was largely caused by the American policy mix of the early eighties: a tight monetary policy combined with an expansionary fiscal policy drove up the American interest rate and, consequently, paved the way for massive US$ appreciation.

The detrimental effects of this policy would not have occurred, of course, if all major nations had followed suit. They did not, however, and they only half-heartedly attempted to counter the exchange rate fluctuations and balance of payments shifts by means of central bank intervention. In addition, the American ideology of the period was that the situation should be left to the markets. Nevertheless, as the American trade deficits kept increasing, a protectionist attitude gained ground.

At the Plaza Meeting in New York in 1985, the G5 countries, i.e. the United Kingdom, the United States, Japan, Germany and France, agreed that the US$ was overvalued and expressed their determination to effect a depreciation by united efforts including exchange market intervention. They succeeded. The US$ depreciated against the DEM and the JPY. The Plaza Meeting is now considered a milestone on the path to a system of international coordination under floating exchange rates.

The US Congress, however, was not willing to follow up on this by reducing American public sector deficits. Instead, it put pressure on major trade surplus countries such as Japan and Germany to make them adopt expansionary fiscal policies.

The attempt was not successful, so instead the United States forced through a further depreciation of the US$ and thus it subjected its trade partners to considerable competitive pressure. In late 1986 Japan and Germany intervened to protect their export industries and, finally, in 1987 the depreciation of the US$ was halted. The defectiveness of the Plaza agreement had been revealed by these events, which showed the lack of unity when it came to agreeing on the 'right' exchange rates.

At the Louvre Meeting in 1987 another attempt was made by the Group of Five. The Group set up target zones for exchange rates but did not make them public. The participating countries expressed their readiness to defend the zones through intervention. During the subsequent eight months exchange rates were reasonably stable within the zones. At the end of this period, however, the United States was forced to adopt a tight monetary policy in order to defend the US$.

The target zone philosophy is a fixed exchange rate system hybrid. As was pointed out above, monetary policy in such a system has to give priority to external goals instead of internal ones. The lack of success of the Louvre Meeting is the specific result of the lacking willingness of the participating countries to commit themselves whole-heartedly to exchange rate stability. In brief, the success of international coordination after 1985 has been very limited.

Some important lessons should be drawn from the post-1973 period. First and foremost, countries have not yet been prepared to allow fully flexible exchange rates. During the period, the system has been one of dirty floating, in which central banks have, to some extent, interfered with the development in exchange rates through exchange market intervention. Of course, the degree of monetary autonomy has been higher than it was in the Bretton Woods period, but it has not been wholly directed towards internal goals. The major countries have not renounced intervention, so international reserves are still necessary. Due to the predominant role of the American economy, the US$ is still the most important reserve currency, which means that even after 1973 the international economic system has the features of asymmetry, although they are less pronounced than before.

The period after 1973 contrasts sharply with the previous Bretton Woods system. The well-defined rules of an asymmetrical game which included an anchor country have been replaced by internationally uncoordinated economic policy, generally speaking. The Bretton Woods system broke down because the rules of the game were not observed, i.e. for lack of coordination. Likewise, the major global imbalances after 1973 have to be ascribed to lack of international coordination.

14.4.3 European economic policy under German leadership

The violent exchange rate fluctuations in the post-1973 period inspired Germany and other European nations to embark on a new fixed exchange rate system. The resulting cooperation first took the form of *the snake in the tunnel*, which allowed a ± 2.25 per cent deviation from parity rates, which were adjusted rather frequently. In 1979 the system was replaced by the European Monetary System, which is still in operation.

The intention underlying this system is one of creating a symmetrical system in which all member countries are obliged to adjust fiscal and monetary policies and, ultimately, exchange rate parities. The so-called *divergence indicator* was designed to single out countries whose exchange rates diverted and which consequently had to take corrective action.

In practice, the EMS turned out to be an asymmetrical construct with Germany as the anchor country and the other participants adapting to her monetary policies. Germany was, and is, fit for this role, not just because of the importance of her economy but particularly because the German Bundesbank is strongly committed to price stability, which is a constitutionally defined goal reflecting the post-First World War memory of hyperinflation. When divergency indications have occurred, Germany has shown little inclination to pursue monetary policies in order to adjust exchange rates. Instead, other countries have been obliged to apply their monetary instruments to defend their exchange rates against the DEM (see Groes and Thygesen 1992). Germany being the anchor country, some member countries have tried to fight inflation by leaning against the DEM and, in so doing, lending credibility to anti-inflation policies. The Danish fixed exchange rate policy pursued from 1982 onwards is one example of this.

The German unification of 1990 has provided one example of how a fixed exchange rate system may come under pressure. The unification caused vast increases in public expenditure but it was not financed through taxes and, as a result, the expansionary fiscal policy triggered an inflationary tendency. Of course the Bundesbank reacted by forcing up German interest rates which were immediately transmitted to those of its partner countries. The high real interest rates placed the partners in straitjackets during the 1992–94 recession. The resulting expectations that internal goals would be given priority translated into devaluation expectations. One indication of these expectations was the fact that the partner countries did not make sufficient use of interest rate policy as spot market exchange rates hit the margins of intervention. According to EMS rules, both countries involved have to take action in such a situation—and if the DEM is involved, the result will be an increase in German money supply, which conflicts with the monetary goals of the Bundesbank.

In the autumn of 1992 violent waves of speculation forced the £ sterling and the ITL to leave the system and other countries to adjust their parities. In 1993 renewed speculation, this time against the FRF and the DKK, put the EMS under considerable pressure and it only survived because the intervention limits were expanded to ± 15 per cent.

14.4.4 EMU planning in the EU

The EU has for many years bolstered plans for an Economic Monetary Union (EMU). The *Werner Plan* of 1970 suggested that an EMU should be established before 1980. The establishment of the EMS in 1979 was a moderate step in this direction. The next crucial plan was formulated in the *Delors Report* of 1989, in which the EMU is outlined in some detail. The single market was to be supported by irrevocably fixed exchange rates and the indispensable joint monetary policy. Fiscal policy was to be coordinated and the EMU to be accomplished over a number of stages. The governments of the EU countries agreed on this plan at the Maastricht Summit in December 1991. With minor modifications the Maastricht Treaty has since been ratified by the EU countries. British and Danish provisos include the introduction of a common currency in the third stage of the EMU.

According to the plan, the EMU will be established over an extended period of time. In the initial phase, the harmonization of the economic development of the participating countries will be given priority, including inflation rates and public sector deficits in particular. The European Monetary Institute (EMI), which consists of the governors of the EU central banks, has been established as a precursor of a European central bank. The aim of the EMI is to promote monetary cooperation in order to stabilize prices. In 1996 a qualified majority will decide whether half of the EU countries do in fact have 'their economies under control'. The criteria that would have to be satisfied in order for a country to qualify are the following:

- Its domestic inflation rate must be no more than 1.5 per cent above the average rate of the three member countries with the lowest rates.
- Its interest rate level must be no more than 2 per cent above that of the same three nations.
- Its government debt must be no more than 60 per cent of GNP.
- Its budgetary deficit must be no more than 3 per cent of GNP.
- It must have observed the normal intervention limits over the past two years and not have begun a devaluation of its currency.

The purpose of these criteria is to prevent the premature membership of countries that are not yet fit for participation and, hence, might destabilize the EMU. The 'healthy currencies' of countries that meet the criteria will have their exchange rates firmly locked and the exact date of introduction of the common currency, the ECU will not be decided until then. If the vote in 1996 shows that there is no agreement that half the countries are ready for the EMU, then the decisive phase will not begin until 1999 with participation being decided half a year ahead. During the decisive phase, the European Central Bank is to be established, whose primary objective will be the securing of price stability. It will be independent of national governments as well as of EU institutions. The explicit statement of the bank's objectives and independence in the Maastricht Treaty should be seen as an attempt to engender confidence in exchange rate stability. Several investigations conclude that central bank independence will further the success of anti-inflation policy. The transition from the EMS to the EMU will also mark the shift from an asymmetrical DEM-dominated system to a symmetrical one in which monetary policy is based on the economic development in all of the EU member countries.

The crucial issue is whether the threat of increased macro-economic instability can be traded off against efficiency gains. These include the elimination of the costs of exchange, which at best account for 0.5 per cent of EU GDP (see Commission of the European Communities 1990). Even when the benefits of reduced international transaction uncertainty has been added, the efficiency gains are bound to be moderate. Chapter 13 set up criteria for selecting candidates for a monetary union and on that basis the 15 current EU members are not equally fit for EMU membership. Labour mobility is low among most of the EU members and in several cases business structures differ markedly. Further, fulfilment of (all of) the criteria of convergence seems unlikely to take place until some time in the far future in the case of several countries.

Thus it is an open question whether EMU participation will prove beneficial to all EU members. However, limitations on politico-economic autonomy should be seen in the light of the fact that countries with strongly interrelated economics always face very restricted economic latitude. In particular, renouncing an independent exchange rate policy necessitates increased wage flexibility since a lack of flexibility would periodically leave countries faced with severe adjustment problems.

SUMMARY

1. International coordination is highlighted by analysing the case of a 'split world', the United States and the EU. One crucial point is whether responsibility for the exchange rate (US$/ ECU) is symmetrical or asymmetrical.
2. The United States took responsibility in the Bretton Woods system, Germany in the EMS system—both were asymmetrical in practice.
3. Depending on the structure of the system, monetary or fiscal policy will affect key variables in the two regions differently. In addition, the effects depend on whether the exchange rates are fixed or flexible.
4. The benefits of coordinating international economic policies may be proven by pay-off considerations between unemployment and inflation rates. The countries' dilemma expresses the tendency for non-coordinated countries to choose the common worst possible situation.
5. Arguments may also be formulated against coordination, including incompatibility of national goals, the unlikelihood of shared economic conceptions and strong commitment.
6. Joint floating, or a monetary union, enhances economic efficiency for several reasons.

Coordination necessitates a common monetary policy, i.e. in practice a common central bank system. Conclusions as to fiscal policy are less obvious; it may be uncoordinated and give rise to harmful neighbour effects.

7. Historical lessons include the Bretton Woods system, the EMS system and Group coordination (G5). In all cases, the lack of commitment of the common goals were destructive, and coordination became inefficient. So far, perspectives for a European economic and monetary union appear cloudy as success criteria are only partly met.

REFERENCES

Commission of the European Communities (1990), 'One market, one money. An evaluation of the potential benefits and costs of forming an economic and monetary union', *European Economy*, **44**.

Committee for the Study of Economic and Monetary Union (1989), 'Report on Economic and Monetary Union in the European Community', Luxembourg.

De Grauwe, Paul (1989), *International Money, Postwar Trends and Theories*, Clarendon Press. Oxford.

De Grauwe, Paul (1990), 'Fiscal policies in the EMS—A strategic analysis', Chapter 7 in *International and European Monetary Systems*, Heinemann Professional Publishing, Oxford.

The Economist (1987), 'The limits to co-operation', 26 September, London.

Eichengreen, Barry (1993), 'European monetary unification', *Journal of Economic Literature*, **XXXI**, 1321–1357.

Frankel, J. A. and K. Rockett (1988), 'International macroeconomic policy coordination when policy makers do not agree on the true model', *American Economic Review*, **78**.

Groes, D. and N. Thygesen (1992), *European Monetary Integration. From the European Monetary System to European Monetary Union*, Longman, London.

Hamada, K. (1974), 'Alternative exchange rate systems and the interdependence of monetary policies', in R. Z. Aliber (ed.), *National Monetary Policies and the International System*, University of Chicago Press, Chicago.

Hamada, K. (1976), 'A strategic analysis of monetary interdependence', *Journal of Political Economy*, **84**, 677–700.

McKibbin, W. J. and J. D. Sachs (1991), *Global Linkages. Macroeconomic Interdependence and Cooperation in the World Economy*, The Brooking Institution, Washington, D.C.

McKinnon, R. I. (1993), 'International money in historical perspective', *Journal of Economic Literature*, **XXXI**, 1.

Nielsen, J. U.-M., H. Heinrich and J. D. Hansen (1992), *An Economic Analysis of the EC*, McGraw-Hill Book Company, London.

BIBLIOGRAPHY

Allen, P. R. and P. B. Kenen (1980), *Asset Markets, Exchange Rates, and Economic Integration*, Cambridge University Press, London.

Artus, J. R. and J. H. Young (1979), 'Fixed and flexible rates: a renewal of the debate', *IMF Staff Papers*, December.

Balassa, B. (1961), *The Theory of Economic Integration*, Irwin, Homewood, Ill.

Balassa, B. (1963), 'An empirical demonstration of classical comparative cost theory', *Review of Economics and Statistics*, August.

Balassa, B. (1964), 'The purchasing power parity doctrine: a reappraisal', *Journal of Political Economy*, December.

Balassa, B. (1967), 'Trade creation and trade diversion in the European Common Market', *Economic Journal*, March.

Bhagwati, J. N. (1981), *International Trade: Selected Readings*, MIT Press, Mass.

Bhagwati, J. N. (1985), *Dependence and Interdependence*, MIT Press, Mass.

Bhagwati, J. N. (1992), 'The threats to the world trading system', *The World Economy*, **15**.

Bhagwati, J. N. and T. N. Srinivasan (1983), *Lectures on International Trade*, MIT Press, Mass.

Bilson, J. F. O. and R. C. Marston (1984), *Exchange Rate Theory and Practice*, University of Chicago Press, Chicago, Ill.

Cassel, G. (1923), *Money and Foreign Exchange After 1914*, Macmillan, New York.

Casson, M. *et al.* (1986), *Multinationals and World Trade*, Allen & Unwin, Mass.

Caves, R. E. (1982), *Multinational Enterprise and Economic Analysis*, Cambridge University Press, Cambridge.

Caves, R. E. and H. G. Johnson (1968), *Readings in International Economics*, Irwin, Ill.

Chenery, H. (1961), 'Comparative advantage and development policy', *American Economic Review*, March.

Chenery, H. and T. N. Srinivasan (1988–89), *Handbook of Development Economics*, Vols I and II, North Holland, Amsterdam.

Chipman, J. S. (1965), 'A survey of the theory of international trade', *Econometrica*, July.

Chow, P. (1987), 'Causality between export growth and industrial development: empirical evidence from the NICs', *Journal of Development Economics*, June.

Corden, W. M. (1971), *The Theory of Protection*, Oxford University Press, London.

Darby, M. R. *et al.* (1983), *The International Transmission of Inflation*, University of Chicago Press, Chicago, Ill.

Dornbusch, R. (1976), 'Expectations and exchange rate dynamics', *Journal of Political Economy*, December.

Dornbusch, R. (1989), *Open Economy Macroeconomics*, Academic Press, New York.

Dornbusch, R. *et al.* (1977), 'Comparative advantage, trade and payments in a Ricardian model, *American Economic Review*, December.

Fair, R. C. (1982), 'Estimated output, price, interest rate, and exchange rate linkages among countries', *Journal of Political Economy*, June.

Feldstein, M. (1988), *International Economic Cooperation*, University of Chicago Press, Chicago, Ill.

Findlay, R. and H. Grubert (1969), 'Factor intensities, technological progress, and international trade', *Oxford Economic Papers*, February.

Frankel, J. and K. Rockett (1988), 'International macroeconomic policy coordination when policy makers do not agree on the true model', *American Economic Review*, June.

Frenkel, J. A. (1981), 'The collapse of purchasing power parity in the 1970s', *European Economic Review*, May.

Frenkel, J. A. (1987), 'The international monetary systems: should it be reformed', *American Economic Review*, May.

Frenkel, J. A. and M. L. Musse (1980), 'The efficiency of the foreign exchange market and measures of turbulence', *American Economic Review*, May.

Greenaway, D. and L. A. Winter (1993), *Surveys in International Trade*, Blackwell, Oxford.

Gros, D. and N. Thygesen (1992), *European Monetary Integration*, Longman, London.

Haberler, G. (1936), *The Theory of International Trade*, W. Hodge & Co., London.

Haberler, G. (1949), 'The market for foreign exchange and the stability of the balance of payments: a theoretical analysis', *Kyklos*, September.

Hamis, J. (1984), 'Applied general equilibrium analysis of small open economies and imperfect competition', *American Economic Review*, December.

Houthakker, H. and S. Magee (1969), 'Income and price elasticities in world trade', *Review of Economics and Statistics*, May.

Hufbauer, G. H. *et al.* (1986), *Trade Protection in the United States: 31 Case Studies*. IIE, Washington, D.C.

Hume, D. (1752), 'On the balance of trade', in *Essays*, Vol. I, Reprinted, for example, in R. N. Cooper (ed.), *International Finance: Selected Readings*, Penguin, London, 1969.

Hymer, S. (1976), *The International Operations of National Firms: A Study of Direct Foreign Investment*, MIT Press, Mass.

IMF (Annual), *Annual Report on Exchange Arrangements and Exchange Restrictions*, Washington, D.C.

Johnson, H. (1971), 'Trade and growth: a geometrical exposition', *Journal of International Economics*, February.

Jones, R. W. and P. B. Kenen (1984), *Handbook of International Economics*, Vols 1 and 2, North-Holland, Amsterdam.

Jones, R. W. and A. Krueger (1990), *The Political Economy of International Trade*, Blackwell, Oxford.

Kreinin, M. and L. Officer (1978), *The Monetary Approach to the Balance of Payments: A Survey*, Princeton University Press, New Jersey.

Krueger, A. O. (1978), 'Alternative strategies and employment in LDCs', *American Economic Review*, May.

Krueger, A. O. (1983), *Exchange Rate Determination*, Cambridge University Press, Cambridge.

Krugman, P. (1979), 'Increasing returns, monopolistic competition and international trade', *Journal of International Economics*, 9, 469–480.

Krugman, P. (1980), 'Scale economies, product differentiation and the pattern of trade', *American Economic Review*, 70, 950–959.

Krugman, P. (1982), 'Trade in differentiated products and political economy of trade liberalization', in Bhagwati, J. (ed.) *Imperfect Competition and Response*, University of Chicago Press, Chicago.

Krugman, P. R. (ed.) (1986), *Strategic Trade Policy and the New International Economics*, MIT Press, Mass.

Krugman, P. R. (1992), 'Does the new trade theory require a new trade policy?', *The World Economy*, 15, 423–441.

Lancaster, K. (1957), 'The Heckscher–Ohlin trade model: a geometric treatment', *Economica*, February.

Leamer, E. (1980), 'The Leontief paradox reconsidered', *Journal of Political Economy*, June.

Leontief, W. W. (1993), 'The use of indifference curves in international trade', *Quarterly Journal of Economics*, May.

Leontief, W. (1954), 'Domestic production and foreign trade: the American capital position reexamined, *Economica Internazionale*, February.

Lerner, A. P. (1936), 'The symmetry between import and export taxes', *Economica*, August.

Linder, S. B. (1961), *An Essay on Trade and Transformation*, Wiley, New York.

Llewellyn, D. T. and C. R. Milner (1990), *Current issues in International Monetary Economics*, Macmillan, London.

Machlup, F. (1955), 'Relative prices and aggregate spending in the analysis of devaluation', *American Economic Review*, June.

McKinnon, R. (1963), 'Optimum currency areas', *American Economic Review*, September.

McKinnon, R. I. (1993), 'The rules of the game: international money in historical perspective', *Journal of Economic Literature*, **31**, 1–44.

Meade, J. (1955), *The Theory of Customs Unions*, North-Holland, Amsterdam.

Meerhaeghe, M. van (1992), *International Economic Institutions*, Kluwer, London.

Metzler, L. M. (1942), 'The transfer problem reconsidered', *Journal of Political Economy*, June.

Miller, M. H. and J. Williamson (1988), 'The international monetary system: an analysis of alternative regimes', *European Economic Review*, June.

Mundell, R. (1957), 'International trade and factor mobility', *American Economic Review*, June.

Mundell, R. (1968), *International Economics*, Macmillan, New York.

OECD (1985), *Costs and Benefits of Protection*, Paris.

Officer, L. H. (1978), 'The relation between absolute and relative purchasing power parity', *Review of Economics and Statistics*, November.

Owen, N. (1983), *Economics of Scale, Competitiveness, and Trade Patterns within the European Economic Community*, Oxford University Press, Oxford.

Papell, D. (1988), 'Expectations and exchange rate dynamics after a decade of flotation', *Journal of International Economics*, November.

Posner, M. V. (1961), 'International trade and technical change', *Oxford Economic Papers*, **13**, 323–41.

Rugman, A. (1976), 'Risk reduction by international diversification', *Journal of International Business Studies*, September

Salvatore, D. (1986), 'Oil import costs and domestic inflation in industrial countries', *Weltwirtschaftliches Archiv*, Band 122, Heft 2, 281–291.

Salvatore, D. (ed.) (1987), *The New Protectionist Threat to World Welfare*, North-Holland, New York and Amsterdam.

Salvatore, D. (1990), *Theory and Problems of International Economics*, McGraw-Hill, New York.

Samuelson, P. A. (1939), 'The gains from international trade', *Canadian Journal of Economics and Political Science*, **5**, 195–205.

Samuelson, P. A. (1948), 'International trade and the equalization of factor prices', *Economic Journal*, June.

Samuelson, P. A. (1949), 'International factor price equalization once again', *Economic Journal*, June.

Samuelson, P. A. (1956), 'Social indifference curves', *Quarterly Journal of Economics*, February.

Samuelson, P. A. (1962), 'The gains from international trade once again', *Economic Journal*, December.

Stopler, W. F. and P. A. Samuelson (1941), 'Protection and real wages', *Review of Economic Studies*, November.

Vernon, R. (1966), 'International investment and international trade in the product cycle', *Quarterly Journal of Economics*, May.

Viner, J. (1937), *Studies in the Theory of International Trade*, Harper and Bros, New York.

Williamson, J. and C. Milner (1991), *The World Economy*, Harvester, New York.

INDEX